Ecumenical perspectives
on baptism,
eucharist and ministry

Ecumenical perspectives on baptism, eucharist and ministry

Edited by Max Thurian

Faith and Order Paper 116

World Council of Churches, Geneva

Cover design: Nelly Witte-Brooymans
ISBN No. 2-8254-0758-5
© 1983 World Council of Churches, 150, route de Ferney,
1211 Geneva 20, Switzerland
Printed in Switzerland

CONTENTS

PREFACE

NIKOS NISSIOTIS

A measure of uneasiness, doubt and fatigue became evident in ecumenical circles during the last decade. What is the use of theological study and discussion for restoring visible church unity amongst the divided church communions? Work on traditional issues of ecclesiology in the ecumenical movement has become an item of open criticism on the part of many prominent, active and impatient ecumenists. They have challenged its relevance in the face of the more urgent need of the churches to act together in addressing contemporary socio-political problems.

At the same time, a number of academic theologians have regarded the ecclesiological work in ecumenical circles as not being adequately theological, or as escaping the real theological issues by attempting a kind of a superficial interconfessional approach to extremely difficult and delicate ecclesiological issues. In conservative ecclesiastical circles, in almost all of the churches, there is the suspicion that a certain kind of interconfessional syncretism has crept into ecumenical theological work.

Because of such criticism, and also because of the lack of spectacular inter-church ecclesiological agreements, particularly amongst the major confessional families, and the continued absence of official full communion between them, a great many church members, especially young people, tend to see in this ecclesiological debate a stagnation threatening the whole of the ecumenical enterprise. Consequently, many of them have sought church unity outside the so-called "official" expressions or channels of ecumenism. Some have entered groups emancipated from

---

• Nikos A. Nissiotis is Moderator of the Faith and Order Commission.

church authorities as new charismatic expressions of genuine and practical ecumenism.

I

The Faith and Order document on "Baptism, Eucharist and Ministry" can offer at least a partial response to these criticisms. Certainly it cannot satisfy any one of these groups entirely, especially those which have had no immediate sharing or experience as church representatives in the difficult work of restoring visible church unity on the basis of serious and consistent doctrinal reflection.

We should not deceive ourselves. There is no authentic, stable and permanent church unity possible without doctrinal agreement. All other enthusiastic approaches have only a limited value and, even risk creating further confusion, however effective they may appear for the moment. Of course, no one should object to a variety of steps being taken towards reuniting church bodies, by applying different practical methods for securing communion in sacraments, preaching and missionary action. Nevertheless, we should always seek basic agreement in matters of faith and church discipline if we are seriously concerned with organic and visible church unity.

Furthermore, this fundamental agreement in matters of faith is not limited to some ecclesiological items, but includes the whole content of the apostolic faith. That is why the text of Faith and Order on "Baptism, Eucharist and Ministry", on which the different authors comment in this book, should not be regarded as a text in isolation. This ecclesiological study is a part of the related effort to "Giving Account of the Hope that is in Us," which had been the previous Faith and Order theme concluded at its Bangalore Assembly (1978). It also makes an inseparable contribution to the Commission's major projected study "Towards a Common Expression of the Apostolic Faith Today". At the same time, it also helps to ground church unity, which is not an end in itself, but rather a living witness and dynamic service in the world linked with its process of renewal, as is indicated by the other major Faith and Order study, "The Unity of the Church and the Renewal of Human Community".

One should keep in mind this broad interrelationship of study themes, when evaluating the text "Baptism, Eucharist and Ministry" (BEM). All of them aim to make unity an instrument of the Church in its service to the world. It becomes immediately evident how important the BEM text is in this connection. There can be neither a common expression of the apostolic faith nor a concerted action of the churches in the world without agreement on these three basic ecclesial events which sum up church life and give it coherence and continuity.

II

In accord with this importance and perspective of the BEM text, the authors of the articles in this collection point out: first, the need of agreement on matters regarding a common confession of faith as the necessary prerequisite and background for all kinds of special agreement on particular ecclesiological issues; second, the most important issues of the agreement achieved on baptism, eucharist and ministry, as well as the difficult issues which are still under debate; and third, the crucial question of how the churches receive the text in its present state and what steps should be undertaken on their part following this reception.

The converging lines of the different confessions are illustrated by the contributors. They are of imperative character, because they demonstrate that they are the developments of the one and the same apostolic faith and church tradition. This signifies that where the substance of faith is faithfully kept and practised within an ecclesial communion, there one can proceed in elaborating further specific elements of agreement. It is only on the basis of the one apostolic faith and tradition that agreement on BEM appears as a normal outcome of the common and unshaken inheritance in which churches share. This basic act of joint confession validates the past dimension of the apostolic faith as our common root. It also opens the future for our mutual converging attitudes on specifics of church life and confession in a fresh way.

In the light of this approach, *baptism* is studied in the document of BEM as the unifying first event in all churches. At the same time, there is an exploration into some of the dividing issues in a new way, (e. g. of infant and adult baptism and the relationship between confirmation and chrismation). The same is true of a new converging approach, as one can easily see by reading the text together with the corresponding commentaries in this edition.

The *eucharist* text is also analyzed by the authors, underlining essential agreement on the main items of the apostolic faith regarding different aspects of the memorial, thanksgiving, and real presence in the eucharist. It affirms the constitutive elements of this sacrament that help us in keeping, manifesting and growing together into the unity of the one Church. We agree on the eucharist as the centre not only of church life but also of world history and as the foretaste of the Kingdom. This discloses our common roots in the one faith of the *ecclesia* and its visible, concrete manifestation as we gather together to break the communion bread in our particular church communion. Certainly, the celebration of the eucharist on this ground of the one unshaken faith also reveals the importance of the place and the meaning of the office of the celebrant. It thereby makes a vital connection with the ministry as well as with baptism, especially in connection with confirmation or chrismation and ordination.

The *ministry* seems to be the most delicate and controversial issue. But it becomes immediately clear that on this very sensitive and difficult problem also both the text and the commentaries show a way out of the traditional divisions by endorsing notions like the one on *episcopé,* the charismatic eucharistic meaning and the eschatological dimensions of the ministry. The difference between sacerdotal and non-sacerdotal ministry persists; as well as the differences between its sacramental and non-sacramental character, the personal or communal understanding of the apostolic succession, and the ordination of women. Again, it is very interesting to follow how the new approach to these unresolved problems contributes towards achieving a major possible agreement in the prospective work in the future. The churches are called now to try to reach a convergence on the ministry within the major reality of the one apostolic faith and the renewing church *diakonia* in the world.

What then does it mean for our common future, now that this text of BEM has been unanimously adopted for referral to the churches by the Faith and Order Plenary Commission at Lima (January 1982), and by the Central Committee of the World Council of Churches in Geneva (July 1982)? Especially important is the "reception" of this document and its use in re-establishing church unity among separated confessional bodies. Though not binding on any church because the text does not pretend to be a new confession of faith, reception here signifies: first, recognition of basic agreement in the one apostolic tradition and biblical inheritance; and second, approval of this basic agreement as the first very important step towards a final consensus in these crucial matters. The commentaries on the significance of reception refer to the need for creating a new ecumenical ethos amongst the churches. The new steps to be taken towards this end are also explicitly given in the final commentaries in this volume.

III

The above remarks should not lead the reader to believe that the BEM text is a radically new one in the history of the ecumenical movement, and especially of Faith and Order. I would like to underline the fact that this text is fundamentally composed in its first draft of earlier authoritative WCC, and especially Faith and Order, documents since 1927. The distinctive value of this document consists not only in the fact that it reflects the findings of previous bilateral church dialogues and Faith and Order studies, but also in that it organically intergrates the thoughts and actions of the churches sharing in one fellowship of love and spiritual communion under the guidance of the Spirit on their way towards continuous renewal and visible unity.

While the core or nucleus of this text reflects the work up to now of Faith and Order within the WCC, it illustrates at the same time a new and fresh way of approaching the centuries-old debate on these three dividing issues among the Christian confessions. Now the BEM text, as a result of genuine ecumenical dialogue within the fellowship of the WCC and in mutual appreciation of one another's church tradition and charismatic life, presents the converging lines of the faith of the separated church communions on baptism, eucharist and ministry.

Only in this way can one explain why separated church confessions, from the extreme Catholic side to the extreme Protestant one, can now together and in full agreement state items of faith on BEM which were not possible even a few years ago. That is the new understanding of "consensus" in a positive sense, i.e. confirming in common our basic elements of faith. We are being drawn into an act of *"consentire"*, in the sense of being in a preliminary agreement by confessing in common the roots of our faith which are to be found in the Bible and the church life throughout the centuries. It is what in Greek one can characterize by the term *"koine synainesis"* which is a *pleonasm* (*koine* and *syn*), and which represents what undergirds the BEM text.

Following these remarks, I may be permitted to make three short observations:

1. Because of this new way of approaching the issues, one should not expect to read a new confessional text similar to those used by separated churches. No one will be satisfied looking at this text solely from one's own confessional stance. It requires a conversion of heart and mind in order to confirm one's own confessional roots anew and together with the other confessions within the one church and biblical tradition.

2. Consequently, one should not try to find in this text one's own confessional faith on BEM fully stated or expounded, for all differences among the confessions are purposely not exhasustively treated.

3. A great deal of the fuller ecumenical approach has been rightly attributed to the responsible and more active participation of Roman Catholic and Eastern Oriental Orthodox scholars in the actual drafting of the documents during the years after the WCC Fifth Assembly. Special consultations had been organized by Faith and Order for achieving this purpose.

Certainly, the BEM text marks a new way of approach that represents the actual growth in the ecumenical movement. Though it is a major event in the process towards visible unity — and one understands for this reason why it has been greeted in ecumenical circles and by the international press with such enthusiasm — we must guard ourselves against any kind of triumphalism and self-justification. We must in all humility present this text as a help to the churches in their dialogues for restoring their own unity. Its significance will depend on the reception and the use that the churches make of it.

****

Concluding this short preface, I would like to extend my thanks to the authors who have contributed by their articles to a fuller understanding of the BEM text. They are among the many persons who have shaped this text by their strenuous work during several years. To all of them, and to those who have worked with them and whose work does not appear in this volume, a warm word of thanks. I may be allowed to name three of them in this connection: the former and present Directors of the Faith and Order Secretariat,

Dr Lukas Vischer who during his long and faithful service, was involved in most of the initiatives taken towards the realization of this plan of study, and Professor William Lazareth, who has worked towards its completion during recent years; and Fr Max Thurian, the editor of the present symposium, who has worked diligently since 1979 in chairing a revision committee on the editing of the text.

INTRODUCTION

WILLIAM H. LAZARETH
AND MAX THURIAN

The Fourth World Conference on Faith and Order, held in Montreal in 1963, was a turning point in the history of the Faith and Order Commission of the World Council of Churches and, it is fair to say, also in the history of ecumenical theology. The subsequent course of the quest for unity was profoundly influenced by the themes dealt with and the conclusions reached by the conference: conception of the Church; relation between Scripture, Tradition and the traditions; the ministry of the Church and the ministries; worship, baptism and eucharist.

After Montreal, and in particular at the Faith and Order Commission meeting in Bristol in 1967, it was clear that it was no longer possible to continue simply juxtaposing and comparing the different doctrinal and ecclesiological traditions. A start had to be made on writing texts showing the doctrinal convergence of the churches throughout the history first of the Faith and Order movement, then of the World Council of Churches, particularly during the first forty years of the Faith and Order Commission. A sufficient series of theological points of agreement could be discovered and noted. The final reports of the various assemblies and official conferences contained enough common doctrinal material to permit the drafting of convergence texts with a view to agreements, and eventually consensus, among the churches.

After Bristol, a first draft statement on the Eucharist was produced (soon to be followed by a second). Following a well-defined theological plan, this statement made use of passages from major

---

• William H. Lazareth is Director of the Faith and Order Secretariat. Fr Max Thurian is Study Adviser to the Faith and Order Commission.

assembly and conference reports. At a meeting in Geneva in 1970, a similar initial draft statement on baptism was produced, and at a meeting in Marseille in 1972 another on ministry. The texts of these initial draft statements are given in an Appendix at the end of this volume.

The subsequent evolution of these texts was monitored by a group of theologians, which in 1977 became the Steering Group on Baptism, Eucharist and Ministry. After the Accra meeting in 1974, the three texts were sent to the churches for their comments and corrections. These were taken fully into account by the Steering Group in preparation for the meetings in Bangalore (1978) and finally in Lima (1982). It was at Lima that the convergence text *Baptism, Eucharist and Ministry* was envisaged as a unity and regarded unanimously by more than a hundred theologians as ripe for sending to the churches for official response (see the Preface to *Baptism, Eucharist and Ministry*).

The section on the eucharist had evolved in a fairly consistent way from 1967 to 1982. The section on baptism had undergone fairly radical recasting. The inital draft on ministry had had to be replaced by a much longer text at the Marseille meeting in 1972, which was then slimmed down to more modest dimensions after 1979.

The theological essays in this volume seek to clarify certain aspects of the Lima document. Since their authors participated more or less uninterruptedly in the evolution of the convergence texts, they are eminently qualified to throw light on their contents.

As has already been pointed out, the present document would not have been possible without the preparatory labours and the findings of the 1963 Faith and Order Conference in Montreal. The Lima text in its entirety is based on the Word of God as contained in Scripture and as understood in the communion of the Church of all ages and all places. This point was dealt with in depth in Section II of the Montreal conference.

It is possible for us today to escape from the impasse in which the division of the sixteenth century had left us as regards the sources of Christian truth and doctrine. On the Catholic side, it was often affirmed that there were two sources of revelation: Holy Scripture and the Tradition of the Church. Certain truths, the most essential ones, could be found in the Bible; others, also necessary but not found expressed in Scripture, could be found in the Tradition of the Church.

Thanks to its Constitution *Dei Verbum,* the Second Vatican Council delivered Catholic theology from this oversimplification. The Council declared:

> Sacred Scripture is the speech (Word) of God as it is put down in writing under the breath of the Holy Spirit. And Tradition transmits in its entirety the Word of God which has been entrusted to the apostles by Christ the Lord and the Holy Spirit. It transmits it to the successors of the apostles so that, enlightened by the Spirit of truth, they may faithfully preserve, expound and spread it abroad by their preaching. Thus it comes about that the Church does not draw her certainty about all revealed truth from the Holy Scriptures alone.[1]

When the Council speaks of "Scripture alone" it seems to mean the Bible in isolation, viewed as a collection of texts fallen from heaven and requiring no ecclesial reading and understanding.

In the same direction and almost contemporaneously, the 1963 Montreal conference strongly criticized the principle of "Scripture alone" as illusory, preferring instead a dynamic concept of the relations between Scripture and Tradition. It declared:

> Thus we can say that we exist as Christians by the Tradition of the Gospel (the *paradosis* of the *kerygma*) testified in Scripture, transmitted in and by the Church through the power of the Holy Spirit. Tradition taken in this sense is actualized in the preaching of the word, in the administration of the sacraments and worship, in Christian teaching and theology, and in mission and witness to Christ by the lives of the members of the Church.[2]

According to these ecumenical texts, Tradition is the life of the Gospel and the Spirit in the Church. The living tradition of the Church cannot be opposed to Scripture. Without this Tradition, Scripture could never have reached us or would remain incomprehensible to us. The Tradition is the Holy Spirit explaining the Gospel to the Church. On the other hand, without Scripture, the Tradition would have neither norm nor limit: without the necessary control of a written Word, everything would be possible in the speech and life of the Church. The living Tradition of the Church is where the freedom and diversity of the gifts of the Spirit are manifested, under the custodianship of the written Word which attests to us the first tradition and transmission of the Gospel, source of the life of the Church in faith. The living Tradition authorizes us to accept all that is not contrary to the witness of Holy Scripture, all that manifests the life of the Gospel in the Church guided by the Spirit. We have to heed all that the Holy Spirit has enabled the Church to explore more deeply in the history of salvation and in the life of Christians. The Tradition brings us advances in the heart's understanding which, insofar as they enable us to understand more deeply the initial truth contained in the Word of God attested by Scripture, should be welcomed and not neglected. There have, of course, been discordant develpments of this foundational truth. The criterion of truth will always require the Church to reject what is contrary to the truth of Holy Scripture and to welcome what glorifies the Word of God.

We are influenced, of course, by our interpretation of Scripture, by our appraisal of Tradition, by our intellectual, spiritual and confessional upbringing. But if we really seek to read the Bible ecumenically, listen attentively to the spiritual experience of others and approach in friendship every human being who desires faithfully to serve Christ, this will certainly require the pledge of a freedom and an objectivity in receiving the Word of God which are by no means illusory and which may perhaps open up new roads towards unity. In this reading of Scripture in the light of the Tradition, it is also right to distinguish clearly between that which is necessary from the standpoint of the essential faith, and that which is optional from the standpoint of piety, in accordance with the old theological principle: 'Unity in things necessary, liberty in things doubtful, charity in everything.'

This ecumenical view of relations between Scripture and Tradition was summed up by a consultation of Faith and Order and the Vatican Unity Secretariat held in Venice in June 1978 in the distinction it made between *the normative, apostolic period* and *the building period of the Church*, that of the church fathers, the creeds, the first liturgies and of the great ecumenical councils.

The essential elements of the Christian mystery are known to us through the witness of the apostolic community, transmitted in the scriptures. These are the fruit of the Gospel and of the action of the Spirit in the primitive Church. On the one hand, they bear witness to the apostolic Church's understanding of the mystery of Christ. On the other hand, however, the truth they transmit could be fully grasped only in the context of the life of that early community faithful to the teaching of the apostles, to the fellowship of the brethren, to the breaking of the bread and to prayer (cf. Acts 2:42). ... After *the normative, apostolic* period, the Church, bearer of the Spirit but engaged in history, saw itself led to make more explicit the faith it had received from the apostles. What it lived in its liturgy and bore witness to, sometimes to the point of martyrdom, it had to express in terms which would allow it to safeguard its unity and give an account of its hope. At that time it was immersed in a particular culture, permeated with the concepts of Greek philosophy, and subject to various political situations. However, this effort to find in this new cultural and historical context an adequate expression of its faith was an essential contribution to the course of its history. In formulating the faith it enriched the Christian heritage. In fact the Spirit then led the Church to make explicit the elements necessary for its communion with the apostolic faith.

This *building period* is that of the Fathers, of the creeds, of the birth of the great liturgies, of the great Councils. The conciliar definitions about God-in-Trinity and the person of Christ Jesus, particularly, gave the Church a steady vision of the points that are at the very heart of its understanding of the Christian mystery. Certainly in every age the Church lives and grows in the Holy Spirit and thus builds itself up in charity and faith. Moreover, since their divisions, the churches have provided themselves with either conciliar decrees or confessions to which they attach a real authority. But this authority remains always subject not only to the authority of Scripture but also to that of those universally received documents which concern the centre of faith and which the Church holds from this period, known for this reason as its building period.[3]

NOTES

1. *Dei Verbum* No. 9, ET from *Documents of Vatican II*, ed. Austin P. Flannery, Eerdmans, Grand Rapids, 1975.
2. *Montreal Report*, Section II, para. 45, p. 52.
3. Towards a Common Confession of Faith, *Faith and Order Paper* 100, Geneva, WCC, 1980 p.3-4.

UNITY IN FAITH

Lukas Vischer

"Visible unity in one faith and in one eucharistic fellowship" —
this is how the goal of the ecumenical movement is defined both in
the Basis of the World Council of Churches and in the By-Laws of
the Faith and Order Commission. The conviction underlying this
definition is clear. The unity of the Church becomes visible in the
common *confession of the apostolic faith* and in the *celebration of
the eucharist*. If there is to be an advance towards visible unity between the churches which are still divided today, they must turn their
attention energetically towards these two requirements.

The three texts presented by the Faith and Order Commission seek
to make it easier for the churches to do this. They are summaries of
what theologians from different traditions are able to say together
today about baptism, the Lord's Supper and the ministry. It is some
years since the texts were first submitted to the churches for comment, and they have now been revised in the light of the comments
received. They enable the churches to see clearly, therefore, the
agreement which has been steadily growing in the ecumenical movement through the years, and which robs some past controversies of
their validity or at least of their sharpness.

But what significance does this agreement on baptism, Lord's Supper and ministry have for "visible unity in the one *faith*"? The three
texts would seem at first sight to be concerned, above all, with "visible unity in one *eucharistic fellowship*". Nor is the Faith and Order
Commission itself unaware of this. In presenting these three texts it is
certainly not claiming to have already answered the question of the

---

• Formerly Director of the Faith and Order Secretariat, Lukas Vischer is at present in
charge of the Protestant Office for Ecumenism in Switzerland.

one apostolic faith. The fact that it has for some years now been working on another project, on the question of how the churches can confess and proclaim together in a way appropriate to our contemporary situation, the faith of the apostles in accordance with the witness of the Church of all ages — in itself shows that it makes no such claim. The first phase of this other project — under the title "Accounting for the Hope that is Within Us" — was an attempt to give a common account of the basis of the Christian hope. It had been initiated at the Commission's meeting in Louvain (1971) and it culminated in "A Common Account of Hope" adopted unanimously at the Commission's meeting in Bangalore (1978). The second phase, initiated in Bangalore, is entitled "Towards the Common Expression of the Apostolic Faith Today". How is the apostolic faith confessed in all ages to be received and confessed by the churches together today? That is the problem and task now being tackled. In the first phase, the starting point for the study was, logically enough, the witness of the Church in the contemporary world. Now, however, we have to turn our attention to the question: How can the confession which has ensured the unity of the Church from generation to generation be developed as basis for unity in our present age?

Are we to infer from this other study that the convergence on baptism, Lord's Supper and ministry has no implications whatever for the "unity in the one faith"? Not at all! There is an inseparable connection between unity in faith and unity in the eucharist. This conviction is reflected in the preface to the Commission's three texts. There the churches are asked to state what consequences follow, in their view, from the convergence on baptism, Lord's Supper and ministry for the visible unity of the Church in one faith. The tacit assumption of this request to the churches is that the agreement on baptism, Lord's Supper and ministry is, in some sense, also an expression of the apostolic faith, with consequences therefore, for visible unity in the one faith.

Is it possible to define more precisely the relationship between these two levels of unity?

Conflicting concepts

If we are to achieve an answer to this question, it is vital to remember that there is no unanimity among the churches about what is meant by unity in the one faith or how it is to be expresed. Three observations are especially important in this connection.

Firstly, there is a difference in the *degree of agreement* which the individual churches consider to be indispensable. Whereas some would limit explicit agreement to a few basic affirmations, others are inclined to widen the area of agreement required. The latter require recognition not only of the ancient church creeds but also of later doctrinal decisions, such as conciliar decisions, the confessions of the sixteenth and seventeenth centuries, and so on. Depending on how much agreement is required in each case, the churches adopt different attitudes to the question of permissible diversity in understanding and proclaiming the faith. If the churches seriously want to set their sights on the goal of visible unity, therefore, one of the points on which agreement is needed is the degree of agreement visible unity requires.

A second difference relates to the significance of *written confessions*. While there are many churches which take for granted the view that unity in the faith must find expression in formal confessions, there are others which insist that the apostolic faith is at least equally attested by the Church's worship and life. Most churches assume that exemplary expression was given to the apostolic faith in the ancient church creeds. To these some would add other formulations of the faith and perhaps also consider that the faith must be confessed today in new forms, as indeed it must be in every generation. But however they may differ in detail, they are nevertheless governed by the conviction that the common faith achieves visibility, above all, in agreed statements. The others, however, question whether this assumption is really valid. In the life of the Church, the role actually played by written confessions is surely only a secondary one. Solidarity in faith is surely expressed in other quite different ways — in ways of worship, in the liturgy, in prayers, in spirituality, in ethical attitudes, in stories taken from the history of the Church. The list could be continued almost indefinitely. Misunderstandings often arise in ecumenical discussion because of our different views of formal confessions. Even if partners in the dialogue agree to produce common statements, they may still be completely at cross purposes because, in the last analysis, they do not assign the same significance to these agreed statements.

The third and final difference to be mentioned here concerns the *function* of formal confessions of faith in the life of the Church. Various functions could be mentioned here. In almost all the churches, the confession of faith has its place in worship, especially in the celebration of baptism and the eucharist. Here it enables the assembled community to focus attention on its faith and to confess it together. But the confession also has a function in preaching and instruction. It reminds the Church of the essence of the message which it must pass on in its preaching and teaching. This function comes to the forefront when ordinands are required to assent to the confession of faith at their ordination. Finally, the confession of faith plays an important role when the Church is required to take decisions in which truth must be distinguished from error. To the extent that a church attaches any importance at all to the confession of faith, none of these functions will be completely absent. But they differ in the choice of the function to which priority is assigned. While some mainly stress the dimension of liturgical doxology in the confession of faith, others regard the confession primarily as a basis for faithful transmission of the gospel in preaching and teaching. In the former case, the confession is completely embedded in the liturgical event, whereas in the latter, it also has a life outsides the service of worship, indeed is sometimes quite independent of worship altogether. Confessions of faith which have been designed for catechetical purposes are not usually recited in worship, or only in exceptional cases.

What is the significance of these differences for the question under consideration? Quite clearly the decision taken on these three matters will mean differences in the view taken of the relation between "unity in the one faith" and "unity in one eucharistic fellowship". Two tendencies can be identified.

Some take the view that, while indeed making an important contribution to unity in the one faith, the texts on baptism, eucharist and ministry represent in the last analysis no more than a first step. It is clearly still necessary to reach agreement on the one apostolic faith. The Faith and Order Commission's texts are indeed important for the common answers they offer to certain themes or aspects of the apostolic faith. But the question as to whether the churches share the same faith is decided *at a different level*. Here agreement is required on the main contents of the kerygma transmitted in the tradition. There must be common reflection on the confesssions of faith. But whatever our detailed view of the task may be, there can be no doubt that it goes much further than the agreement on baptism, the Lord's Supper and ministry — is indeed even independent of it.

Others tended to a contrary view: namely, that in reaching agreement on baptism, eucharist and ministry, agreement has also been reached on the apostolic faith. Baptism, the Lords' Supper and church structure are not independent themes, separated or separable from the apostolic faith. On the contrary, everything the Church must confess and proclaim is already contained in them, expressed or at least indicated in them. In a certain sense, baptism, the Lord's Supper and the church structure willed by Christ are a summary of the Gospel. They are like a mirror in which the faith of the Church can be recognized. Agreement here, therefore, is *already implicitly agreement in the understanding of the Gospel.* Further steps may certainly be required. The existing agreement must be made fruitful for preaching and instruction. However difficult this task may be, though it amounts in the last analysis to no more than the development of what has already been achieved. The still-divided churches would be well-advised, therefore, to start living in accordance with the agreement proposed by the Faith and Order Commission. The more they let it guide their steps, the more they will discover that, basically, they are already one in the apostolic faith. The truth of the old maxim *lex orandi lex credendi* will be confirmed.

Two important approaches

What are we to think of these two tendencies? Each is inadequate and open to criticism.

In the first place it must be insisted that the question of the one faith has in fact already been raised in the question of baptism, eucharist and ministry. The entire Faith and Order Commission study is based on this assumption. The apostolic faith is confessed not only by words but also *in and through the sacraments and structures of the Church.* The apostolic faith is not a theory or system to be understood and transmitted from generation to generation. It is of its very essence, rather, to be experienced and understood only in the fellowship of those who believe. God has called this fellowship in Christ. He upholds it throughout the centuries by the power of the Holy Spirit. But it is not something constantly created *de novo.* On the contrary, it has been profiled from the very beginning by certain sacramental structures assigned to it by the risen Christ himself. It consists of members who have received baptism and in this way been led into a new life. It is a fellowship which experiences the presence of Christ afresh over and over again in the eucharistic meal. It recognizes a ministry whose task is to gather it together around the Word and sacrament. It can really understand and confess the apostolic faith only as it lives *in* these structures; indeed, in a real sense, it has *already* confessed that faith by committing itself to these structures. It has been created as a confessing community. Even before it ever opens its mouth to formulate the message, therefore, it has always already confessed the apostolic faith, or even denied it.

The basic structure of baptism, Lord's Supper and ministry all issue in one and the same goal. They unite the members in common thanksgiving. They bring home what was revealed in Christ and give opportunity for the community to invoke the Spirit to make the promise of Christ good for today. Through these structures the Church is led to hear and confess the gospel.

How the Church deals with these structures is crucial, therefore, for the unity in the one faith. The agreement achieved by the Faith and Order Commission is extremely important in this context. The three texts show the churches how to find their way back from their present divisions to that fundamental unity which is the precondition for hearing and confessing the Gospel. In the Eastern liturgy, the confession is preceded directly by the exhortation: "Let us love, that we may together confess the faith!" Basically, the three texts on baptism, eucharist and ministry are simply a summons to the churches to be united in this mutual love. By clearing space again for this fellowship given and willed by Christ, they will also be re-enabled to confess the apostolic faith.

Having said that, it is certainly necessary to make the second point. Important though the basic sacramental structures are, they cannot on their own suffice to guarantee the unity in the apostolic faith. Although the agreement on baptism, the Lord's Supper and ministry is already itself a common confession of faith, the question still remains: *How can the message entrusted to the apostles be interpreted, proclaimed and transmitted by the churches together today?* This question cannot be answered on the basis of the agreement on baptism, the Lord's Supper and ministry alone. While this agreement is undoubtedly one of the pre-conditions for the answer, it is not itself the answer. If we are to confess the one faith together, an effort which goes beyond this agreement is needed.

In particular, unity in the faith must be demonstrated in the proclamation of the Gospel. For it is when the Church begins to interpret and proclaim the message entrusted to it that the danger to its unity becomes acute. It then has to understand clearly what the Gospel means in the specific situation in which the Church finds itself. It must try to read and understand the "signs of the times". On the basis of its faith in the crucified, risen and returning Lord, it must recognize what is to be said to that situation and what ethical consequences must be drawn. Profound differences can then arise. Above all, the ways can divide when the Church is faced with a new question to which no answer is already available in the Tradition. The story of divisions in the Church is the story of divergent interpretations which proved impossible to reconcile and which hardened into creeds or "confessions".

If unity in the one apostolic faith is to be maintained and demonstrated afresh again and again, therefore, new ways must be found which make it possible for us to agree on the interpretation of the Christian faith. For the apostolic faith is certainly not just a fixed number of statements which can be handed down to others. It is a living message intended to be heard and proclaimed afresh, again and again. The Church must therefore be a community which is constantly wrestling with questions. At the same time, however, it must also be prepared to undertake the risky venture of giving common answers to these questions. The sacramental structures remind the Church of the source of its being and life. The ancient church creeds set before it the exemplary response of the early centuries. But if it is to be enabled to respond today with a common answer, it has to turn afresh to the living Word. The Church must seek to learn from the scriptures what it has to say today. It will seek to listen also to the answers given by previous generations through the centuries. It realizes, however, that its task remains unfulfilled so long as it does no more than repeat these answers. Only as it examines the questions raised by the contemporary situation can it really proclaim the apostolic faith. Just as the Church of the early centuries was a conciliar fellowship, so the Church continues to be a conciliar fellowship which reinterprets and confesses anew. This commitment to agreed knowledge and understanding is the necessary condition to be fulfilled if the faith and convictions of individual church members, for all their legitimate diversity, are to be held together in unity.

But what is the significance of these two approaches for the churches which are invited to respond to the texts presented to them by the Faith and Order Commission? The challenge is not the same for all the churches.

It is undoubtedly the churches which attach only *secondary importance* to the sacramental structures of fellowship which are primarily challenged here — that is, the Reformation churches who were led by the experience of the sixteenth century to subject themselves resolutely both in worship and in daily life to the authority of the Word of God as attested in the Scriptures. The importance of this experience is in no way impugned in the Faith and Order Commision's texts. The question these texts do raise, however, is whether the Reformation churches, in emphasising the living Word, do not under-rate the significance of the sacramental structures of fellowship. The Church is not constantly being completely reborn of the Word alone. The very moment it turns to the Word, it is already indelibly marked by these sacramental structures; the celebration of the sacraments makes it receptive to the Word. Baptism and the Lord's Supper are not only secondary signs confirming the Word. They also, at the same time, lead up to the Word. A great deal depends, therefore, on the way a church deals with the sacramental structures. Neglect of them deprives the proclamation of the basis which sustains and protects it. The Commission's texts are a summons to rectify this situation, an invitation to give more room to the sacramental structures in the life of the Church and to let their full significance shine out more clearly. In this connection, one of the most important statements in the entire document perhaps is the recommendation that the eucharist should be celebrated regularly, at least every Sunday.

But is the challenge only directed to this address? It may be tempting for the churches which have always attached greater weight to the sacramental structures to think so. They may welcome the Faith and Order Commission's texts because these invite the Reformation churches to move in their direction; it could be seen as a first step, to be followed later by others. Views of this sort have already been expressed. But they are based on a misunderstanding. The texts on baptism, eucharist and ministry also address a challenge to churches in the "catholic" tradition. The question here is basically the same: it concerns the relationship between the living Word and the sacramental structures of the Church. How far is the unity of the Church really based on the sacramental structures? The experience of the Reformers and of the Reformation churches also counsels caution and restraint in this respect. The living Word becomes truly free only when the Church takes the step in the direction of common confession. Unity in the sacramental structures *can* be a dead unity. The Gospel needs to be proclaimed together concretely today. The Faith and Order Commision's text can only lead to unity, therefore, when the churches are ready to create, here and now, a fellowship in which it will be possible for them to examine together what the Spirit of God has to say to the Church today. Only the readiness for this contemporary expression of the faith will make clear the real significance of baptism, Lord's Supper and ministry in the life of the Church.

Implications for the study on the common expression of the faith

From what has already been said, it is not difficult to understand the importance of the decision of the Faith and Order Commission to turn to the question of the "common expression of the apostolic faith today". What can be said about this study? Five thoughts on this are offered in conclusion.

1. It should firstly be emphasized that this new project is very closely connected to the study on "Baptism, Eucharist and Ministry". It is the organic continuation and complement to that earlier study. The new project must build on the already achieved agreement on baptism, the Lord's Supper and ministry. It must not lose sight of the fact that that agreement is already a first common expression of the apostolic faith. Not that the common expression we seek of the apostolic faith is to be simply deduced from it. As we have already seen, the new project must go much further than that. At the same time, however, it must not be undertaken independently of the agreement already achieved. For even though the common expression of the apostolic faith contains far more than what is confessed in worship and the liturgy, it is nevertheless rooted in Christian worship and has its place there.

2. The continuation of work on the texts on baptism, eucharist and ministry must therefore be regarded in principle as part of the new project. The three texts still leave many questions open. They propose a provisional common view of the three themes. But real agreement will only be achieved when the churches feel prepared to let this common understanding lead them to common practice or at least to a practice which is explicitly recognized as mutual. In other words, the texts call for reforms on the part of all the churches. There will be innumerable questions in this connection. To what extent must the practice of the churches be uniform? When does the moment of mutual recognition arrive? If in some sense it is true that the agreement on baptism, eucharist and ministry is a common expression of the apostolic faith, every step towards agreement in the life of the churches is obviously at the same time a contribution to the new project.

Nothing specific is said in the texts of the way the apostolic faith should be confessed in baptism, eucharist and ordination. One of the first steps in the new project would certainly have to be a clarification of this question and a closer approach to an answer. At its Lima meeting, the Faith and Order Commission summoned the churches to recognize the *Niceno-Constantinopolitan Creed* as a fundamental confession of the Church. But this proposal certainly requires further clarification. There is certainly a great deal to be said in favour of the suggestion that the churches should gather together around this creed which is still the one most universally recognized. But what would such a "gathering around" mean? What questions still need clearing up before this creed can really be regarded as a common confession? Can an appeal to recognize this creed disregard the different views taken of it? Would recognition mean the regular recitation of this creed — perhaps of this creed alone — in Christian worship? Or could we conceive the confession of the apostolic faith in Christian worship taking a variety of forms?

3. Another question to which the new study will need to turn is that of ways and means of confessing the apostolic faith together in the contemporary world in all its diverse situations. On the one hand, the churches seek to come closer together in the ecumenical movement; on the other hand, they are in danger of becoming divided again as they confront the questions of our time. The project must provide some help to enable them to deal with these questions together. Can they do this by working at the common interpretation of the ancient church creeds — the *Niceno-Constantinopolitan Creed* in particular? Perhaps to some extent, yes. But they will soon discover that these creeds do not furnish all the pointers they need for their common response. Questions arise today which had then not even entered the purview of the Church. The project must therefore be ready for new answers which, if certainly not in contradiction to the ancient church creeds, cannot nevertheless be deduced from them.

4. The project must take into account the diverse situations in the contemporary ecumenical movement. The common expression of the faith which it seeks to achieve will in principle have to allow room for a diversity of expressions. It is of the very essence of the apostolic faith to be able to enter into the different cultures. The final outcome of the project, therefore, can hardly be a uniform statement valid uniformly for the Church in all situations. On the contrary, the common expression of the faith will be distinguished by the tension

between common statements and statements which are, at first sight at least, different. It was never possible in the history of the Church to escape this tension, but it is more inescapable than ever today.

What is it, however, which holds the Church together in this diversity of confessional action? A number of different factors may be mentioned: the witness of Scripture, the celebration of Christian worship (above all, baptism and the eucharist), the common tradition in which the Church lives and to which it must give account of itself. And, we surely have to add: the readiness to account to each other for their proclamation and to learn from each other's account.

In this connection, the importance of the sacramental structures of fellowship once again becomes clear. If the churches really allow the agreement on baptism, the Lord's Supper and ministry to influence their life profoundly, they will be all the better equipped to deal with this tension between the common ground in our expression of the apostolic faith and the differences in the way it is expressed.

5. The aim of the project must be to create the basis for a conciliar fellowship in which the churches not only mutually recognize one another but also confess the apostolic faith together in ever new ways. This calls, on the one hand, for sufficient agreement in our understanding of the faith to make explicit mutual recognition and fellowship possible. On the other hand, we also need conciliar structures in order to be able to practise the unity of faith and proclamation. If these structures are to become a reality, work must begin on them *now*. Conciliar fellowship is not just a far-distant goal in some indefinite future. On the contrary, it is a task we are already being called to today. The churches must come together so that unity in the one faith may grow among them. They need the conciliar fellowship in order, on the one hand, to achieve a common view of the creeds of the ancient Church and, on the other hand, by wrestling together with the Scriptures and by reflection on the Tradition, to find the answers we need to the questions of our time. The project will also have to give some thought, therefore, to ways and means whereby this conciliar fellowship may already begin to take shape now.

BAPTISM FROM ACCRA TO LIMA

GUNTER WAGNER

The Lima (1982) text on Baptism is the Accra (1974) "agreed statement"[1] in a considerably revised form. The factors which have contributed to the revision include the response of the churches[2] to the document emerging from Accra, the Louisville Consultation on Baptism[3] 1979, which dealt especially with the debate on infant baptism and believers' baptism, and the continued effort of the Working Group to integrate all responses, including those of the members of the Faith and Order Commission made before and during the Lima meeting. The development of the text between Accra and Lima need not be traced step by step and in each detail; the text must — and will — speak for itself. However, a comparison of the Accra and Lima versions might help us to understand the revised version and the significance of the changes; and a concluding reflection on the recognition of both forms of baptism (here from the perspective of a Baptist) might help us to focus not only on where we now stand, but also on how we can possibly move forward, facing the challenges involved in this sensitive issue — an issue of increasing concern among and within the churches.

• Gunter Wagner is Professor of New Testament in the Baptist Theological Seminary of Ruschlikon (Switzerland).

* The author wishes to dedicate this chapter to Eduard Schweizer, member of the Faith and Order Commission 1968-1975, on the occasion of his seventieth birthday in April 1983. In Accra he reminded the Commission: "Jesus is certainly going ahead, and from wherever we may come to follow him, he will go before us to the same centre, to the coming of the kingdom of God." After Lima we are even more hopeful that one day we will all find ourselves as followers of Jesus Christ *at the centre* — even on this still divisive issue of baptism.

I. From Accra to Lima

1.1 It deserves to be mentioned, first of all, that the general substance of the Accra document (= A) has been preserved in the Lima text (= L), with one notable exception: the paragraph on "Eucharistic Sharing", spelling out one of the "Implications of Baptism" (A§6), has been omitted altogether.[4] This is most regrettable and hard to understand (and as far as I can see, the Lima text on the "Eucharist" does not repair the damage.) At the same time, four new paragraphs have been added, three of which contribute to the exposition of the meaning of baptism: one deals with the various images of baptism as found in the New Testament (L§2), a second with conversion, pardoning and cleansing as part of the baptismal experience (L§4), and the third sees in baptism the sign of the kingdom of God and of the life of the world to come (L§7). The fourth new paragraph (L§11) is based on one of the agreements reached in Louisville[5] and deals with the development of believers' and infant baptism in the practice of the Church.[6]

1.2 Besides the omission and the additions just mentioned, there are a number of changes, first noticeable in the outline and arrangement of the material. Both documents begin with the two headings of "The Insitution of Baptism" and "The Meaning of Baptism", the second one being considerably enlarged in the Lima text, not only by those three new paragraphs, but also by treating "The Gift of the Spirit" and "Incorporation into the Body of Christ" separately and by including in the latter (L§6) the substance of A§5 ("Bond of Unity"). The more recent treatment, then, results in a very welcome accentuation of the *meaning* of baptism. A second accent is on the heading, "Baptism and Faith", which appeared in the Accra document under "The Meaning of Baptism." The three paragraphs under this heading make use also of A§7, "Commitment and Witness to Christ", so that all material which once appeared under the third heading of the Accra paper, "Implications of Baptism", has either been dropped or redistributed. The challenge implied in the meaning of baptism, namely its dynamic toward unity, eucharistic sharing and a committed fellowship — all of which was spelled out in the Accra document — is, however, not completely lost; but it is no longer thematized and seems to have given way to a poised and synthesizing reflection on *Baptism and Faith*. Does this shift reflect a sort of consolidating, rather than venturesome, mood on the part of the churches whose responses have led the Working Group in such direction?

The remaining fourth and fifth headings of the Lima text, "Baptismal Practice" and "Celebration of Baptism", drastically rearrange what one could read under the three last headings of the Accra statement.[7] One is struck by the reduction of five paragraphs from Accra to one (plus "commentary") from Lima: *Confirmation* (A§§15-19; L§14)[8] seems to be a problem. And this, too, calls for reflection because one needs to consider its potential for the whole process of Christian initiation; and the unity of Christian initiation, in turn, is of the greatest importance for inter-church relationships. On the whole, one might say, the changes in the outline and arrangement of the material in the Lima text over against the Accra statement lead one to a better grasp of the meaning of baptism; a prominent place is given to the question of the relation between baptism and faith; and the paper's thrust appears to be toward the mutual recognition of baptism, rather than toward the mutual acceptance at the Lord's Table on the basis of our common baptism.

1.3 Other changes on the way from Accra to Lima can be recognized when one looks at the texts, paragraph by paragraph, following the numbering of the Lima document. Before we do this, we may proudly report that one paragraph has remained the same word by word. It is L§17 (= A§9), which reads in its entirety: "Baptism is administered with water in the name of the Father, the Son and the Holy Spirit." The silver medal in the paragraphs' contest for survival goes to L§22, which improves the style of A§8 by saying: "Baptism is normally administered by an ordained minister, though in certain circumstances others are allowed to baptize." Bronze is to be awarded L§23: it drops Christmas from the enumeration of the "great festival occasions" to which "the sacrament is appropriate" and omits the pedestrian explanation why Easter and Pentecost are such meaningful dates (contrast A§20).

L§1 The institution of baptism

A§1 put the emphasis on the "dominical institution," "origin" of baptism in the earthly life of Jesus and its ancient practice in the Church. L§1 strikes the reader by including sentences which seem to belong under the heading of the *meaning* of baptism, rather than its *institution*. Such arrangement, however, does not appear to be an oversight; for one's understanding of the meaning of the rite determines also one's description of its institution: Baptism is "rooted" in the total Christ event and is a gift of the triune God (A§1 "Christ's gift";

but see A§3). Next to Matthew 28:18-20, the living tradition of the Church, practising baptism as "a rite of commitment," receives its due weight. It may be hoped that theologians strongly advocating the "trinitarian approach" and exegetes with their historical-critical interpretation of Matthew 28:18-20 will find the new text more acceptable.

L§2 The meaning of baptism

The response of the churches to the Accra document revealed notable agreement concerning the meaning of baptism:

"It can be summarized in the following three sentences which are interdependent:
— The central meaning of baptism is incorporation in Christ, and participation in his death and resurrection.
— In baptism, the Spirit of Pentecost both gives and is given, so that we are united to Christ and with each other.
— Baptism is fundamental and constitutive for membership in the body of Christ and cannot be conceived apart from faith, personal commitment and life-long growth."[9]

In the Lima text the meaning of baptism is expounded with much more care than was the case in Accra. First of all, it is pointed out that the one reality of baptism is reflected in the New Testament writings through a great variety of images. This general characterization of the rite prepares for the following exposition, which goes beyond "Accra" and still cannot claim to be exhaustive. Two thoughts come to mind here: (1) Does not the variety of biblical images encourage a greater variety in our use of symbols in the celebration of baptism? L§§ 18-19 seem to be sensitive to this question. (2) If there is such an obvious variety of images, what then is the relationship between the reality symbolized and the symbol as such? Does the reality coincide with the symbolic action? Or does it precede or follow it? Are symbol and reality truly congruous?

L§3 Participation in Christ's death and resurrection

A§2 offered "the key to a common understanding" of "the central meaning of baptism" (as evidenced in the above title), and that key was a concept of Jesus' own baptism as having been comprised of his whole life from the Jordan to the resurrection. The idea was based on an earlier Faith and Order study which made Jesus' baptism constitutive for the understanding of Christian baptism.[10] This approach was eventually found unacceptable: one cannot condense Jesus' baptism, his life, death, resurrection, the manifestation of the Spirit at the Jordan and at Pentecost into a kind of super-baptism, in which we are made to share. While "Accra" made Jesus' baptism *begin* at the Jordan and *continue* in his passion, "Lima" says that his baptism "led Jesus along the way of the Suffering Servant..." From here, our baptism could have been understood as our commitment to discipleship. In fact, the last version of the text, circulated before Lima, began with the sentence: "Baptism means following in the way of Jesus Christ"; but this was changed in the present text. A last-minute attempt at Lima to restore the pre-Lima version did not find the approval of the three-man jury on the platform. If baptism means a "sacramental" participation in the death and resurrection of Jesus Christ, how do we participate in the *life* of Jesus?[11] Sacramentally or by discipleship? Or is this the wrong question? In any case, through baptism "into Christ" we are united with the Crucified and the Risen One. If this results in more than being "forgiven" (A§2), if through baptism "the power of sin is broken" and the "baptized are no longer slaves to sin, but free," does not this language require an existential interpretation? Romans 6, which is being used here, contains that existential element. The text of Lima rightly distinguishes between "a new life in the power of the resurrection" and our "ultimate" resurrection still in the future. The distinction has important consequences for the eschatological orientation of baptism, for its proleptic character, and for its dynamics issuing in a process of growth. The document comes back to this aspect of the meaning of baptism.[12]

L§4 Conversion, pardoning and cleansing

This new paragraph is self-explanatory. It is true to a constitutive element in baptism that can be traced from the time of John the Baptist onward, and it is certainly in harmony with the "classical" text of Romans 6: baptism and conversion go together (however differently the churches may interpret the words "implies" and "implications"). The "baptismal experience" provides "a new ethical orientation"[13] — *hopefully*, one is inclined to say, when one remembers the contemporary dictators, tyrants, torturers and ruthless exploiters among the baptized!

L§5 The gift of the Spirit

The parallel in A§3 was an extremely compact paragraph with rather abrupt sentences, and the Lima text tries to disentangle it. L§5 omits the problematic sentence: "The Spirit both gives and is given in baptism"; but retained in L§14 is the phrase from A§15 which states that baptism "signifies and effects both" participation in Christ's death and resurrection and the receiving of the Spirit — adding, however, that baptism *in its full meaning* does it. The word *full* here mystifies the reader and continues to do so as it crops up later in L§10 ("the full significance of the one baptism") and the L§12 "Commentary" ("the full fruit of baptism"). Such language points to a lack of clarity. Commenting on A§§3 and 15 (= L§§5 and 14) G. Wainwright says:

> I suspect that some of the deepest divisions in the area of Christian initiation concern the anthropology and theology of *signs*. How far does the performance of signs *produce* the reality which they signify? How far is any such production instantaneous, and how far is it spread over a future time-span? How far, on the other hand, does the performance of signs *presuppose* already the existence of the reality signified? In what measure must the reality be present before the signs are allowed to express it?[14]

For the time being L§5 gets around the difficulty with the ingenious (and true) sentence that "the Holy Spirit is at work in the lives of people before, in and after their baptism," thus avoiding the establishment of a fixed time of the reception of the Spirit. L§14 also shows some flexibility in the question. Employing New Testament language, the gift of the Spirit is called a "seal" and "the first instalment of their inheritance as sons and daughters of God", thus highlighting again (cf. L§3) the eschatological orientation of the spiritual life of the baptized.

L§6 Incorporation into the Body of Christ

This paragraph combines parts of A§§3 and 5 and offers new formulations. There is a significant omission from A§3, namely: "Baptism is a gift of God's redeeming love and *is received by those who believe in Jesus Christ*."[15] The latter phrase would not cover infant baptism and cannot be maintained in a paragraph that dwells on our "one baptism," "common baptism" and "baptismal unity"; however, the characterization of baptism as "a sign and seal of our discipleship" has been kept, though with the addition of the word "common". Does this mean that every baptized person *is* a disciple or that there is something like a corporate discipleship of the Church?

"Through their *one* baptism..." (A§5) has been changed into "Through their *own* baptism..." Indeed, in the response of the churches there was the warning: "We must beware of shouting baptismal unity, baptismal unity, where honestly there is no more than a common use of words and language." And one is bound to ask: "Is it in fact 'the one baptism,' when understandings and practices vary as widely as they do?"[16] Still, the Lima text rightly continues to speak of the "one baptism," quoting Ephesians 4:4-6: Christian baptism is one because it is baptism "into Christ"; and, as such, it unites the baptized with Christ and his body, "with the Church of every time and place" (A§5 said "into the life of the Church Universal").

Because baptism "unites us to Christ *in faith*" (A§5"... in the context of faith", evidently with the believing community in mind), it is "a basic bond of unity." The Lima text is more reluctant than the Accra version to imply unity as a fact based on the rite. The "one baptism" is no *deus ex machina*. "Baptismal unity" is "given *in Christ*" (L§15); "*genuine* baptismal unity" needs to be "*recovered*" (L§6 Commentary); it is "within a fellowship of witness and service" that "*the full significance* of the one baptism as the gift of God to all his people" will be "*discovered*" (L§10). L§6 looks forward to the time "when baptismal unity is realized in one holy, catholic, apostolic Church."

We must not allow our affirmation of baptismal unity to remain empty talk;[17] for all churches "baptism into Christ constitutes a call... to overcome their divisions and visibly manifest their fellowship" and the common commitment of all their members.

L§7 The sign of the Kingdom

The importance of the orientation of baptism towards the future has already been observed in L.3. Many replies of the churches pointed to the necessity of stressing the eschatological dimension of baptism. "Lima" simply edited a summary of such responses made at Crêt-Bérard.[18]

L§§8-10 Baptism and faith

These three paragraphs correspond to A§§4 and 7. L§8 begins with a sentence from A§7 which reads: "Baptism is both God's gift and human *commitment*..." This has now become: "Baptism is both God's gift and *our* human *response to that gift*." In other words, like the omission mentioned above under L§6, the sentence is made to fit infant baptism in which the infant does not *commit* him/herself, but the Church can *respond*. One should note the use which L§12 makes of this shift in its new "Commentary": "The differences between infant and believers' baptism become less sharp when it is recognized that both forms of baptism embody God's own initiative in Christ *and express a response of faith made within the believing community*" However, the problem is still there: all churches acknowledge "the necessity of faith for the reception of the salvation embodied and set forth in baptism." Whose faith? Could it possiby be the Church's if the infant is to be the subject of the "reception"? The following sentence is equally difficult: "Personal commitment is necessary for responsible membership of the body of Christ." Is there an *un-responsible* membership? In which sense then could an infant be a "full" member of the body?

L§9 dwells on the orientation of baptism towards the future and meets the request for an elaboration of the idea of "growth into Christ." The response consists of a reference to 2 Cor. 3:18 and of a reminder that the life of the Christian is an ongoing struggle and a life of service empowered by an eschatological hope. This is to be welcomed. The language remains hazy, though, at two points: (1) What does it mean that "Baptism is *related*... to a life-long growth..."? Why not simply say: "Baptism marks the beginning of..."? At several points in the document one has the impression that certain terms, like faith and baptism, are stretched to cover more than they can at a closer look.[19] (2) "In this new relationship..." What is the antecedent? Wasn't A§4 clearer: "In faith and obedience..."?

The real subject of L§10 is baptism and new creation, and it makes one's heart rejoice (pardon me for this outburst!). In some sense it continues the thought of L§4, but at the same time it makes clear that baptism is not a private matter for self-centred pietists caring about their own salvation, but rather a highly "public" event, for people who begin to care about their witness, in word and deed, to "Christ, the Liberator of all human beings." Couldn't we agree on this, and wouldn't this wake up our churches? The first sentence of L§10 shows that one can speak about what the New Testament calls "new creation" without being presumptuous: "As they grow in the Christian life of faith, baptized believers demonstrate that humanity can be regenerated and liberated."[20]

L§§11-13 Baptism of believers and infants

The Accra document was optimistic enough to think that one could expect mutual recognition of baptism because of its "uniqueness" and because of the agreement that it is an "unrepeatable act" (A§22). The responses of some churches demonstrated that the co-existence of infant and believers' baptism is a real possibility; for others, complex issues remained yet unsolved.[21]

The Louisville Consultation has addressed itself to most of these questions and has provided some answers.[22] The "five significant points of agreement" read:

> 1. The acceptance that believers' baptism is the most clearly attested practice of baptism in the New Testament, together with the recognition that infant baptism has developed within the Christian tradition and witnesses to valid Christian insights.
> 2. The statement that the personal faith of the recipient and continuous participation in the life of the church are essential for the full fruit of baptism. In believers' baptism the believing community has played its part in the nurture of that personal faith, whilst in infant baptism, the supportive believing community surrounding the infant will nurture the child's personal faith as it moves toward discipleship.
> 3. The recognition in all the group reports that both forms of baptism require a similar and responsible attitude towards Christian nurture and a serious development of the concept of the Christian catechumenate.
> 4. The reminder that the pressures of contextuality have always borne in on the understanding and practice of baptism and that in these present days contextuality requires radical thinking by both groups as to what form of baptism they practise and why.
> 5. The conviction that indiscriminate baptism is seen as an abuse to be eliminated.[23]

The influence of these agreements can be seen most clearly in L§§11-12 and 21.[24] L§11, which is new, considers the fact that in the course of history two different practices of baptism have developed, and it acknowledges that "baptism upon personal profession of faith is the most clearly attested pattern in the New Testament documents."

L§12 restructures drastically the contents of A§12-14. Instead of characterizing infant baptism and believers' baptism separately, L§12 constantly switches back and forth between the two, trying to show how much they have in common and how their differences are somehow variations of the same theme: Both forms of baptism have their setting in the Church as the community of faith, and in both there is the response of faith. "In both cases, the baptized person will have to grow in the understanding of faith." All baptism is grounded in the grace and faithfulness of God in Christ. The comparatively lengthy and at times repetitious "commentary" L§12 calls attention to the need of Christian nurture in both traditions and leads to the question of whether both forms of baptism could be recognized as "equivalent alternatives for entry into the Church."

A few of the changes from the Accra text may bear quick comment: according to A§12 Baptists saw baptism as "the crowning moment and goal of the faith which turns to the Lord." Evidently it was not clear that the sentence meant to present baptism as the climax of conversion (when faith "turns to the Lord") rather than the goal of the pilgrimage of faith.

A§14 made the strong statement: "... in the baptism of infants, the rite does not take the place of faith, but demands it." It is weakened in L§12: "When an infant is baptized, the personal response will be offered at a later moment in life." And a new point is made in the "Commentary": "The differences between infant and believers' baptism become less sharp when it is recognized that *both* forms of baptism embody God's own initiative in Christ *and express a response of faith made within the believing community*." And finally, "The practice of infant baptism emphasizes the corporate faith *and the faith which the child shares with its parents*." The way from Accra to Lima has led us back to the assertion of the *faith of infants*. Consequently, while A§14 could point to the need of personal faith "if the fruits of baptism are to be known...", L§12"Commentary" reads"... for the *full* fruit of baptism." The word *full* is as vague as the meaning of the sentence, "The infant is born into a broken world and shares in its brokenness", in its context.

L§13 agrees in substance with A§22: Baptism is an unrepeatable act, and re-baptisms must be avoided.[25] The Lousiville Consultation reported:

> We all reject the notion of "re-baptism," for we all regard Baptism to be the unrepeatable act of commitment to the Lordship of Christ and of incorporation into his body.

At the same time it observed that

> in the Baptist tradition personal confession of faith is the necessary mark of a believer. Therefore, infant baptism is not generally recognized by Baptists.

...a serious difficulty arises when a person baptized in infancy applies for "believers" baptism. Paedo-baptists will regard such an act as rebaptism and therefore invite the person to renew his or her baptism vows through confession and partaking in the eucharist. Most Baptists, on the other hand, will admit such a person to believers' baptism, thereby implicitly regarding his or her infant baptism as no baptism. They would also consider it a violation of the individual's freedom of conscience if the request for believers' baptism were denied.[26]

In other words, there is agreement in the rejection of re-baptism, but still one church's "sacramental integrity" stands against another church's "sacramental integrity." The Lima report expresses the hope that practices which *might be interpreted* as "re-baptism" will stop "as the churches come to fuller mutual understanding and acceptance of one another and enter into closer relationships in witness and service."

L§14 Baptism — chrismation — confirmation
There is agreement that "Christian baptism is in water and the Holy Spirit"; there is disagreement "as to where the sign of the gift of the Spirit is to be found". "Baptism *in its full meaning* signifies and effects" participation in Christ's death and resurrection and the receiving of the Spirit. In other words, besides baptism there is no need for a *later and separate* chrismation and confirmation. There is no need of interposing another rite between baptism and admission to communion. In fact, the eucharist is the best occasion for a reaffirmation of baptismal vows. L§14 with its "commentary" brings clarity into the rather complicated Accra text (A§§15-19). One wonders, though, why the present text does not deal with "confirmation" as an occasion for a confession of faith, in which one baptized in infancy offers his/her personal response to the Gospel. L§12 says: "When an infant is baptized, the personal response will be afforded at a later moment in life." Does the Church make no (liturgical) provisions for it? L§8 recognizes that "personal commitment is necessary for responsible membership of the body of Christ." Does the Church not celebrate a fundamental act of personal commitment to Christ?[27]

L§§15-16 Towards mutual recognition of baptism
We shall deal with the important question of the recognition of both infant and believers' baptism under II.1

L§§17-23 The celebration of baptism

Concluding the sketchy survey of the development of the text between Accra and Lima, we need to note a few more changes related to reflections on the "celebration of baptism."

L§18 no longer recommends *immersion* as strongly as was the case in A§21: the reference to the normal practice of immersion "in the early centuries" and the suggestion that immersion would *"enhance the symbolism of the liturgy"* have disappeared from this paragraph; instead the new[28] paragraph 19 appeals to the practice "in the early centuries" to signify the gift of the Spirit (through the laying on of hands, by anointing or chrismation) and adds the sign of the cross — "the recovery of such vivid signs may be expected to *enrich the liturgy*". It always seems to be a question of *what use* one wants to make of ancient traditions! Still, the appeal to enrich baptismal liturgies needs to be heeded; and both paragraphs, including the new "commentary", which calls attention to other facets of water symbolism, make helpful suggestions.

Listing those elements which should have a place in "any comprehensive order of baptism," *L§20* replaces the acknowledgement of God's initiative (A§10 (a) by "proclamation" (which, naturally, should include the former); the profession of faith includes "the Holy Trinity" (A§10 (d): "and the affirmation of allegiance to God: Father, Son and Holy Spirit"); "the use of water" is added (to mention that may seem superfluous, but it is not; see L§21 (c); the last "element," the declaration of the new identity, links the status of the "sons and daughters" (A§10 (a): "child") of God and their being "witnesses to the Gospel" with their being "members of the Church." The concluding sentence of §20 is particularly interesting since it expresses the unity of Christian "initiation" as preserved by "some churches." Because of its inherent significance, it is good that the observation belongs to the text rather than to a "commentary".

L§21 is an adaptation of A§11 due to the expanded exposition of the "meaning of baptism" in L§§2,4 and 7. The "commentary" illustrates the unquestionable significance of "the socio-cultural context" for the understanding of the meaning of baptism, the "translation" of this meaning into vastly different settings, and the resulting need for a creative adaptation of the liturgy of baptism. One must not underestimate the importance of the subject[29] — after all, neither Jesus nor the Church invented the rite of water baptism, for it was a culturally "given" religious practice. The questions, therefore, hinted at in the "commentary" lie right at the historical beginnings of our "sacramental" ritual.

On *L§§22-23* we need not say more than was said under 1.3 above.

II. A Baptist response

2.1 We have postponed a comment on L§§15-16, "Towards Mutual Recognition of Baptism", because we should like to respond in the context of some broader reflections. Yet first it should be recorded that obviously some progress in regard to a mutual recognition has been made since the time of Accra because L§15 (unlike A§23) begins with the statement that "churches *are increasingly* recognizing each other's baptism. . ."[30] New is also the suggestion of an explicit expression of mutual recognition by the churches. In A§24 those who baptize infants were asked to "guard themselves against the practice of apparently indiscriminate baptism and (to) take more seriously their responsibility for the nurture of baptized children to mature commitment to Christ," and this sentence is preserved in L§16. However, the suggestion made to Baptists that they "consider afresh the values in responsible infant baptism" (A§24) has been replaced by the recommendation that they "may seek to express more visibly the fact that children are placed under the protection of God's grace" (L§16). I hasten to add, though, that the challenge which the document as a whole presents to Baptists goes far beyond the question whether they are willing to continue or to introduce a service of the blessing of children. In a sober mood the Lima text recognizes that "mutual baptismal recognition" has not ended the "actual dividedness" of the churches, yet it also expresses the view that "the need to recover baptismal unity is at the heart of the ecumenical task" (L§6 "Commentary"). Concretely, Baptists are asked whether they will refrain from *what others consider as* re-baptism (L§13), and whether they will regard infant baptism and believers' baptism as *"equivalent alternatives"* (L§12 "Commentary").

The latter will not be easy for any church, despite the definition in L§12 "Commentary" which seems to suggest that churches other than Baptist baptize people "at any age". This may be true in regard to adult converts, but — so far — it is not generally true as regards *the choice of the parent* to postpone the baptism of their children. Infant baptism *and* believers' baptism as truly *equivalent* alternatives side by side in one and the same church, and even local congregations, pose indeed profound questions not only about the meaning of the rite but also concerning the nature of the Church itself.

2.2 The reader of the Lima text discerns three explicit or implicit *models of baptism,* which we shall simply call Models A, B, and C.[31] *Model A* is represented by "baptism upon personal profession of faith" (L§11), i.e. baptism which is administered only to "those able to make a confession of faith for themselves" (L§12 "Commentary"); in this case "a personal confession of faith will be an integral part of the baptismal service" (L§12). The rite is viewed as an occasion for *personal* "commitment to the Lord who bestows his grace upon his people" (L§1), one in which "confession of sin and conversion of heart" take place and "a new ethical orientation" is "part of their baptismal experience" (L4). Thus baptism becomes "a sign and seal" of personal discipleship (L§6).

Model B is represented by infant baptism which is considered "not complete without the sealing of the baptized with the gift of the Holy Spirit and participation in holy communion" (L§20). Such practice "emphasizes the corporate faith and *the faith which the child (= infant) shares with its parents"* (L§12 "Commentary"). There is no need of a later personal profession of faith which would make the initiation complete, rather "an infant is considered to be a believer."[32]

Model C is represented by baptism understood as part of a *process* of initiation in which baptism at an early age is followed later by personal confession and commitment (L§15). "...Christian nurture is directed to the eliciting of this confession" (L§12). Parents, guardians, and the Church are ready "to bring up the children in the Christian faith" (L§11). Personal faith and commitment are *"essential* for the full fruit of baptism" (L§12 "Commentary") and *"necessary* for responsible membership of the body of Christ" (L§8). (Admission to the eucharist normally presupposes some rite of "confirmation".)

2.3 Although *Model A* has increasingly found support outside Baptist circles, Baptists have had sufficient reason to re-think their position. This process of self-reflection has led at times to a rediscovery of a variety within the Baptist tradition, at other times to a fresh recognition of aspects of baptismal theology and practice, which we had overlooked so far. The response of Baptists to the *ecumenical* problem posed by the different models exhibits a very broad range of position,[33] but it seems fair to say that there is (a) a growing recognition of the *sacramental* character of baptism,[34] (b) a greater awareness of the need of *Christian nurture*, or growth, before and after baptism,[35] (c) a concern about *the place of the child* in the Christian community[36] and the practice of *Infant Dedication and Thanksgiving*,[37] (d) the desire to strengthen *the visible unity of the rite of initiation*,[38] (e) an increasing readiness to draw practical consequences from the recognition of *the reality of the faith of believers baptized in infancy*,[39] (f) an acknowledgment that *"infant baptism witnesses to valid Christian insights"*[40] — but what has *not* come about is a straightforward acceptance of infant baptism as Christian baptism,[41] nor is it to be expected in the future. We have to face the fact that in the ecumenical "infant baptism-believers' baptism" debate neither side has succeeded in convincing the other of the rightness of its position.

Model B impresses Baptists as being a true competitor of *Model A;* both maintain the unity of the rite of initiation; without a delay, baptism leads directly to eucharistic communion — a view which is thoroughly biblical (Gal 3:27f; I Cor 11: 12f; 10:15-17) and has been clearly expressed in L§14 "Commentary" (b).[42] If infants are baptized, one can hardly think of any valid theological reason not to proceed with infant communion; in fact, refusal of infant communion is tantamount to the "ex-communication" of infants who belong to the Body of Christ. A baptism that leads directly to eucharistic communion is truly "complete" and does not need to be complemented by any other rite such as "confirmation".

Baptists have basic difficulties with the concept of *faith of infants*, and they are still convinced that "the act of God in baptism is such ... that it must be met, at the time of baptism, by an undoubtedly personal response of faith from the one baptized (cf. Rom 10:9ff.)."[43] They keep raising the question whether it is hermeneutically legitimate to transfer biblical statements relative to the meaning of baptism from the existential setting of a mature convert to the life-setting of the infant. E. Schlink once called the understanding of baptism as God's act *or* as an act of human obedience "the deepest difference" that divides the churches in the baptismal debate.[44] This is no longer true.[45] Today the deepest difference lies between a "sacramental objectivism" and an emphasis on the faith-reception of the sacrament in the sense in which L§15 speaks of "personal faith and commitment" (cf. A§7; L12). [46]

The latter distinction applies also to what the Lima text has to say about baptism and faith (§§8-10): the faith setting which the Church provides is important for its practice of baptism and for the growth of the infant to a responsible faith — and yet that faith setting is no substitute for "the personal faith of the recipient of baptism" (L§12 "Commentary"; A§§13-14).

Since it is unlikely that all of Christendom will be converted to accept *Model A* or *Model B*, though one seems to recognize a growing polarization in their direction, *Model C* may still prove to become the bridge leading eventually to an ecumenical understanding of Christian initiation, which will not eliminate Models A and B, but will give a definite and important place to *confession/confirmation* in such a way that infant baptism will parallel believers' baptism (L§15). The trend toward such a comprehensive view of *Christian initiation* was strong between 1968, when the first Faith and Order consultation on "Baptism, Confirmation and Eucharist" took place, and 1971, when the Faith and Order Commission met in Louvain; at the latter meeting E. Schlink called this concept of "initiation" *a break-through* provided it does not ignore the once-for-all nature of baptism. [47] However, already in Accra 1974, the concept of "initiation" did not receive the full attention it deserves, and in the Lima text the potential ecumenical significance of confirmation has certainly not been highlighted. This weakness of our document and the growing trend toward infant communion (Model B), understandable as it is, detracts further from confirmation and a comprehensive concept of initiation in which Baptism began to develop an interest. [48]

2.4 In conclusion one might say that the strong effort made in the Lima text to use "faith" as the bracket around both forms of baptism will probably not prove to be *the* bridge between the two traditions; however, it will take us a long part of the way in our common pilgrimage as churches. The expectation that an increasing number of churches will look at infant baptism and believers' baptism as "equivalent alternatives" will probably reopen the debate about *the nature of the Church*. Given the different understandings of *the nature of the sacramental act* in both traditions, true "equivalency" can hardly be expected; but a "co-existence" of both forms seems feasible provided we can still relate our thinking and our practice to a comprehensive understanding of Christian initiation as a process —

which inevitably means the incompleteness of its parts, but if there is to be mutual recognition all parts call for equal attention.[49] In the near future that "equal attention" needs to be given not only to Baptism and Eucharist but also to *confirmation/the catechumenate* as suggested by the Louisville Consultation[50] and advocated in an eloquent way by Michael Hurley, S.J., whose proposal deserves the attention of all churches.[51]

In L§13 "Commentary" there is the intriguing phrase, *"As the churches come to fuller mutual understanding and acceptance of one another and enter into closer relationships in witness and service..."* Perhaps, here lies a key: as we all experience the ecclesial life of our partner churches we begin to move toward one another. Baptists will appreciate the emphasis on responsible infant baptism and all efforts to lead baptized children to mature commitment to Christ (L§16). They in turn do well to continue going in the direction indicated above (2§3 A) knowing that we must carry the burden of historical divisions (cf. L§11) together[52] and trusting that Christ will unite us through faith and commitment to him and to one another.

NOTES

1. "One Baptism, One Eucharist and a Mutually Recognized Ministry", *Faith and Order Paper* No. 73, 1975.
2. See the summary in "Towards an Ecumenical Consensus on Baptism, Eucharist and Ministry", *Faith and Order Paper* No. 84, 1977, pp.6-8.
3. For complete documentation see "Louisville Consultation on Baptism", *Faith and Order Paper* No. 97, 1980 (= *Review and Expositor* LXXVII/1, winter 1980). The Louisville consultation was held in response to a recommendation made at Crêt-Bérard (*Faith and Order Paper* No. 84, p.7), where some forty theologians met to study the reactions of the churches to the Accra documents. For the integration of the "five significant points of agreement" recorded in Louisville, see below under L§§11-13.
4. There is only a passing hint at the connection between baptism and the eucharist in L§14 Commentary (b).
5. *Faith and Order Paper* No. 97, p.101.
6. It should not be overlooked that some of the "commentaries" which L has added contain new material (L§§6, 12, 13, 14, 18 and 21).
7. A complete synopsis of the Lima and Accra documents would relate the paragraphs as follows:

L§1 = A.1	L§4 new
L§2 new	L§§5-6 with "commentary" = A§§3,5
L§3 = A.2	A§6 omitted in L

L§7 new
L§§8-9 = A§4 and first sentence of §7
L§10 = A§7
L§11 new
L§12 with "commentary" = A§§12-14
L§13 with "commentary" = A§22
L§14 with "commentary" = A§§15-18
L§15 = A§23

L§16 = A§24
L§17 = A§9
L§18 with "commentary" = A§21
L§19 = A§19
L§20 = A§10
L§21 "commentary" = A§11
L§22 = A§8
L§23 = A§20

8. The first sentence of A§19 is taken up in a different context: L§19.
9. "Towards an Ecumenical Consensus on Baptism, Eucharist and Ministry", *Faith and Order Paper* No. 84, 1977, p.6.
10. *One Lord, One Baptism* (Faith and Order Commission Paper No. 29), London, SCM Press, 1960, 53f. For other literature on this notion, see G. Wainwright, "Christian Initiation in the Ecumenical Movement", *Studia Liturgica* 12, 1977, p.74.
11. In the response of the churches to "Accra", the question was raised: "Since baptism means participation in Christ's suffering, what is the place of suffering in our understanding of baptism?" (*Faith and Order Paper* No. 84, 1977, p.8).
12. For the eschatological orientation of baptism, see §§5, 6, 7, 9, 10 and 21, all of which represent changes in comparison with the "Accra" text.
13. For an emphasis on "ethical implications", see also L§10, which is new in comparison with the parallel in A§7.
14. *Studia Liturgica* 12, 1977, p.75.
15. For a corresponding change see the first sentence of L§8.
16. G. Wainwright, *Studia Liturgica* 12, 1977, p.76. The question, "How 'one' is the 'one baptism'?" is raised not only by Baptists; cf. G. Wagner, "Wie 'eins' ist die 'eine Taufe'?", *Oekumenische Rundschau* 22, 1973, pp.395-400.
17. "In many times and places, for instance in Latin America today, suffering for Christ is inflicted by authorities who are themselves baptized but use their power to maintain oppression. What is the role of baptism in a situation of social injustice? Should it not provide a bond of unity which excludes oppression? Does it indeed contribute to putting 'an end to all human estrangement'? Or does it, as some critics of the churches say, allow unjust structures to persist? What does it mean that baptism has often been imposed with force, thus becoming in some instances an instrument of colonization and a symbol of subjection to the colonized?" (*Faith and Order Paper* No. 84, p.8). Doesn't this problem weigh at least as heavily as any offence caused by so-called "re-baptisms"?
18. *Faith and Order Paper* No. 84, p.7.
19. Though it might seem to work in the opposite direction, the use of the word "full" mainfests a similar lack of precision (as noted above under L§5).
20. Contrast A§7: "By this growth, baptized believers should manifest to the world the new race of a redeemed mankind."
21. At Crêt-Bérard they were summarized in the following main questions: "(1) What authority can be claimed for the different practices of Christian initiation? (2) What is the relation between the faith of the individual and the faith of the Christian community? (3) What are the ecclesiological implications of the two forms of baptism; and when they are practised in the same church, what is the ecclesiological significance of that fact? (4) What is the implication of the practice of churches which use a form for infant baptism which was originally intended for believers' baptism? (5) What is the theological significance of the service of the

blessing of infants which is increasingly practised in the churches, including those which traditionally practice infant baptism?" *Faith and Order Paper* No. 84, p.7.

22. *Faith and Order Paper* No. 97, Group Reports on "Authority-Justification" (for Believers' Baptism, for Infant Baptism) (pp.103f.), "Sacrament-Faith" (pp.104f.), "Ecclesiology" (pp.105f.), "Contextuality" (pp.106-108).

23. *Faith and Order Paper* No. 97, pp. 101f.

24. *Faith and Order Paper* No. 97, p.103.

25. L§6 above has provided the theological basis for the dictum of L§13.

26. *Faith and Order Paper* No. 97, pp.105f.

27. Note that L§15 also presupposes a later affirmation of the Church's confession at infant baptism, an affirmation "by personal faith and commitment".

28. But see already A§19.

29. It was recognized at the Louisville consultation; see *Faith and Order Paper* No. 97, pp.106-108.

30. Cf. Nils Ehrenström, Mutual Recognition of Baptism in Interchurch Agreements. *Faith and Order Paper* No. 90, Geneva, 1978.

31. With qualifications, they could be called "The Baptist Model", "The Orthodox Model", and "The Process Model".

32. *Faith and Order Paper* No. 97, p. 105 (reference is made to the Orthodox tradition).

33. For a survey, see T. Lorenzen, "Baptists and Ecumenicity with Special Reference to Baptism", *Faith and Order Paper* No. 97, pp.21-45; "Baptism and Church Membership: Some Baptist Positions and Their Ecumenical Implications", *Journal of Ecumenical Studies* 18, 1981, pp.561-574. For a somewhat different response among the Disciples of Christ, cf. W.D. Carpe, "Baptismal Theology in the Disciples of Christ", *Faith and Order Paper* No. 97, pp.89-100; on why the Disciples of Christ "were... able to revise their position" in the American "Consultation on Church Union", see G.F. Moede, *Oneness in Christ*, Princeton, Minute Press 1981, pp.78-80.

34. Report of Theological Conversations Sponsored by the World Alliance of Reformed Churches and the Baptist World Alliance 1973-77. Geneva, WARC / Washington, BWA, 1976, p.11; J.F. Matthews, *Baptism: a Baptist View*, London, The Baptist Union, 1976, p.19; *Faith and Order Paper* No. 97, pp.104f.; Rechenschaft vom Glauben, Bad Homburg, Bund Ev.-Freikirchlicher Gemeinden, 1977, p.9; Schlussbericht des Gespräches zwischen dem Bund Evangelisch-Freikirchlicher Gemeinden in Deutschland und der Vereinigten Evangelisch-Lutherischen Kirche Deutschlands, Theologisches Gesprach (Kassel), 5-6/1981, pp.13f.

35. Report of Theological Conversations... p.16 (thesis 8); *Faith and Order Paper* No. 97, p.101 (2,3), p.105 (VI); cf. N. Clark, "The Theology of Baptism", in *Christian Baptism*, ed. by A. Gilmore, London, Lutterworth Press, 1959, p.326: "For no baptism can lack its proleptic element, and every baptism points forward for its completion and fulfilment."

36. *The Child and the Church: a Baptist Discussion*, London, Carey Kingsgate Press, 1966; *Faith and Order Paper*, No. 97, p.106.

37. *Faith and Order Paper* No. 97, p. 106 (VI.B.2); *Praise God: a Collection of Resource Material for Christian Worship*, compiled by A. Gilmore et al, London, The Baptist Union 1980, pp.129-136: "Infant Dedication and Thanksgiving."

38. Praise God... p.137; cf. also G.R. Beasley-Murray, *Baptism in the New Testament*. London, Macmillan, 1962, pp.393-395.
39. G.R. Beasley-Murray, *Baptism Today and Tomorrow*. London, Macmillan/New York, St Martin's Press, 1966, pp. 167f. One of the consequences is that "many Baptist churches admit other Christians, baptized as infants, to the Lord's Supper on the basis of their personal faith in Christ and when they are in good standing with their own churches, a practice which is a *de facto* recognition of their Christian status." (Report of Theological Conversations... p.14, cf. p.17, para. 11. Another one is the practice of "open membership", i. e. the reception of applicants as members if their infant baptism was followed later by a personal confession of faith; cf. Documents Concerning Baptism and Church Membership: a Controversy among North Carolina Baptists", by G.M. Bryan et al. (*Perspectives in Religious Studies. Special Studies Series* No. 1; Association of Baptist Professors of Religion 1977 passim; Report on Theological Conversations... p.17 (para. 11); G. Wagner, "Taufe und offene Mitgliedschaft", Blickpunkt Gemeinde (Kassel), 6/1980, p.4.
40. *Faith and Order Paper* No. 97, pp. para. 101, 104. Cf. Report of Theological Conversations... p. 16 (para. 6): "The Reformed emphasis on the priority of God's grace in baptism and the Baptist accent on man's active participation in the baptismal event are, in a sense, complementary and as such contribute to ecumenical rapprochement."
41. It seems that A. Gilmore, *Baptism and Christian Unity*, London, Lutterworth Press, 1966, comes closest to it. The often cited example of the attitute of Baptists who have joined the Church of North India (see also L.12 "Commentary") does not mean that those Baptists consider infant baptism an "equivalent" alternative to their believers' baptism; for details see T. Lorenzen, *Faith and Order Paper* No. 97, pp.23f.
42. Cf. also J.M.R. Tillard, "New Roman Catholic Insights on Baptism," *Mid-Stream* XVIII, 1979, pp.433f., 436, 439.
43. Report of Theological Conversations... p.12.
44. *Die Lehre von der Taufe*. Kassel, Johannes Stauda Verlag, 1969, p.140.
45. See Report of Theological Conversations... p.11; *Faith and Order Paper* No. 97, pp.104f.
46. On this issue see also J. Moltmann, *The Church in the Power of the Spirit*. London, SCM Press, 1977, pp.228, 239f.
47. *Faith and Order Paper* No. 60, 1971, p.31.
48. Report of Theological Conversations... p.13; Praise God... p.137; H.O. Russell, "The Relationship Between the Faith of the Individual and the Faith of the Community in Baptism, the Blessing of Children and Confirmation: a Baptist Perspective", *Faith and Order Paper* No. 97, p.85; see also the Report, *ibid.* p.105. On the concept of "initiation" see *Studia Liturgica* 12, 1977, 65-206; *Structures of Initiation in Crisis*, ed. by L. Maldonado and D. Power, New York, Seabury Press, 1979; *Concilium* 122 (2/1977).
49. So already the document on "Baptism, Confirmation and Eucharist" presented at Louvain (K. Raiser, Hrsg., Lowen, 1971. Stuttgart, Evangelischer Missionsverlag, 1971, S.35; Beiheft zur *Oekumenischen Rundschau* 18/19; *Faith and Order Paper* No. 59, pp.35-53).
50. The "five significant points of agreement" at the Louisville consultation include "the recognition in all the group reports that both forms of baptism require a

similar and responsible attitude towards Christian nurture and a serious development of the concept of the Christian catechumenate" (*Faith and Order Paper No. 97*, p.101).

51. "Baptism in Ecumenical Perspective", *One in Christ* 14, 1978, pp.106-123. "The promotion of this catechumenate in the Roman Catholic Church can help the process of church renewal and baptismal renewal in various ways. In the first place, it will give new emphasis to the unity of the three sacraments of Christian initiation and, therefore, to the anomalousness of first communion before confirmation. Secondly, it will highlight the radical character of Christian initiation; so much so that infant baptism by contrast may appear to be a step of no very great consequence. The task of reviewing the theology and practice of infant baptism will, therefore, become still more urgent. Thirdly, it will show the nature of the church to approximate rather closely to that of a 'gathered community' or 'basic community'. It will, therefore, give new point to questions about the structure of the local church. Fourthly, it cannot but lead to a reduction in the number of those individuals calling for rebaptism. Fifthly, and lastly, it should be noted that the new Roman *Rite of Christian Initiation* includes, despite its title, a chapter devoted to a 'Rite of Initiation for Children of Catechetical Age' i.e. of those 'who have reached the age of reason and are able to be taught'" (pp.121f.).

52. Cf. the first among the "five significant points of agreement": *Faith and Order Paper* No. 97, p.101, also the group report on "Contextuality," *ibid.*, pp.106-108.

CONVERGENCE ON BAPTISM

Lewis S. Mudge

The first article on the Baptism convergence statement has dealt mainly with the genesis of that document. This essay will be largely concerned with its content as finished work, and with its consequences. Some reference to the process by which the Baptism document took form, of course, will be illuminating in understanding its character as a theological statement. But the object of this analysis will be to look at the text as it now stands, and to put some thoughts in order about what the reception of this document by the churches might permit to happen next.

We must not, whatever we do, underestimate the achievement involved in having brought the Baptism, Eucharist and Ministry convergence statements (henceforth abbreviated "BEM") to the point at which they have now arrived. What is that point? A vote by the Plenary Commission on Faith and Order that these three documents, taken together as the "Lima Text", are sufficiently "mature"to be sent to the WCC member churches, and other bodies, for response to a series of searching questions. Not this time are the churches asked to suggest amendments (although this is certainly not ruled out), but rather to say, authoritatively, to what extent they "can recognize in this text the faith of the church throughout the ages." They are asked to consider what consequences the text can have for their own relations to other churches, what guidance it can provide for their own life and worship, and what the text means for the next steps in Faith and Order. In particular, they are asked to think about the relation of the Lima consensus document to the long-range Faith and Order project "Toward the Common Expression of the Apostolic Faith

---

• Lewis S. Mudge is Dean of McCormick Theological Seminary (Chicago).

Today". To have reached a convergence about which such questions can confidently be asked is itself a momentous achievement. It will be even more so if the churches, in their responses, indicate that this convergence, whatever its shortcomings, helps open the way toward a common articulation of the apostolic faith itself.

It is important to have said all this at the outset. The explication of such a text as this turns, to a great extent, on our perception of the process in which it plays a part. Taken in and of itself, the Lima Text remains what I have elsewhere called a "fragile bridge of words between worlds". To have been part of the drafting process at various stages, as the writer has been, is to have been struck by how very precariously some of these sentences work their way between — and indeed in, with, and among — historic confessional positions, as well as the theological idiosyncrasies of individual drafters! It is not the ingenuity of the words themselves that counts. It is the proof they bear that Protestant, Anglican, Roman Catholic and Orthodox theologians can meet, write such sentences together, and call the result "mature" enough to invite their colleagues all over the world to consider steps towards each other which will require a new level of ecumenical confidence. One can venture an analogy from the scientific world. If another group of theologians should, with the same effort, with the same prolonged and careful consideration, try to write such a document, we now have confidence that it could, like a scientific experiment, be done again, and again. Not that some new "bridge of words" would be identically the same. But the ecumenical situation is now such that we know we can do this together because we have done it. That is the point.

1. Genesis of the Lima text

The Baptism, Eucharist and Ministry texts are profoundly inter-related. Several facts about the common history of these documents are important for understanding the moment in the dialogue we have reached today.

As the reader already knows, the proposal with which the drafting process began was that sentences and paragraphs should be extracted from authoritative ecumenical documents (actions of WCC Assemblies, agreements of Faith and Order conferences, and the like), and strung together into continuous prose. In the attempt to do this, two discoveries were quickly made. First, that the extracted materials depended for their sense on their original contexts and did not lend themselves to re-use without considerable editing and fresh composition. And second, that in the ecumenical documents existing at the time (the early seventies) both Roman Catholic and Orthodox thought tended to be under-represented. The earlier ecumenical documents still provided an indispensable baseline, but it could be seen that an opportunity was at hand for a new departure in ecumenical drafting, in which Protestant, Roman Catholic, and Orthodox thinkers would share on an equal basis.

It may also be true — different observers would no doubt have different views — that the issues dividing us over the doctrine of baptism in particular were not fully identified at the outset. If the tension between infant baptism and believers' baptism existed among Protestants, it was not felt to be fundamental to the dialogue on this subject across the full breadth of Christendom. As it turned out, this observation was both right and wrong. The infant baptism and believers' baptism question was helpfully reframed, in part because of the Roman Catholic and Orthodox presence, toward the conviction that the two practices could be held within a common theological understanding. But the question of the fundamental elements of Christian initiation and their divergent relations to each other in the different confessions and communions, proved to have broader implications than many first realized.

It may also be important to point out that, from the Faith and Order Commission meeting in Accra (1974) onward, the Baptism text underwent fewer changes by far than either the Eucharist text or the Ministry text. Possibly this was because controversy over the nature of baptism as such — as opposed to its place in the whole sequence of initiation — was felt by many to be some distance from the centre of ecumenical debate. Questions about the eucharist, and, above all, concerning ministry, simply occupied the lion's share of attention both in the commission and in the churches, and therefore in the consciousness of those with responsibility for drafting. But the consequence, for this observer, was that the Baptism text reached the Lima meeting in some ways further from "maturity" than the other two.

I believe that the "maturity" achieved at Lima must be understood as relative to that ecumenical moment. Certainly the final redaction dealt with most, if not all, of the remaining textual infelicities. And several questions, including that of the relation between baptism and name-giving as practised in different cultures, were introduced helpfully for the first time. But the unsolved question of the relation between baptism and confirmation, or chrismation, which is to say the relationship between baptism, eucharist, and the common life under the oversight of a mutually recognized ministry, began to appear deeper than it had before.

2. The theological character of the Baptism document

The Baptism document, of course, must speak for itself. It is possible here only to exhibit its structure, and to pick out certain formulations which seem particularly significant.

On the authority of Matt. 28:18-20, and on the basis of its universal practice in the Church from apostolic times to the present, baptism is said to have been instituted by God and given to the Church as a gift. Other biblical references, in rich array, are invoked to set forth the "meaning" of baptism through "images" which, though many, are affirmed to point to a single "reality." Thus baptism is "participation in Christ's death and resurrection" (Rom. 6:3-5; Col. 2:12-13; 3:1; Eph. 2:5-6); it is "conversion, pardoning, and cleansing" (Mark 1:4; Heb. 10:22; 1 Pet. 3:21; Acts 22:16; 1 Cor. 6:11); it is "the gift of the Spirit" (Mark 1:10-11; Acts 2; 2 Cor. 1:21-22; Eph. 1:13-14); it is "incorporation into the Body of Christ" (Eph. 4:3-6); it is "the sign of the kingdom".

The last-mentioned of these categories is no doubt the least developed. Throughout the drafting of the BEM documents pressure was felt, quite properly, to relate their subject-matter to the concrete witness of the Church in the world: in such matters, for example, as justice and peace. The drafters attempted to do this without either interrupting the flow of exposition or introducing matter bound to be seen by some as extraneous, hortatory, or ideological. The "sign of the kingdom" is thus mentioned here without elaboration or specific application. But we are to understand that this reference points us forward to Paragraph 10 of our text where we read that "...baptism has ethical implications which not only call for personal sanctification, but also motivate Christians to strive for the realization of the will of God in all realms of life". We are prepared by these words for the fuller outworking of ethical themes in the Eucharist and Ministry texts.

The next main section of the Baptism document is devoted to "Baptism and Faith." Here groundwork is laid for the important observations which follow a page later in the treatment of "Baptismal practice". Paragraph 8 has been carefully shaped to apply equally to all variants of baptismal practice, whether "infant baptism," "believers' baptism," or some combination of the two.

Baptism is both God's gift and our human response to that gift. It looks toward a growth into the measure of the stature of the fullness of Christ (Eph. 4:13). The necessity of faith for the reception of the salvation embodied and set forth in baptism is acknowledged by all churches. Personal commitment is necessary for responsible membership of the Body of Christ.

With this foundation, the document deals skilfully with the classic differences of baptismal practice in Protestantism. The fact that the differences are of "practice", and no longer of "faith", is the heart of the matter. Paragraphs 11 through 13 are thus free to show that the same faith receives different articulations, or is seen from different points of view, in the practices of the different churches. The churches no longer need be fundamentally divided over this point. Indeed it is observed that there are churches in which both "infants'" and "believers'" baptism are practised according to the situation.

The description of the different practices nonetheless needed to be carefully done. The paragraphs in question were interestingly volatile through the drafting process until the final hours of the shaping of the text. The problem was not continuing theological disagreement. It was that of stating the situation correctly, yet with economy of means. The drafting effort finally issued in the forthright sentence which now opens Paragraph 11: "While baptism upon personal profession of faith is the most clearly attested practice in the New Testament documents, the possibility that infant baptism was also practised in the apostolic age cannot be excluded." (By general agreement, our inability to "exclude" infant baptism from the apostolic age rests upon references to the baptism of some particular person "and all his house".) There follows a discussion of the "variety of forms" which the practice of baptism has assumed.

11. ... Some churches baptize infants brought by parents who are ready, in and with the Church, to bring up their children in the Christian faith. Other churches practise exclusively the baptism of believers who are able to make a personal confession of faith....
12. Both the baptism of believers and the baptism of infants take place in the Church as the community of faith. When one who can answer for himself or herself is baptized, a personal confession of faith will be an integral part of the baptismal service. When an infant is baptized, the personal response will be offered at a later moment of life. In both cases the baptized person will have to grow in the understanding of faith.

The commentary on this paragraph makes several observations which nail down the point:

> The differences between infant and believers' baptism become less sharp when it is recognized that both forms of baptism embody God's own initiative in Christ and express a response of faith made within the believing community.... The practice of infant baptism emphasizes the corporate faith and the faith which the child shares with its parents.... The practice of believer's baptism emphasizes the explicit confession of the person who responds to the grace of God in and through the community of faith and who seeks baptism.... In some churches which unite both infant-baptist and believer-baptist traditions, it has been possible to regard as equivalent alternatives for entry into the Church both a pattern whereby baptism in infancy is followed by later profession of faith and a pattern whereby believer baptism follows upon a presentation and blessing in infancy. This example invites other churches to decide whether they, too, could not recognize equivalent alternatives in their reciprocal relations and in church union negotiations.

Paragraph 13 then states with stark simplicity: "Baptism is an unrepeatable act. Any practice which might be interpreted as re-baptism must be avoided."

The treatment of "Baptismal Practice" now turns to a second bundle of questions: those centring upon "Baptism — Chrismation — Confirmation". Here, it may be said, lies the area in which most work still needs to be done if agreement on baptism is to lead, as it logically should, towards mutual recognition of members. The movement of the dialogue from a fundamentally "Protestant" context into one involving Anglicans, Roman Catholics, and Orthodox inevitably raises questions of the whole "rite of initiation", of the parts of which it is thought to be composed, and of the relation of the initiation process to admission of the person to the Eucharist.

The controlling theological question is that of the relation between baptism and the receiving of the Holy Spirit. The mystery of Christ's death and resurrection is inseparably linked with the event of Pentecost. So, too, with the participation in these mysteries of the one baptized. As our text affirms, "Baptism in its full meaning signifies and effects both" participation in Christ's death and resurrection and the receiving of the Spirit. The problem lies in the different ways the churches mark the moment of the gift of the Spirit. Do they liturgically signify that the gift is given in the act of baptism itself, or is this gift associated with some rite performed at a later moment, such as confirmation or chrismation? The Commentary on this point is most carefully articulated, and one can do no better than quote the key sentences: When the signs occur within a single liturgy, they express the fundamental conviction that incorporation into Christ and participation in His Spirit are inseparable. However, when the sign of the Spirit becomes separated from water baptism and does not occur until later in the life of the recipient, a serious problem arises, since it seems that incorporation into Christ is separated from full life in the Spirit. This is the inherent problem of a sacramental interpretation of confirmation.

The non-sacramental interpretation of a later rite of confirmation can also pose serious questions. Its pastoral practice often overshadows that of baptism, creating the impression that confirmation, not baptism, incorporates a person into the community. If such confirmation is interposed between baptism and admission to communion, the ground for this action must be questioned. If baptism, as incorporation into the body of Christ, points by its very nature to the eucharistic sharing of Christ's body and blood, the question arises as to how a further and separate rite can be interposed between baptism and admission to communion.

The questions raised here involve more than meets the eye. In a brief pair of paragraphs titled "Toward Mutual Recognition of Baptism", we read that "churches are increasingly recognizing each other's baptism as the one baptism into Christ...." This practice of mutual recognition is encouraged: "Whenever possible, mutual recognition should be expressed explicitly by the churches." The problem, of course, is what this means. Logically, mutual recognition of baptism means mutual recognition of members, and mutual recognition of members is hard, in the end, to distinguish from full communion. Obviously, the churches are not yet ready to go that far. And, if this is so, what does "mutual recognition of baptism" mean? It is at least, as our text says, "an important sign and means of expressing the baptismal unity given in Christ". The final part of this article will return to this issue with some reflections on the way ahead.

Meanwhile the Baptism text moves to its final main section, "The Celebration of Baptism". The completed form of the text stresses the power of the symbolism of water without entering upon the vexed issue of whether the amount of water used or the manner of its use is relevant to the ecumenical recognition of a given practice. Stress is also laid upon marking the gift of the Spirit by some sign within the baptismal rite itself: the laying-on of hands, anointing or chrismation. Even the sign of the cross recalls the promised gift of the Spirit.

In the light of the issues raised a few paragraphs earlier, the sentence ending Paragraph 19 seems an understatement: "The recovery of such vivid signs will enrich the liturgy." In fact, such recovery bears on the question of communion between the churches as such.

The Lima meeting stepped back from any suggestion that the list of elements offered in Paragraph 20 constitutes a recommended liturgical order. It is merely, as the text says, an account of that which should "find a place" within any "comprehensive order of baptism". Lima was also responsible for the addition, redundant in view of what has gone before yet full of portent in this location in the document: "Some churches consider that Christian initiation is not complete without the sealing of the baptized with the gift of the Holy Spirit and participation in holy communion."

The baptism document moves towards a conclusion with a rather elaborate discussion, considering the generally spare style of the whole, of problems arising in certain cultural contexts. The issues call for little comment, for they speak for themselves. On the one hand, confusion between Christian baptism and name-giving rituals in certain cultures not only obscures the distinctive meaning of baptism but unhappily encourages church authorities to insist that "Christian" — i.e. biblical or European — names be chosen, thus alienating new Christians from their cultural roots. And the "indiscriminate" baptism practised by the majority churches in European or American situations understandably gives the baptism of infants, who are generally the ones involved, a bad name, especially among those already committed to the baptism of believers.

Two comments about "normality" in baptismal practice are reserved for the end. Baptism is "normally" administered by an ordained minister, "although in certain circumstances others are allowed to baptize". And baptism is "normally" administered during a regular act of worship of the congregation.

3. The path ahead

The churches are now, in effect, asked to say what the existence of the BEM texts means to them. The request asks for response "at the highest appropriate level of authority," but leaves to the churches' discretion the level at which action is to be taken as well as the kind of action called for. It also leaves the churches to decide how profound a question is being put to them. They must decide, in effect, what they will take the question, theologically and practically, to mean. In one way, this approach makes sense. Different churches in different situations will indeed respond in different ways. If taken seriously, the BEM texts will provoke a spectrum of reactions from which we will learn much about the "status quaestionis" of baptism in the ecumenical movement. But, on the other hand, even taken together with the planned introductory paragraphs, the Baptism document gives surprisingly few hints of the kinds of questions which might be asked: i.e. it has little to say, except by implication, of the role baptism has already played in Faith and Order dialogue, and therefore of the sorts of issues on which this document might be expected to throw light.

Let us step back for a moment and review the short but interesting history of the ecumenical discussion of baptism. One finds, by and large, a series of rather cursory references to the subject in the documents of early Faith and Order meetings and WCC Assemblies. The eucharist has almost always been identified as the sacrament of unity. The one baptism has then been said, without much elaboration, to have implications for the one eucharist. Interest in baptism as a sacrament of unity in its own right has been much more recent. With Nils Ehrenstrom, in his booklet *Mutual Recognition of Baptism in Interchurch Agreements*,[1] one wonders why awareness of the importance of this matter was so long in coming.

It may be significant to name three possible reasons for the change in awareness we are now seeing.

(1) In the predominantly "Protestant" period of ecumenism, i.e. before the great growth of Orthodox and Roman Catholic participation, the conflict between adherents of infant and believers' baptism seemed to involve such sharp mutual denials that this arena of discussion seemed singularly unpromising. Today two things have happened. The ecumenical centre of gravity has changed, and, as we have seen earlier in this article, the old baptismal debate among Protestants has begun to be solved by means of a broader view of Christian initiation taken as a whole. Perhaps we are ready now for a new phase of the dialogue. If so, the BEM text will play a significant part.

(2) Prior to Vatican II, the Roman Catholic Church maintained a practice which made this discussion seem just as unpromising as it had within Protestantism: the practice of "indiscriminate conditional baptism", that is to say, the custom of rebaptizing converts from other church bodies using a formula that placed in doubt the validity of the baptism they had already received. The Vatican II

pronouncements on baptism, in the *Decree on Ecumenism* and in *Lumen Gentium*, not only condemned this practice but, as we will see, made statements about Christian baptism as such which have given the discussion new potential for advancing the cause of unity.

(3) And now, many ecumenical documents are moving beyond references to the unitive potential of our acknowledgement of the one baptism to efforts of various kinds to make mutual recognition of our respective doctrines and practices of baptism explicit and, occasionally, to tie such mutual recognition to the search for mutual recognition of members. Nils Ehrenstrom, in the booklet already mentioned, has usefully collected illustrative documents from around the world. In one case, that of the Consultation on Church Union in the USA, the attempt to link mutual recognition of baptism to mutual recognition of members is relatively far advanced.

The root problem which emerges in all this discussion is the one that for years has fascinated unity dialoguers: how can we detect, and how do we talk about, the presence of the one Church of Jesus Christ in the midst of the divided churches? The discussion of baptism at Vatican II illustrates the point. The Council's baptismal pronouncements, especially when seen in the context of the meeting's predominant ecclesiology, raise ecumenical expectations which the juridical form of the Roman Church is unable to fulfill. *Lumen Gentium* states that baptized persons are incorporated into the Church. *The Decree on Ecumenism*, speaking of non-Catholics, declares, "All those justified by faith through baptism are incorporated into Christ." As Gerald Moede writes in his article "Ecumenical Pressure and the Mutual Recognition of Baptism/Members",[2] "When the word 'incorporate' is utilized, it is difficult to see how the Body of Christ can be avoided. And if they belong to the Body of Christ, one can scarcely deny that they belong to the church, 'which is his body.'".

The ecclesiology presupposed here, of course, is the *communio* or *koinonia* ecclesiology of the Council, in which the Church is described, in the words of Avery Dulles, as "an instrument for the redemption of all." Before being an institution, the Church is a "spiritual community." The juridical and social manifestations of communion, as Dulles points out, though important, are derivative, not primary. The *communio* into which all Christians are baptized is this spiritual body. In this sense baptism is the fundamental sacrament of unity, prior to and transcending ecclesiastical divisions.[3] But, at the

same time, the *Decree on Ecumenism* points to the incompleteness of
the sanctifying and unifying grace flowing from an act of baptism,
even if validly perfomed, unless it is lived out in communion with the
Roman Catholic Church. In the words of the *Decree*:

> Baptism, therefore, constitutes a sacramental bond of unity linking all
> who have been reborn by means of it. But baptism, of itself, is only a
> beginning, a point of departure, for it is wholly directed toward the acquir-
> ing of fullness of life in Christ. Baptism is thus oriented toward a complete
> profession of faith, a complete incorporation into the system of salvation
> such as Christ Himself intended it to be, and finally, toward a complete
> participation in Eucharistic communion. The ecclesial communities
> separated from us lack that fullness of unity with us which should flow
> from baptism, and we believe that especially because of the lack of the
> sacrament of orders they have not preserved the genuine and total reality
> of the Eucharistic mystery.

It is not merely the Roman Catholic Church, but all the churches,
which must wrestle with the anomaly that one can be "incorporated into the Body of Christ" only through membership, in the sense of enrolment, in some specific church body. Thus baptism, which should confer membership in the Church as such, only does so in combination
with the fulfilment of whatever requirements some particular church
may lay down. It is helpful to suggest, as the Baptism convergence text
does, that no further rite be interposed between baptism and admission
to the eucharist. But this suggestion does not reach the fact that
"membership", as different churches understand it, has as much to do
with the sociological assumptions operative in the history and present
context of the body in question as with that body's baptismal theology.
For Roman Catholics, membership is communion with the Roman see.
For Presbyterians, it is the right to participate constituionally in ecclesiastical governance. For bodies in the "free church" tradition, it is
voluntary adherence to and participation in a local worshipping congregation. The whole Troeltschian spectrum of assumptions about the
relation between the Church and the social order around it — the ways
in which one Church may replicate and reinforce the social patterns of
its environment while another may oppose these patterns with structures of its own — must be understood if we are to grasp the way
"membership" works in practice. If agreement on the doctrine of baptism is to lead to "mutual recognition of membership", steps will have
to be taken which lie outside the scope of the convergence statement as
we have it now.

In his book *And yet It Moves: Dream and Reality of the Ecumenical Movement*,[4] Ernst Lange wrote of the period of Louvain that "consensus on the theology of baptism is more apparent than real" (p.47). He added: "Agreement on the theology of baptism (has) proved relatively easy only because baptism (has) been isolated from its contexts." This, as we have seen, is still true. We know, as Lange pointed out, that "Water baptism, anointing or the imposition of hands as symbolizing the gift of the Holy Spirit, and first communion, together constituted integral parts of one liturgical event in the early Church." But we are not sure what to do with our knowledge.

Does it follow that the convergence on baptism is only as potent as our ecumenical progress on other fronts permits it to be? From one point of view, the answer is yes. Not only is our reponse to the convergence on baptism closely tied to whatever progress proves to have been made on such matters as eucharist and ministerial orders, which, of course, is why BEM comes as a single, three-part, text, but recognition of each others' baptisms in the name of the Trinity must involve some degree of accord on the Trinitarian theology in question. But in another sense, the answer may be, "not entirely". Why?

Agreement on the nature of baptism should, in its own right, put a certain ecumenical pressure on us. If we were to take seriously the insistence of the present document that Christian initiation is a continuous process and that no rite should be interposed between baptism and admission to communion, we would by implication have relativized all our limited, socio-confessional, ideals of "membership". We would be on the way to an understanding of "membership" in the body of Christ which would challenge the autonomy of our dialogues on eucharist and ministry, as well as our particular confessional understandings of these matters. An embodiment of the "given unity" we so like to talk about would be in process of formation in our midst. There would be more reason to believe that our understanding of the Gospel could triumph over the sociological forms in which we are still imprisoned.

The ecumenical pressure on us would increase if the churches were to adopt the recommendations of the Baptism text in their actual practice, and if they were to affirm that adherence to the theological understanding of baptism in the text is sufficient for full mutual recognition, not only of their respective baptisms but of their processes of Christian initiation as a whole. It would, in fact, be very difficult to distinguish such a state of affairs from "full communion".

Clearly this is not going to happen tomorrow. But the development of our common thinking on Christian initiation offers an approach to communion which can supplement our work on eucharist and ministry. It can strengthen the latter work by offering a converging approach to the same goal. By encouraging such steps as the renunciation of rebaptism or conditional baptism of persons baptized in other churches, or the composition of a common liturgy of initiation, work on the implications of the Baptism text could bring us closer to the time when we can decisively act on the insights that it embodies. And, unquestionably, by raising the question of what we mean by the Trinitarian formula into which we baptize, this dialogue propels us towards the coming Faith and Order study of our unity in the one Apostolic faith.

NOTES

1. *Faith and Order Paper* 90, Geneva, WCC, 1978.
2. *Mid-Stream*, Vol. XVII, No. 3, July 1978, pp. 246f.
3. References to Dulles in Moede, *op. cit.*, pp. 244f.
4. Eerdmans, Grand Rapids, 1979.

CHRISMATION

CYRILLE ARGENTI

I. Introduction: the title

We entitle this paper "Chrismation" and not "Confirmation". The latter term only appears in church history in the period of the Gallic councils of Riez (439) and Orange (441), and it was only in 458 that Pope St Leo the Great became the first to speak of "the sacrament of confirmation".[1] Thereafter the celebration of this latter would be separated from and observed at an interval of some years from baptism. The reason for this was the splitting of the rite of immersion-anointing into two parts: one celebrated by the priest and the other by the bishop in person. Separated in this way from the celebration of baptism, the "sacrament of confirmation" would invite the criticisms of the Reformers, who could then deny its dominical institution.

In contrast to this, the term "chrismation" recalls the evangelical origin of the sacrament, i.e. the anointing (in the Greek *chrisma*) or chrismation of the Lord Jesus himself by the Holy Spirit "descending upon him like a dove", "when he came up out of the water" (Mk 1:10). This anointing manifests him as God's "Anointed" (in Greek, *Christos*). This is attested, the next day, by Andrew, the "first called", who tells his brother Simon: "We have found the Messiah" which means Christ (Anointed) (Jn 1:41). This continuity between immersion, or baptism, and anointing, or chrismation, cannot be broken without falsifying the meaning of both. The reader is therefore asked to leave aside the problems which arose subsequent

---

• Cyrille Argenti is Priest of the Greek Orthodox Parish in Marseille.
Translator's note: Biblical texts are quoted from the Revised Standard Version unless otherwise stated; JB = Jerusalem Bible.

to the splitting of the rite in the West and to adopt the perspective of the Christians of the first four centuries.

II. Chrismation in the Old Testament

The importance of the rites of the Old Covenant for deeper understanding of the Christian mysteries has been very well described by Jean Daniélou:

> Recent studies on the history of liturgical origins... have established the fact that we must not look to Hellenistic culture for the origin of the Christian sacraments as people have been so willing to do for the last fifty years, but rather to the liturgy of Judaism, to which they are directly related. We must therefore ask ourselves the question: what significance did the signs used in the Jewish liturgy hold for the Jews of the time of Christ and for Christ himself? It is also quite evident that the mentality of the Jews and of Christ was formed by the Old Testament. Consequently it is in studying the significance for the Old Testament of the different elements used in the sacraments that we have the best method of discovering their significance for Christ and the Apostles...
>
> This reference to the Bible has a double value. First of all, it constitutes an authority justifying the existence and the form of the sacraments by showing that they are already prefigured in the Old Testament and that they are the expression of constant modes of the divine action, so that they... appear as the expression of the very design of God. Moreover these references to the Bible give us the symbolism in which the sacraments were first conceived...[2]

1) According to the Mosaic law, anointing is used for consecration to the priesthood

We read in Exodus: "The Lord said to Moses ... You shall bring Aaron and his sons to the door of the tent of meeting, and wash them in water ... and you shall take the anointing oil and pour it on his head and anoint him" (Ex. 29:4,7). We note already the linking of immersion and anointing. The purpose intended by this rite is indicated in the following chapter (30): "Take the finest spices" (v.23) — it is therefore a fragrant oil — "you shall make of these a sacred anointing oil" (v.25) — the words used by the LXX Greek version are: "chrisma hagion" — "you shall anoint Aaron and his sons, and consecrate them, that they may serve me as priests" (v.30). Chrismation is therefore intended to consecrate priests. This is confirmed by Leviticus: "The anointed priest..." (Lev. 4:5). Moses presents Aaron and his sons and washes them *in* water (Lev. 8:6). "Moses took the anointing oil (v.10)... he poured some of the anointing oil on Aaron's head, and anointed him, to consecrate him" (v.12). As for the high priest, on whose head the anointing oil has been poured (Lev. 21:10, *tou élaiou tou christou*), "the consecration of the anointing oil of his God is upon him" (*to hagion élaion tou christou tou théou ép'autô*: v.12).

We understand, therefore, why Psalm 133 (132) speaks of "...the precious oil upon the head, running down upon the beard, upon the beard of Aaron, running down on the collar of his robes" (v.2).

2) Subsequently chrismation will be used to consecrate kings

This is the case of the first king of Israel, Saul. "Samuel took a vial of oil and poured it on his head, and kissed him and said, "Has not the Lord anointed you (made you christ) to be prince of his people Israel" (1 Sam. 10:1). "Then the spirit of the Lord will come mightily upon you, and you shall prophesy with them and be turned into another man" (v.6). "And the spirit of God came mightily upon him, and he prophesied among them (the prophets). And all who knew him before saw how he prophesied with the prophets" (v.10). Anointing, chrismation, is therefore accompanied by the gift of the Spirit, who not only consecrates Saul as king, but also makes him a prophet.

Anointing will have the same function when David is crowned king: "Samuel took the horn of oil and anointed him in the midst of his brothers; and the Spirit of the Lord came mightily upon David from that day forward" (1 Sam. 16:13).

Similary in the Psalms, anointing is the seal of a holy kingship: "The kings of the earth set themselves... against the Lord and his anointed" (Ps. 2:2); "... the Lord will speak to them in his wrath... I have set my king on Zion, my holy hill" (v.6); "The Lord said to me, 'You are my son, today I have begotten you (v.7)... I will make the nations your heritage'" (v.8). Psalm 18: "Great triumphs he (the Lord) gives to his king, and shows steadfast love to his anointed, to David and his descendants for ever" (v.50). Psalm 20: "The Lord will give victory to his anointed" (v.7). Psalm 45: "Your throne, o God, endures for ever and ever. Your royal sceptre is a sceptre of equity" (v.6). "You love righteousness and hate iniquity. Therefore God, your God, has anointed you with the oil of gladness" (v.7). Psalm 89: "I have found David, my servant, with my holy oil I have anointed him (v.20)... He shall cry to me, 'Thou art my Father, my God and the Rock of my salvation'. And I will make him the first-born, the highest of the kings of the earth" (vv.26-27). "I will

establish his line for ever and his throne as the days of the heavens"
(v.29)... "Once for all I have sworn by my holiness... His line shall
endure for ever (vv.35-36)... But now thou hast cast off and rejected,
thou art full of wrath against thy anointed" (v.38). Psalm 132: "For
thy servant David's sake do not turn away the face of thy anointed
one" (v.10).

3) The anointed was therefore first a priest, then a king, but
also a prophet; his anointing (or chrismation) was not only an
anointing with oil but essentially an unction by the Spirit of God.
Quite naturally, therefore, chrismation by oil and by the Spirit
will become in the book of Isaiah the distinctive sign characterizing the "Servant" of God, God's 'Chosen One', the Anointed *par
excellence*, that is to say the awaited Messiah or Christ, who will
be at once priest, king and prophet: Is. 61:1-3: "The Spirit of
the Lord is upon me, because the Lord has anointed me (*échrisè
mé*) to bring good tidings to the poor, ... to bind up the broken-
hearted ... to comfort all who mourn... to give them ... the oil of
gladness."

The essential, however, is not the anointing with oil, but the
anointing with the Spirit: "Behold my servant, whom I uphold, my
chosen, in whom my soul delights: I have put my Spirit upon him, he
will bring forth justice to the nations" (Is. 42:1). And again: "There
shall come forth a shoot from the stump of Jesse, and a branch shall
grow out of his roots. And the Spirit of the Lord shall rest upon
him" (Is. 11:1). (This verse is followed by the celebrated messianic
prophecy of Is. 11:1-9.)

In short, anointing by the Holy Spirit will be the distinctive mark
of the priest-king-prophet, the Chosen One and Servant of God, the
awaited Saviour, and is the reason for his title of Messiah, Anointed,
"Christos".

III. Chrismation in the New Testament

We shall not be surprised, then, that the last and greatest of the
prophets of the Old Covenant, who will also be the forerunner of the
New, recognizes God's Chosen One by his chrismation by the Holy
Spirit: "He who sent me to baptize with water said to me, 'He on
whom you see the Spirit descend and remain, this is he who baptizes
with the Holy Spirit.' And I have seen and have borne witness that
this is the Chosen One of God" (Jn 1:33-34). That is why Andrew,
the first-called, will tell his brother Simon (Peter): "We have found

the Messiah (which means Christ)" (Jn 1:41). The evangelist uses the Greek word *christos*, past participle of the verb *chrio*, I anoint).

Let us accordingly recall the event which inaugurates the New Covenant and which — with the triumphant entry into Jerusalem, the crucifixion and resurrection — is the only one narrated by all four evangelists. St Mark with his habitual conciseness relates it as follows: "In those days Jesus came from Nazareth of Galilee and was baptized by John in the Jordan. And when he came up out of the water, immediately he saw the heavens opened and the Spirit descending upon him like a dove; and a voice came from heaven, 'Thou art my beloved Son; with thee I am well pleased'" (Mk 1:9-10).

It is therefore at the moment when he came up out of the water, that is to say *immediately* after his immersion (in Greek: "baptisma") that his anointing in the Spirit was revealed, that is to say his chrismation manifesting him as Christ.

Thus the two events, immersion in water and unction by the Spirit, are directly linked and are inseparable. They are nevertheless distinct and successive: (1) John baptizes Jesus; (2) When Jesus comes up out of the water, the Spirit in the form of a dove descends on him while the voice of the Father designates the Anointed as his Son, as in Psalm 2 quoted above, though here, of course, the anointing, the chrismation, is that of the Lord Jesus. And the Son became man to give human beings that Spirit which rests on him from all eternity, and who is the Gift of God — "God given" — of which Jesus will speak to the Samaritan woman.

If he, then, is the Anointed, he became man to transmit his anointing to human beings. *The chrismation of the disciples is the very reason for the incarnation of the Son.* This will be accomplished on the day of Pentecost, when the Lord Jesus "raised to the heights by God's right hand, ... received from the Father the Holy Spirit, who was promised, and what you see and hear is the outpouring of that Spirit" (Acts 2:33; JB).

He first had to be "raised to the heights". But to be exalted he first had to "go away" by death: "But because I have said these things to you, sorrow has filled your hearts. Nevertheless I tell you the truth: it is to your advantage that I go away, for if I do not go away, the Counsellor will not come to you; but if I go, I will send him to you" (Jn 16:6-7). It is the same idea as we find expressed in chapter 7:37-39, "On the last day of the feast... Jesus stood up and proclaimed.... 'He who believes in me, out of his heart shall flow rivers of living water.' Now this he said about the Spirit which those who believed in him were to receive; for there was no Spirit as yet because Jesus had not yet been glorified" (Jn 7:37-39; JB). He would not be glorified until he had passed through passion, death, burial. Hence his cry on the eve of his death: "Father, the hour has come, glorify thy Son."

In short, death, burial, resurrection necessarily had to precede Pentecost. There could be no Pentecost without death and resurrection. Nevertheless death and resurrection are not themselves Pentecost, but prepare for it. Similarly baptism must preceed chrismation, yet baptism is not chrismation. Immersion in water — baptism — is a figure of the death and burial of Christ — "Are you able to be baptized with the baptism with which I am baptized?" (Mk 10:38) — and engrafts us on to the Crucified and Risen Christ: "...all of us who have been baptized into Christ Jesus were baptized into his death. We were buried therefore with him by baptism into death.... For if we have been united with him in a death like his, we shall certainly be united with him in a resurrection like his" (Rom. 6:3-5). Anointing, chrismation, is a figure of Pentecost and conveys to us the Gift of God, the Holy Spirit. That is what St Paul tells us: "It is God himself who assures us, and you, of our standing in Christ, and has anointed us, marking us with his seal and giving us the pledge, the Spirit, that we carry in our hearts" (2 Cor. 1:21-22; JB). Is it not probable that this anointing was not only spiritual but was carried out, as in the time of Moses and David, with fragrant oil and aromatic balsam? This would explain Paul's phrase in the next chapter: "We are the aroma of Christ to God" (2 Cor. 2:15). This metaphor would be very strained and artificial unless it recalled a rite familiar to Christian readers; it is by chrismation that we are the aroma of Christ. That is also suggested by St John in his first letter (1 Jn 2:27): "But the anointing which you received from him abides in you, and you have no need that anyone should teach you; as his anointing teaches you about everything, and is true, and is no lie, just as it has taught you, abide in him."

It is evident that the terms used by St Paul and St John have quite a different ring if today's sacrament is designated by the same word, "chrisma", chrismation, as that used by the apostles to denote the anointing by the Spirit. When furthermore, according to Orthodox custom, the ritual action is punctuated by the phrase: "The *seal* of the Gift of the Holy Spirit", it immediately recalls the letter to the

Ephesians (1:13): "In him you... have believed,... were sealed with the promised Holy Spirit, which is the guarantee of our inheritance", and Eph. 4:30: "And do not grieve the Holy Spirit of God, in whom you were sealed for the day of redemption."

This seal of the Holy Spirit, this gift of the Holy Spirit, is very clearly conferred *after* baptism on two occasions related for us by the Acts of the Apostles. Here, however, it is a matter not of anointing with oil, but of laying on of hands by the apostles.

(a) *Acts 8:12-17*: "But when they (the Samaritans accompanying Simon the magician) believed Philip as he preached good news about the kingdom of God and the name of Jesus Christ, they were baptized, both men and women.... Now when the apostles at Jerusalem heard that Samaria had received the word of God, they sent to them Peter and John, who came down and prayed for them that they might receive the Holy Spirit; for it had not yet fallen on them, but they had only been baptized in the name of the Lord Jesus. Then they laid their hands on them and they received the Holy Spirit."

(b) *Acts 19:1-7*: "Paul... came to Ephesus. There he found some disciples. And he said to them, 'Did you receive the Holy Spirit when you believed?' And they said, 'No, we have never even heard that there is a Holy Spirit.' And he said, 'Into what then were you baptized?' They said, 'Into John's baptism.' And Paul said, 'John baptized with the baptism of repentance, telling the people to believe in the one who was to come after him, that is, Jesus.' On hearing this, they were baptized in the name of the Lord Jesus. And when Paul had laid his hands upon them, the Holy Spirit came on them."

Let us note that (1) baptism in the name of the Lord Jesus implies subsequent reception of the gift of the Holy Spirit ("Into what then were you baptized?" Implying: "If you had been baptized in the name of the Lord Jesus, you would have received the Holy Spirit") (2) the gift of the Holy Spirit is nevertheless received on the occasion of an act distinct from the immersion: the laying on of hands by the apostle. And this action is necessary. For in fact (a) although the Samaritans had already been baptized by Philip, the Spirit "had not yet fallen on them, but they had only been baptized in the name of the Lord Jesus" (Acts 8:16); (b) although Paul himself had just administered baptism "in the name of the Lord Jesus" to John's disciples in Ephesus, he had to lay hands on them for the Holy Spirit to come on them (Acts 19:7).

One problem nevertheless remains. In 2 Cor. 1 and 1 Jn 2, the gift of the Spirit appears to be linked, as in the Old Testament, with a chrismation, that is to say with anointing with aromatic oil, whereas in the two events narrated in Acts, the Spirit descends on the occasion of an imposition of hands by the apostles Peter, John or Paul. Hence the question immediately suggests itself whether in the apostolic period the gift of the Spirit was conferred by anointing or by laying on of hands.

The question arises all the more pointedly because the second letter to the Corinthians which we have quoted as an example of chrismation, was no doubt written in Ephesus, at the very period when Paul was laying hands on John's disciples.

When St Peter (1 Pet. 2:9) tells the faithful: "You are... a royal priesthood (*basileion hiérateuma*)", and the Book of Revelation reminds us that Jesus Christ "made us a kingdom, priests to his God and Father" (1:6), or again that the Lamb "made them (the saints) a kingdom and priests to our God" (5:10), it is clearly apparent that the New Covenant has extended to the whole of the Christian people the priesthood and royalty which in the days of the Old Covenant the Spirit of God conferred only on priests and kings by anointing with oil. From this to the assumption that this anointing itself was conferred in apostolic times to all the baptized, is but a step which the passages quoted (2 Cor. and 1 Jn) justify us, it would seem, in taking. One can then presume that as soon as Christian communities began to multiply even hundreds of kilometers from the place of residence of the nearest apostle, the idea arose of replacing imposition of hands by the apostles by an anointing performed by presbyters, a chrismation in conformity to the well-established Jewish tradition of anointing priests and kings.

Be that as it may, anointing or chrismation administered immediately after emerging from the waters of baptism, and conferring the gift of the Holy Spirit, is solidly attested in the universal Church from the third century of our era, as will be shown in the next section.

IV. Chrismation from the second to the fourth century

1. In Lyons (St Irenaeus)

Born in Smyrna (c. A.D. 125), St Irenaeus, bishop of Lyons, writing about A.D. 175, already refers to Chrismation in his "Presentation of the Apostolic Preaching": "The Son, inasmuch as he is God, receives from the Father, that is, from God, the throne of eternal kingship and the oil of anointing more abundantly than his companions. The anointing oil is the Spirit by which he is anointed, and his companions are the prophets, the just, the apostles and all who receive participation in his kingship, that is to say, his disciples" (n. 47). Jesus' chrismation is therefore the Holy Spirit, and his disciples receive it by participation. The rite, however, is not described.

2. In Carthage

(a) Tertullian

The earliest description of chrismation which has come down to us is no doubt that given about the year 206 by Tertullian (160-240) in his treatise *De baptismo*. It is obvious that he is describing a well-established rite, which means that he attests the tradition of the Church of Carthage in the second century. Here is what he writes (VI-VIII):

> Not that we obtain the Holy Spirit in the water,[3] but being cleansed in the water, under the Angel,[4] we are prepared for the Holy Spirit (VI).
>
> After this, having come out from the bath, we are anointed thoroughly with a blessed unction, according to the ancient rule, by which we were wont to be anointed for the priesthood with oil out of an horn. Wherefore Aaron was anointed by Moses; whence Christ is named from Chrism, which is "anointing", which, being made spiritual, furnished a name for the Lord, because he was anointed with the Spirit of God the Father: as it is said in the acts. For of a truth against Thy Holy Child, Whom Thou hast anointed, they were gathered together in that city. So in us also the anointing runneth over us bodily, but profiteth spiritually... (VIII).
>
> Next to this, the hand is laid upon us, calling upon and inviting the Holy Spirit, through the blessing.... Then that most Holy Spirit cometh down willingly from the Father upon the bodies that have been cleansed and blessed, and resteth upon the water of Baptism, as though remembering His ancient abiding place, who in the form of a dove descended upon the Lord.... For as, after the waters of the flood, whereby the former iniquity was purged, after the baptism (so to speak) of the world, the herald dove sent forth from the ark, and returning with an olive branch,... announced to the world the appeasement of the wrath of heaven.... By the same ordering of spiritual effect, doth the Dove of the Holy Spirit fly down upon our earth, that is, our flesh, when it cometh forth from the laver

after its former sins, bringing to us the peace of God, sent forth from the heavens, wherein is the Church, the prefigured ark (VIII).[5]

The theology of chrismation, as taught by all Orthodox tradition down to our own days, is already perfectly expressed in this passage: the gift of the Spirit, prepared for by the saving immersion, is received by the anointing. The anointing which gave the Lord his name of "Christ" when he came up out of the water, is given to us by him when in our turn we all come up out of the waters and receive the chrismation which makes us "christ-ians". Note the double rite, anointing with oil *and* imposition of hands.

(b) St Cyprian

Fifty years later St Cyprian sums up the meaning of chrismation in the words: "The newly baptized ought to appear before the heads of the Church to receive the Holy Ghost by invocation and the imposition of hands and to be made perfect by the seal (*signaculum*) of the Lord'.[6] The word *signaculum* exactly corresponds to the Greek term *sphragis*, seal, imprint; it denotes anointing in the form of a cross.[7]

3. In Rome (Hippolytus)

Hippolytus about 215, at more or less the same period as Tertullian, attests the baptismal tradition in Rome in a very precise and detailed way, in Chapter 21 of *The Apostolic Tradition*.[8] After describing the triple immersion, each immersion accompanied by a confession of faith in each of the divine Persons, he writes:

And afterwards, when he comes up[9] he shall be anointed by the presbyter with the oil of Thanskgiving, saying: I anoint thee with holy oil in the Name of Jesus Christ. And so each one drying himself with a towel they shall now put on their clothes and after this let them be together in the assembly" (ecclesia).

And the Bishop shall lay his hand upon them invoking and saying: O Lord God who didst count these worthy of obtaining the forgiveness of sins by the laver of regeneration, make them worthy to be filled with Thy Holy Spirit[10] and send upon them Thy grace, that they may serve Thee according to Thy Will: (for) to Thee (is) the glory, to the Father and to the Son with (the) Holy Ghost in the holy Church, both now and ever and world without end. Amen.

And after this pouring the consecrated oil (from his hand)[11] and laying his hand on his head, he shall say: I anoint thee with holy oil in God the Father Almighty and Christ Jesus and the Holy Ghost.

And sealing him on the forehead he shall give him the kiss (of peace).

Despite a few differences of detail, in particular the double anointing, the rite is the same as in Carthage: triple immersion, anointing, imposition of hands. The gospel expression "on coming up out of the water" underlines that the chrismation which immediately follows the immersion is an anamnesis of the chrismation by the Dove of Jesus "coming up out of the water" (Mk 1:10).

4. In Egypt (Euchologion of Serapion)

Serapion was Bishop of Thmuis in lower Egypt before 339. He was a contemporary of St Athanasius. The *euchologion*, or collection of prayers, which bears his name and no doubt consists of prayers which he used, testifies to traditions much earlier than Serapion himself. Gregory Dix[12] considers that they reflect Egyptian tradition at the beginning of the third century. Their style and theology in fact have a very much more primitive ring than those of the contemporaries of St Athanasius.[13] The chrismation prayer which we are about to quote is therefore probably not very much later than the texts of Tertullian and Hippolytus already referred to. It is entitled "Prayer in regard to the Chrism with which those who have been baptized are being anointed".[14]

> God of hosts, the helper of every soul that turns to thee and that cometh under the mighty hand of thy only-begotten,[15] we invoke thee to work in this chrism a divine and heavenly energy through the divine and unseen powers of our Lord and Saviour Jesus Christ, in order that they who have been baptized, and who are being anointed with it with the impress (*ektupoma*) of the sign of the saving cross of the only-begotten, by which cross Satan and every opposing power was routed and triumphed over, they also, as being regenerated and renewed through the washing of regeneration, may become partakers of the gift of the Holy Spirit, and being made secure by this seal, may continue steadfast and unmoveable....

The bath of baptism regenerates and renews. It is a "rebirth". The anointing allows "participation in the gifts of the Spirit". It is administered by a consecrated oil and applied like a seal by a cruciform action: these are undoubtedly the essential elements of the universal tradition of the Church of the early centuries.

5. In Jerusalem (St Cyril)

We do not, as far as I know, possess any witness to the tradition of the Church in the East on our subject earlier than the Catecheses of

St Cyril of Jerusalem (348). These, however, evidence a fully developed theology of chrismation which will remain the expression of Orthodox faith down to the present day and clearly testify to a firmly established rite already ancient in the days when St Cyril explained it to his catechumens. He devotes the whole of his 21st Catechesis to it (Catechesis 21 or Third Mystagogic Catechesis).[16]

And He (Christ) having bathed in the Jordan and the Holy Spirit descended personally upon Him, Like resting on Like. And you also when you came out of the pool of the sacred water, you received the anointing, the sacrament (mark) of that with which Christ was anointed, I mean to say, the Holy Spirit.... (1089A).

Christ was not anointed by an oil or by a physical perfume given by the hand of men. But the Father, Who established Him in advance as Savior of the whole universe, anointed Him with the Holy Spirit, as Peter says: Jesus of Nazareth whom God anointed with the Holy Spirit (Acts 10:38) (1089A).

This capital text contains three ideas:

(a) Chrismation, being given at the moment when the baptized "comes out of the pool of the sacred water", is the immediate sequel of baptism.

(b) It constitutes "the mark with which Christ was anointed". That is to say, chrismation of the baptized is the anamnesis of Jesus' anointing.

(c) And this anointing is the Holy Spirit. Daniélou admirably expresses the thought of St Cyril when he writes: "In the same way as baptism configures us to Christ dead and risen again, so Confirmation configures us to Christ anointed by the Holy Spirit".[17] That is precisely why it is appropriate to call it chrismation.

By our faith and burial in the baptismal waters, we personally appropriate today the resurrection of human nature realized once and for all by Christ and offered to all men on the glorious Sunday when the Risen Christ showed himself to his apostles. Similarly by faith and chrismation we personally appropriate today the gift of the Spirit. The Spirit rests eternally on the Son, but his presence on his human nature was manifested by his chrismation when he came up out of the waters of Jordan. He was given to the Church and offered to all men on the glorious Sunday of Pentecost.

St Cyril expresses this idea as follows:

And in the same way as Christ was truly crucified, truly buried, truly risen again, and as it has been granted to you in Baptism to be crucified with

Him, buried with Him, risen again with Him in a certain imitation, so it is with the chrism. He was anointed with the spiritual oil of exultation, that is to say, with the Holy Spirit, called the Oil of Exultation because He is the source of spiritual joy; and you, you have been anointed with perfumed oil, and become participants in Christ (1089A-B).

Here St Cyril develops an idea already expressed in Serapion's prayer: the oil of chrismation is a consecrated oil. For he goes on to say:

But beware of supposing this to be plain ointment. For as the Bread of the Eucharist, after the invocation of the Holy Ghost, is mere bread no longer, but the Body of Christ, so also this holy ointment is no more simple ointment, nor (so to say) common, after the invocation, but the gift of Christ; and by the presence of his Godhead, it causes in us the Holy Ghost.... and while the body is anointed with visible ointment, the soul is sanctified by the Holy and life-giving Spirit (III,1089 B15).

In the realistic conception which the Orthodox hold of the sacraments, the material element — water, oil, bread, wine — is not so much "the visible sign of an invisible grace" as the vehicle which bears the Holy Spirit. It is understandable, therefore, that very early[18] the Christian East could dispense with the presence of the bishop at chrismation and in that way not separate its celebration in time from that of baptism: the bishop invokes the Spirit on the oil, which becomes as it were an extension of his hand, and in the absence of the bishop, the presbyters can celebrate chrismation when the baptized person "comes up out of the water". The East will thus be able to avoid the dilemma which will present itself to the Western Church in the early fifth century, either of ignoring the necessary role of the bishop, the living symbol of church unity, or of splitting the baptismal rite by breaking the unity of immerison and anointing and thus ignoring the anamnesis of Jesus' chrismation "when he came up out of the water".

As regards the necessity of chrismation, St Cyril underlines it (1092 C2): "Having become worthy of this holy Chrism, you are called Christians (*christianoi*, christ-ians) making the name truly yours by regeneration. Before you were worthy of this grace, you did not truly merit this name, but you were on the way, aiming to become Christians."

Consequently the etymology of the words "christos", "christianoi", and our awareness of it, can play an important part in our conception of the meaning of the sacrament.

6. In Milan (St Ambrose)

St Ambrose was almost a contemporary of St Cyril, for he was consecrated bishop in 373, some 25 years after St Cyril wrote his

Catechesis. The bishop of Milan has left us two fine commentaries on baptism and chrismation, the *De sacramentis* which appears to be a collection of catechetical sermons taken down by a shorthand reporter, and the *De mysteriis*, a treatise composed for publication and with only the literary semblance of a sermon.[19] The content of the two works is very similar, though the second is obviously more polished than the first. We shall accordingly quote the two works in parallel columns. We shall observe firstly that in the time of Ambrose, baptism and chrismation were still celebrated in Milan almost in the same way as in Rome in the time of Hippolytus; secondly, that the meaning given to chrismation in the West at the end of the 4th century was just the same as in Jerusalem in the same period; and thirdly, that chrismation was still administered in the West as in the East, immediately on emerging from the waters of baptism. The only important difference is the personal participation of the bishop in the ceremony, which would soon prove impracticable and would lead in the West to dissociation of the two parts of the baptism-chrismation ceremony. We also note the rite of the washing of feet, which was peculiar to the Church of Milan. The following are some characteristic passages from the two works of St Ambrose:

(a) *First anointing by the bishop*
1. This takes place immediately after emerging from the water.

De sacramentis
II, 24: Therefore thou didst dip, thou camest to the priest (sacerdos = bishop). What did he say to thee? "God the Father Almighty", he saith, "who hath regenerated thee by water and the Holy Ghost, and hath forgiven thee thy sins, himself anoint thee unto eternal life."

De mysteriis
VI, 29: After all this[20] thou didst go up to the priest (sacerdos = bishop). Consider what followed. Was it not that which David said, It is like the ointment upon the head, that ran down unto the beard, even unto Aaron's beard?

2. By chrismation the baptized accede to the rank of the priests and kings of the Old Testament.

IV, I,3: What is the people itself but priestly? To whom it was said, But ye are a chosen generation, a royal priesthood, a holy nation, as saith the Apostle Peter. Everyone is

VI, 30: Understand why this is done,... for this purpose, that thou mayest become a chosen generation, priestly, precious, for we are all anointed with spiritual grace unto

anointed to the priesthood, is anointed to the kingdom also; but it is a spiritual kingdom and a spiritual priesthood.

the kingdom of God and the priesthood.

3. This fragrant anointing makes us "the aroma of Christ" (2 Cor. 2:15).

IV, I,4: In the second tabernacle is the censer also, which is wont to diffuse a sweet savour. So you also are now a sweet savour of Christ; no longer is there in you any stain of sins, any savour of rank error.

VI, 29: This is the ointment of which Solomon also says, Thy name is as ointment poured forth, therefore did the maidens love thee and draw thee (Cant. 1:2). How many souls regenerated today have loved thee, Lord Jesus, saying, Draw us after thee, we run to the odour of thy garments (Cant. 1:3), that they may drink in the odour of the resurrection!

(b) This first anointing by the bishop, immediately after baptism, was followed by the washing of the baptized person's feet by the bishop. This rite was peculiar to the Church of Milan. St Ambrose emphasizes that it was right to do this, even though the Church of Rome did not. After the washing of feet, a second anointing was celebrated by the bishop (*sphragis* or *signaculum*); this constituted the chrismation proper.

III, II,8: There follows[21] the spiritual seal,[22] which you have heard mentioned in the lesson,[23] today. For after the font it remains for the "perfecting" to take place, when, at the invocation of the priest (bishop), the Holy Spirit is bestowed.

VI, II,6: It is God who anointed thee, and the Lord signed thee, and put the Holy Spirit in thy heart. Thou hast therefore received the Holy Spirit in thy heart.

VI, II,7: Therefore God anointed thee, the Lord signed thee. How? Because thou wast signed with the image of the cross itself unto his passion.

VII, 41: Whence the Lord Jesus himself... says to the Church, set me as a seal upon thine heart, as a signet upon thine arm (Cant. 8:6).

VII, 42: Wherefore recollect that thou hast received the spiritual seal, the spirit of wisdom and understanding, the spirit of counsel and strength, the spirit of knowledge and godliness, the spirit of holy fear (Is. 11:2-3), and preserve what thou hast received. God the Father hath sealed thee, Christ the Lord hath confirmed thee, and hath given the earnest of the Spirit in thy heart, as thou hast learned from the apostolic lesson (2 Cor. 1:21-22).

(c) *In the baptismal celebration there is a trinitarian succession (De sacramentis, VI, II, 8)*: "Then, thou hast elsewhere a special work that, while God called thee, in baptism thou art as it were specially crucified with Christ. Then (as an instance of special operation), when thou receivest the spiritual seal, note that there is a distinction of persons, but that the whole mystery of Trinity is bound up together." In other words, St Ambrose appears to associate more particularly the call to the Father, baptism to the Son, and chrismation to the Spirit, without for all that dissociating one Person from the others, or call from baptism, or baptism from chrismation. Distinction without confusion: call, baptism, chrismation are linked, as are Father, Son and Holy Spirit.

The texts we have quoted show clearly:

1. That chrismation was a universal practice of the Christian Church of the 2nd to the 5th centuries.

2. That everywhere in that period it was celebrated immediately on coming up out of the water and consequently constituted an anamnesis of the anointing of the Lord Jesus.

3. That it was everywhere understood to confer the gift of the Holy Spirit as a logical consequence of baptism and its necessary complement.

V. The division of the sacrament in the West in the early 5th century

We have seen in the above section that in Rome in Hippolytus' time, baptism was followed by two anointings:

(1) The first, celebrated when the baptized person "came up out of the water", was performed by the priest.

(2) The second, administered when the baptized person had dressed, was celebrated by the bishop after laying on of hands.

Almost two centuries later in Milan, with St Ambrose, we have found the same two anointings, both celebrated by the bishop:

(1) One immediately after the believer had been "bathed".

(2) The other in the form of *signaculum*, immediately after the washing of feet peculiar to the Milanese rite.

The tradition of two successive unctions after the immersion accordingly appears to have been firmly established in the West.

We can thus appreciate the observations of Fr Edmond Chavaz, in the review *Foyers mixtes*, No 50[24]

In the time of Pope Innocent I (402-417), St Jerome (died 420) and St Augustine (died 430), evangelization had reached the countryside and led to the permanent establishment of priests in villages round the episcopal city. In these satellite centres, the priests celebrated the eucharist. Church unity had lost the symbol constituted by the single Sunday Eucharist presided over by the bishop surrounded by his presbyterium. It had also become impossible to reserve baptism to the bishop, especially since the custom of infant baptism had become general. It had been found necessary to authorize priests to baptize in the satellite centres. The bishops of East and West, however, insisted on reserving to themselves some participation in the rite of initiation in order to show clearly that Church unity around their person had not been weakened. The part retained by the Eastern bishops was minimal; they authorized the priests to accomplish the triple[25] baptismal rite in its entirety, reserving to themselves only the blessing of the chrism, the anointing oil. The Western bishops wanted the sign of unity to be much more striking; many of them were already in the habit of having the first part of the rite accomplished by their assistant priests. Very often it was the priest who administered the baptism and a first anointing of the body of the baptized,[26] in the baptistry, and then, having dressed, the newly baptized were led to the church to receive from the bishop another anointing on the head and laying on of hands. The Western innovation consisted in authorizing priests to accomplish in their parish baptistries what until then had been performed only in the episcopal baptistry (that is to say, the priest alone performed the immersion and the first anointing, while the bishop afterwards performed the second anointing and the laying on of hands). Church unity was thus clearly signified, but the unity of the rite had been split... A new name was given to the separated rite: it was henceforward called "confirmation".

From that time onwards, confusion was to grow in the West about the meaning of what was now regarded as two separate sacraments. St Jerome, for instance, writes,

I do not deny that this is the custom of the churches that the bishop should rush about (*excurrat*) to those who have been baptized by presbyters and deacons far from larger cities, to call down the Holy Spirit by the laying on of hands.... yet it is done rather for the glory of the bishop than for any pressure of necessity. If the Holy Spirit only descends at the mighty imprecation of a bishop, they are most unfortunate who live in farms or villages, or who happen to die in remote spots after being baptized by presbyters or deacons before the bishop can discover them.[27]

Pope Innocent I says exactly the opposite:

That the power of signing with oil and transmitting the Paraclete Spirit is due to bishops alone is not demonstrated by ecclesiastical custom alone, but also by the passage in the Acts of the Apostles which states that Peter and John were sent to transmit the Holy Spirit to those who had already been baptized. [28]

This confusion has persisted in the West until this day. The point of view of Protestants is basically on the lines of St Jerome's: confirmation as a sacrament conferring the Holy Spirit is regarded as useless and non-evangelical, and redundant as a repetition of baptism. Among Roman Catholics considerable uncertainity is perceptible as regards the meaning that should be attached to the sacrament and when it should be administered.

VI. Orthodox tradition in the Middle Ages and today

1. Nicholas Cabasilas

We find once more in the 14th century in the *Life in Jesus Christ* of Nicholas Cabasilas[29] the ideas developed by the Fathers of the second to fourth centuries, with, however, some deepening in Christology and the doctrine of man: "God was not far from men in distance, for he occupies every place, but by dissimilarity; our nature itself moved away from God by differing from him in everything, and had nothing in common, and our nature was merely human. But when flesh was deified and human nature united hypostatically to God — by the incarnation of the Son — ... The same person being divine, yet assuming humanity... abolishes the distance between divinity and humanity, becomes a link between the natures... our nature being deified in the flesh of the Saviour, nothing separates God from the human race any more... except sin. God has overthrown the double obstacle, that is, that of our nature by becoming incarnate and that of our will perverted by malice by allowing himself to be crucified, for it is the cross which has freed from sin. That is why, after baptism, which possesses the efficacy of the Saviour's cross and death, we proceed to chrismation, which is the communication of the Holy Spirit. For the two obstacles[30] being removed,[31] nothing more prevents the effusion of the Holy Spirit on all flesh.[32] 'Jesus' is the Anointed since all ages... before the incarnation. As long as the divinity was not yet communicated, he was the Anointed, remaining in himself. But when he assumed flesh, which received "the fullness of the Godhead"... Christ becomes... an unction: to communicate himself is what it means for him to become an unction and be poured out".[33]

Chrismation thus tends to realize in each of us (according to the "zeal we show to draw upon this treasure"[34]), by the Spirit who is poured out on our flesh, that deification of our nature which was perfectly accomplished in the person of Jesus who is God made man.

Cabasilas sees then the chrismation of the believer — made possible by baptism which prepares for it — the realization of what St Athanasius called the *theosis* of human nature by the incarnation of the Word. From St Irenaeus to Cabasilas, from the second to the 14th century, the same doctrine of chrismation persists and deepens.

2. The celebration of chrismation today in the Orthodox Church

The connection between the immersion of Jesus in the Jordan and the manifestation of the Spirit under the appearance of the Dove, between burial in the water and the gift of the Spirit, between cross and resurrection, on the one hand, and Pentecost on the other, between baptism and chrismation, is so evident that the two sacraments — if one insists on distinguishing them — are habitually administered together even today in the Orthodox Church in the course of the same celebration. It is accordingly by the same prayer that the Church, just before the immersion of the catechumen, asks that he may receive the benefits of baptism *and* those of chrismation.

(a) The benefits of baptism

Grant that he who is baptized in this water may be transformed; that he may put away from him the old man which is corrupt through the lusts of the flesh, and that he may be clothed upon with the new man, and renewed after the image of him who created him: that being buried after the pattern of thy death, he may in like manner be a partaker of thy Resurrection ...

(b) The benefits of chrismation

... and having preserved the gift of thy Holy Spirit, and increased the measure of grace committed to him, he may receive the prize of his high calling, and be numbered with the first-born whose name is written in heaven, in thee, our God and Lord, Jesus Christ.

This prayer underlines both the close connection and the distinction between the paschal mystery in which we share by baptism, and the mystery of Pentecost, in which we share by chrismation.

Immediately after the triple immersion, in the name of the Father, the Son and the Holy Spirit, the priest reads the prayer of chrismation (*euche tou Myrou*):

Blessed art thou, O Lord God Almighty, source of all good things, Sun of Righteousness, who sheddest forth upon them that were in darkness the light of salvation, through the manifestation of thine Only-begotten Son and our God; and who hast given unto us, unworthy though we be, blessed purification through hallowed water, and divine sanctification through life-giving Chrismation; who now, also, hast been graciously pleased to regenerate thy servant that hath newly received Illumination, by water and the Spirit, and grantest unto him remission of sins, whether voluntary or involuntary. Do thou, the same Master, compassionate King of kings, grant also unto him the seal of the gift of thy holy, and almighty, and adorable Spirit, and participation in the holy Body and the precious Blood of thy Christ.[35] Keep him in thy sanctification; confirm him in the Orthodox faith; deliver him from the Evil One, and from the inclinations of the same. And preserve his soul in purity and uprightness, through the saving fear of thee; that he may please thee in every deed and word, and may be a child and heir of thy heavenly kingdom, for thou art our God, the God who showeth mercy and saveth; and unto thee we ascribe glory, to the Father and to the Son, and to the Holy Spirit, now, and ever, and unto ages of ages. Amen.

Immediately after this prayer, the priest anoints the baptized person with the holy chrism, making the sign of the cross on his brow, eyes, nostrils, hands, mouth, ears, chest and feet, saying: "The seal of the gift of the Holy Spirit. Amen."

Then the baptized person is dressed and he makes his entry into the eucharistic assembly to the chant: "As many as have been baptized into Christ have put on Christ.[36] Alleluia."[37]

Conclusion

From the days of Moses and the anointing of Aaron down to the present day and the anointing of our baptized contemporaries, it is the same mystery of chrismation by the Holy Spirit of the Son of God "coming up out of the water", a mystery prefigured in the Old Testament and actualized in the sacrament of the Church, that we celebrate. From St Paul, St Peter and St John down to our days, by way of St Irenaeus of Lyons, Tertullian and St Cyprian of Carthage, St Hippolytus of Rome, Serapion of Thmuis, St Cyril of Jerusalem, St Ambrose of Milan, Nicholas Cabasilas of Thessalonica, it is the same Orthodox Faith and the same Apostolic Tradition that we confess and live in the same Catholic Church.

NOTES

1. Cf. Edmond Chavaz, in *Foyers chrétiens*, Lyons, 1981, no. 50, p.12.
2. J. Daniélou, *The Bible and the Liturgy*, London, 1960, p.6.
3. Tertullian in fact had said in IV (*A Library of Fathers*, Oxford, 1842, trans. C. Dogson, p.259): "Thus the nature of water, sanctified by the Holy One, itself also received the power of sanctifying." But we must not confuse the operation of the Holy Spirit, without which there cannot be any sacrament and by which the water is sanctified and adapted to engraft us on the buried and risen Christ, with the gift which the Holy Spirit makes of himself by the chrismation. Similarly one cannot confuse the fact that at his resurrection Christ "was made alive in the Spirit" (1 Pet. 23:18) — that is, the operation of the Holy Spirit — with the fact that at Pentecost the disciples "were all filled with the Holy Spirit" (Acts 2:4) — that is, the gift of the Holy Spirit.
4. A reference, no doubt, to the pool of Bethesda (John 5:1-18).
5. This text is quoted in: *Le bapteme d'après les Pères de l'Eglise*, texts chosen and presented by A. Hamman, Grasset, Paris, 1962. In C. Dodgson, *op. cit.*, pp.262-264.
6. Letter 77, quoted by J. Daniélou, *The Bible and the Liturgy, op. cit.*, p.119, n. 5.
7. Cf. infra, Serapion: "They who have been baptized and who are being anointed with it with the impress (ektupoma) of the sign of the cross".
8. *The Apostolic Tradition of St Hippolytus*, ed. G. Dix, London, 1937, (1967), p.38; trans. Dom Bernard Botte, Sources Chrétiennes no. 11 bis, p.87.
9. Expression taken from Mark 1:10.
10. Compare with the chrismation prayer in the present Orthodox rite: "Thou who now hast been graciously pleased to regenerate thy servant that hath newly received Illumination, by water and the Spirit, and grantest unto him remission of sins, whether voluntary or involuntary. Do Thou, the same Master, compassionate King of kings, grant also unto him the seal of the gift of thy holy, and almighty and adorable Spirit..."; *Service Book of the Holy Orthodox-Catholic Apostolic (Greco-Russian) Church*, ed. I.F. Hapgood, New York, 1906, p.282.
11. Dom B. Botte observes that "this double post-baptismal anointing, that of the bishop added to that of the priest, is proper to the Roman rite" (*op. cit.*, p.89).
12. *The Shape of the Liturgy*, Glasgow, 1959, pp.162-172.
13. See, for instance, the celebrated invocation of the Logos in the same Euchologion.
14. Cf. Lucien Deiss, *Aux sources de la liturgie*, p.141; Bishop Sarapion's Prayer Book, ed. J. Wordsworth, London 1923.
15. The expression suggests a laying on of hands.
16. Canon Bouvet, *Catechèses baptismales et mystagogiques*, Editions du Soleil levant, Namur, 1962, pp.166-470; E. tr. quoted from J. Daniélou, *The Bible and the Liturgy*, pp.117-118.
17. J. Daniélou, *op. cit.*, p.118.
18. From about 200, according to Mgr L. Duchesne, *Les origines du culte chrétien*, p.321; *Christian Worship: its Origin and Evolution*, London, 1910, p.330.
19. Cf. the commentary of Dom B. Botte in the Sources Chrétiennes edition, no. 25 bis: *Des sacrements. Des mystères*, Ed. du Cerf, Paris, 1961; St Ambrose, *On the Sacraments and On the Mysteries*, ed. J.H. Srawley, London, 1950.
20. That is to say, after the triple immersion.
21. That is to say, after the washing of feet.

22. Signaculum, sphragis.
23. 2 Cor. 1:21-23. Cf. *De Mysteriis* VIII, 42; *op. cit.*, p.141.
24. Lyons, 1981.
25. Confession of faith — immersion — chrismation.
26. Cf. Hippolytus.
27. Quoted by Edmond Chavaz, *op. cit.*, p.12; St Jerome, *Dialogus contra Luciferianos* 9.
28. Edmond Chavaz, *op. cit.*, p.12; cf. Denz-Bann, *Enchir. Symb.*, 98.
29. *La vie en Jésus Christ*, trans. S. Broussaleux, Chevetogue, 1960, Book III. Effects of chrismation in regard to life in Jesus Christ.
30. That of our nature and that of our sin.
31. By baptism.
32. By chrismation. Cf. John 2:28; Acts 2:79. N. Cabasilas, *op. cit.*, p.89.
33. *Ibid.*, p.88.
34. *Ibid.*, p.88.
35. Note the immediate prospect of eucharistic communion.
36. Rom. 6:2.
37. *Service Book of the Holy Orthodox-Catholic Apostolic (Greco-Russian) Church*, ed. I.F. Hapgood, New York, 1906, pp.279ff.

CONFIRMATION IN THE 1980s

DAVID R. HOLETON

> What good can it do to me, after the mystery of baptism, to have the ministration of confirmation? So far as I can see, we have not obtained everything from the font, if after the font we still need something new.[1]

Faustus' fifth-century question about confirmation marks the beginning of the development of a separate theology of the post-baptismal anointing and imposition of hands.[2] Over the centuries Faustus has not been wanting for successors. What has been called a rite in search of a theology has been doing more searching over the past decade than at any time since its appearance. The answers being found are not any closer to producing an adequate resolution to the question now than they were for Faustus or for the Reformers of the sixteenth century. The best can be done at present is to point to the areas of disagreement that highlight the present state of the question. These involve historical, theological, pastoral, ecclesiological and ecumenical dimensions.

The context of the discussion

Historical development

The vast literature of the past decades on Christian initiation has had a profound effect on confirmation. Most discussions on the subject now at least integrate into the broader subject of Christian initiation, something that for most is now commonplace but in the context of the historical treatment of the subject is relatively innovative.

One thing that has become evident from the historical research is that confirmation has rarely had an easy time in its pastoral

---

• David R. Holeton is Professor of Liturgy, Trinity College, Toronto.

observance. The whole medieval canonical tradition revolved around a series of limits before which children had to be confirmed, beginning with a matter of weeks after the child's baptism and culminating — through lack of observance — at seven years. During most of this time infants received the eucharist at the time of their baptism and, where confirmation came to be required before the eucharist could be received, it was often to coerce the laity into receiving a sacrament that was generally ignored. Indeed confirmation was so generally ignored that the rite itself came to be included at the beginning of the pontifical as most candidates for ordination had not been confirmed. The general lack of attention paid to the sacrament was not only a lay phenomenon. Because the sacrament was restricted to the bishop its ministration varied directly with the pastoral concern of the bishop, the size of the diocese and the clemency of the weather. Vast dioceses in inhospitable parts of northern Europe rarely saw episcopal visitations. In many of these its was impossible for even the most conscientious of bishops to travel the entire diocese in the course of a normal episcopate. This again affected the canonical time within which confirmation had to be received as well as the manner of celebration of the sacrament. It was not uncommon for bishops to confirm on horseback as he rode through their dioceses and for canons to require parents living within a particular distance from the bishop's projected route to bring their unconfirmed children to line the roadside so that they could be confirmed as the bishop passed. This practice seems to have been so common that the author of the *Vita* of St Hugh of Lincoln (a not untypical northern European diocese) makes a particular point of the fact that Hugh always dismounted before confirming unlike many of his fellow bishops.[3]

It would be erroneous, however, to see this general disregard for confirmation as simply a series of medieval abuses. In Hispanic countries the sacrament was generally a rite for the very young until the last 10-15 years. It would simply be announced that on a particular Sunday the bishop would be confirming in his cathedral and parents would bring their three to five year olds to be confirmed. Most Hispanic Christians lived out their lives — as communicants — never having been confirmed. In England it was not until the nineteenth century that most Anglicans were communicants, not because they had been confirmed but rather because, in the words of the rubric, "they were ready and desirous to be confirmed". Even in churches of the continental Reformation where confirmation has often attained the place of the most significant rite in a Christian's life, the esteem for confirmation has not always been unclouded. Confirmation was unknown in the Church of Sweden until the beginning of the nineteenth century, and then only appeared as a rite of admission to communion.

The particular concern for confirmation of the past two decades must be analyzed in the context of the entire history of the rite. The premise with which much catechetical literature on confirmation is written is that the rite has inherent meaning and that it ought to be treated as a significant event in itself. This has almost nothing to do with the way confirmation has been treated during most of its history. A simple survey of the popular customs that have been associated with confirmation and those associated with baptism and first communion make it clear that the popular roots are shallow and do not penetrate deeply into the general religious culture. Confirmation ceremonies are generally those of the last two centuries and bear the marks of a heavy-handed rationalism, unlike customs associated with baptism and first communion.

The effect of historical research on the theology of confirmation

The incorporation of confirmation in the spectrum of Christian initiation has produced a theological division over the subject which is becoming increasingly rigid. There are now many who see confirmation as being intelligible only if it is understood as being part of a one-time unitary rite of baptism that through historical and geographical accident has become isolated from that rite both in time and place.[4]

There is essential agreement among those who take this position on confirmation that could be summarized in four points.

1. A sealing in the Spirit is included within the total baptismal synaxis, at least by the early third if not during the course of the second century.
2. This sealing occurs in direct, intimate and inseparable relationship with the Spirit-filled water-event. The water-event, with its sealing, together with the Spirit-filled table-event of the eucharistic thanksgiving, constitutes "baptism in its fullness".
3. The form the sealing takes is that of an oleaginous handlaying and consignation with pneumatic or epicletic prayer.
4. The form, place, and meaning of the sealing have absolutely nothing to do with the physical, social, emotional, intellectual, or

even "spiritual" age of the initiate. The form and meaning of the sealing have rather to do with the fact that the initiate is entering into a Spirit-filled community of faith through the passion, death, and resurrection of Christ, who has himself become the life-giving Spirit by which the community believes and lives.[5]

This understanding has produced revised baptismal rites which restore the integrity of the original rite and attempt to reverse what is seen as a process of sacramental devolution.[6] Underlying this consensus are two important premises. The first is that baptism is normatively for adults; that is, the fullness of the sign of baptism is to be found in the baptism of believing adults. What the church does to infants must be interpreted as being derivative from that norm. (That is *not* to say that churches baptizing infants must desist but rather that when the church baptises an adult it must not be interpreted as an anomalous example of what normally is a sacrament for infants.) The second premise is that there is a disjuncture between church and society — Christianity and civil religion. Both premises give the supporters of this position a certain affinity for a model of the church that antedates the establishment of Christendom. It is therefore easy to appreciate that its advocates are less easy to find within state churches or where folk-religion is well established.

On the other hand there are those who see confirmation as having an integrity of its own and that its separation from baptism is commendable and self-justifying.[7] For those who take this position, confirmation remains a distinct event even if it happens to take place at the same time as baptism. Included in this group are at least three types of people. There are some who see an inherent distinction between baptism and the sealing with the Spirit even in the New Testament. They would suggest that the separation of confirmation from baptism was the natural development as we are dealing with two distinct realities. The second group would see confirmation as a rite of personal commitment, required at some point in the life of the Christian to solemnly mark the point at which one makes a mature commitment to Christ, takes on for one the promises made by one's sponsors at baptism; or to mark the point at which one becomes a full member of the Christian community. The third group would include many of those who have written about confirmation in recent years. They would advocate confirmation as a rite of intensification, of lay ordination or of graduation from catechesis. The distinctions between these groups are not easy to make; there is frequent cross-fertilization of ideas. What would characterize this third segment is that, on the whole, their rationale for confirmation is a novelty amongst the traditional rationales that have been given to confirmation.

This position dominates in a number of very different churches. In some it is to legitimize traditional practices or because the church has inherited a sacramental theology that defines a particular number of sacraments. The position is perhaps more tenacious in traditions that have placed a high value on the individual's public expression of his or her commitment to Christ. This is not always the product of pietism but rather a response to state-churches or places where folk-religion is tenacious. In these situations, where a vast percentage is baptised yet does not practise, confirmation rather than baptism becomes the mark of the Christian. In other situations, where the culture is hostile to Christianity either for political or religious reasons, confirmation plays the role of a public expression of allegiance to what is a religious sub-culture. This is not uncommon in countries where the early teens involve a public ceremony of commitment to the state. The final segment of those who provide a rationale for an independent rite are often those who, having found the unitary rite impossible to implement in their own churches for either political or cultural reasons, are trying to provide some meaning to a rite that otherwise has become pastorally and catechetically vacuous.

What must be made clear, however, is that these basic positions do not characterize mutually exclusive traditions, but can both be found within single churches and religious families.[8] Sometimes the variance is regional or national, but as often it is also evident within the local church.

Appeal to the East

While the question as a whole is a Western one, and rather remote to the Byzantine and Eastern tradition, both Western schools have turned to the East for support, and both claim to find it. Those who take the unitary position look at the practice of baptism, chrismation (and first communion) and find a unitary rite which they see as proof of their claims. However, those who see confirmation as having an integrity of its own look at the same Byzantine and Eastern traditions and see three distinct rites: baptism, confirmation, first communion.

Here orthodox theologians are of little help; first because they themselves are not of a common mind. Some would suggest that even posing the question posits a Western epistomology that is alien to Orthodox sacramental theology.[9] Others use the Western vocabulary without hesitation although it is not always clear that the content is the same.[10] What can be said is that the appeal to the East for a solution to the question has reached an impasse that will not be resolved until serious study has been made of the genesis and use of Western terminology by the Orthodox and Eastern churches.[11] These traditions have much to offer the Western churches as they explore new meanings for Christian initiation — particularly their traditional attitudes towards children as part of the Christian community and their participation (from infancy) in the whole sacramental life of the church. What they cannot offer, at present, is a solution to the question of confirmation as it is being debated in the West.

One area of present historical research that may well contribute much to the question is the serious examination of the Syrian baptismal tradition.[12] Here, what had been traditionally seen as a curious anomaly is proving quite likely to be the oldest Eastern practice; one baptismal anointing only, and that before the water rite. For churches concerned with the development of the tradition, and which are trying to be sensitive to it in their liturgical revisions, this will have a significant effect. The basic impetus of this work would be a re-examination of some basic baptismal imagery. The conclusion of those who have worked on this material is that the primary liturgical image of the Holy Spirit in baptism was originally eschatological. The Spirit marks the Christian for the day of fulfilment, and is the firstfruits of an eternal heritage (2 Cor. 1:21; Eph. 1:13-14; 4:30). The Spirit marked the Christian as God's own, conferring sonship, daughterhood, and the royal priesthood. As the eschatological expectation of the church waned, the primary liturgical image for baptism became that of death and burial. With that basic shift in the primary image of baptism the anointing took place after the baptism and was interpreted as an anointing conferring particular gifts, the water-rite having assumed the images of sonship and priesthood formally associated with the Spirit. The consequence of this re-examination of the imagery would be a greater reluctance to separate in time the work of the Spirit from the water-rite. For in the developed Syrian tradition the Spirit was active, and bestowed himself on the initiates from the pre-baptismal anointing to the concluding eucharist.

The pastoral practice of confirmation

Just as opinion is divided over the meaning of confirmation within particular churches as well as between the churches, so too its practice varies tremendously within as well as between churches. Confirmation is in a state of pastoral crisis in many churches. Churches that had traditionally confirmed children in their early teens are asking serious questions about the advisability of the practice, while others that had confirmed at an earlier age are discovering themselves landed with an entirely new sacrament invented by educators.

Several examples may help illustrate this experience of crisis among the churches. In some parts of the Anglican Communion confirmation had been regarded as a rite of maturity in which the confirmand took upon oneself the baptismal vows made on one's behalf by the godparents when one was an infant. Confirmation usually took place between ages 13-15 and was normally required before admission to the eucharist. Surveys made in the 1950s and 1960s revealed that a significant percentage (sometimes well over 50%) of those who made a mature profession of commitment to Christ and received their first communion never returned to receive communion again; a curious type of "mature" commitment. [13]

In Latin America one priest and professor describes the present practice of confirmation as the invention of European religious educators. Before Vatican II confirmation in Argentina took place at a very early age and was seen as being part of the sequence of baptism — confirmation — eucharist. Now it is related to education and initiation into Catholic Action. It has lost any relationship it ever had with either baptism or the eucharist. It has taken on an independent status and function of its own as the sacrament of education. When the same priest was asked for a bibliography of local books on confirmation he replied that they didn't exist, everything had been imported from Europe.

In Africa adult baptism is as common as the baptism of infants in the Roman Catholic Church. The period of preparation before an adult is baptised is usually three years. When the adult is baptised he or she is given the eucharist for the first time. Confirmation, however, is witheld for a year as a means of obliging the baptizand to continue with another year's catechesis.

These examples can but point to the general pastoral confusion that surrounds the celebration of the rite in the churches today. They also help clarify some questions that need to be posed by the churches on their own pastoral practices and the theological pre-suppositions that underlie them.

Confirmation and the life cycle

There can be little doubt that the convention of relating baptism and confirmation to the life-cycle events of birth and maturation produces a host of difficulties in attaining an adequate grasp of what this one compound sacramental act truly is. The analogies of baptism with physical birth and of confirmation with personal maturity or social majority have become univocal in practice. This requires that baptism be treated as a special sacrament of early infancy and confirmation, correlatively, as the special sacrament of pre- or post-adolescence. This assumption having been entrenched leads into an imperceptible transfer of one's own personal public confession of Christian faith from baptism to confirmation. It leaves baptism as little more than a preliminary if major exorcism of sin, and inflates confirmation into a *de facto* surrogate baptism administered in the midst of adolescent psychosocial individuation crises.[14]

It is not an overstatement to assert that, for the average church member, confirmation has often been given a greater public emphasis than any other liturgical action. In churches where infant baptism has been practised, confirmation has certainly assumed a much more important place in the corporate life of the community than baptism has for centuries. In many churches infants are baptised at small family-only services and confirmation assumes the public dimension that rightly belongs to baptism. This is seen in its extreme in churches which privately baptise any unbaptised confirmation candidates immediately before their confirmation. The catechetical preparation for confirmation, when it is the rite of admission to communion, has been directed at the commitment of the individual, his or her maturity, and the completion of one's religious education rather than on entrance into the eucharistic community where one must play one's role with fellow Christians. This treatment of confirmation puts baptism and the eucharist in a secondary position that no church would support. Yet is is only the natural conclusion to be drawn by those who see the churches dealing with baptism as if it were a matter normally the concern of infants and confirmation for the "mature". This imbalance was even more evident in churches in which it was the practice to separate the service of confirmation from the celebration of the eucharist.

The equation of confirmation and Christian maturity poses other serious problems. Reformation churches that fixed the age for confirmation somewhere in the early teens did so in a culture in which the age of confirmation was usually that at which some other social or legal status was conferred. The child who was being confirmed became an adult in the church with all the responsibilities involved. At the same time the child achieved a civil majority with its corresponding responsibilities. (In England the age of confirmation was related to the time after which godparents were no longer legally responsable for the care of their godchildren; in Europe the age for confirmation was often that at which a person could legally contract marriage.) Today, the age for confirmation remains that of the past, and yet it confers no status of legal majority either in the church or in the state. The young confirmand is refused a vote or the right to take a place on church councils because he or she is not old enough, and no civil authority would allow the person to enter into any legally binding contract (let alone marriage) nor would most states hold the person legally culpable for his/her actions. Confirmation as a rite of maturity is undermined by the churches' refusal to confer with it what would have to be seen as the rights and responsibilities of the mature Christian.

The corollary of the equation, confirmation = Christian maturity, is the equation Christian maturity varies directly with age. This is one of the most pernicious equations to have found a place in Western churches. It has led to children being denied their place in the Christian community, let alone access to the eucharist, and has borne its fruit in an arid cerebral Christianity that ignores the wholeness of the individual person. Such an equation refuses to take seriously Jesus' using a child as a model for the kingdom of God. (Mt. 18:1-4) So too it is a misunderstanding of Jesus' command that all Christians are to become mature (Mt. 5:48) There is a dynamic tension between these two images and their place in the life of the Christian, yet each must be taken seriously and not ignored in favour of the other. In a real sense the churches today are rediscovering that the two are complementary. This is very much the result of what for many churches is the revolutionary idea of accepting children as regular members of the worshipping community.

If this new discovery tells us anything it must certainly be this: age has very little to do with Christian maturity. Through our children we have access to an insight into the Christian message to which as adults we have often been blind. We can see in the child the perfect receiver, unembarrassed and graceful, receiving the unmerited and unearned gift of God's grace. We can see in the child, ever launching out, unafraid, into a perilous world, the model of perfect trust. We can see in the child infectious, effervescent joy, the model of the delight of the saints. These qualities have a tendency to fade in adults. The consequence is that the churches are becoming less certain about designating any particular moment as that at which Christian maturity is attained.

Pastoral experience over recent years would indicate that the early teens are perhaps the least appropriate to designate as a time for a profession of mature Christian faith. At least in North America pastoral experience indicates that significant numbers of children are confirmed who have no evident religious conviction. They are at an age where pleasing their parents is still important and being confirmed is a relatively harmless way in which to do it. Even though they will perhaps admit that they do not even believe in God they are not willing not to be confirmed because of the distress it wil cause at home.

In some countries, particularly Germany and Scandinavia, confirmation as a rite of passage has become fairly engrained in the popular culture. Many young people are confirmed, not because of any religious conviction, but because of the material advantages that accompany the event. Being confirmed brings with it tremendous (for a young person) material benefits, presents that often include tape recorders, televisions and even cars. In some Scandinavian countries there has developed the practice of purely secular confirmations in which those who do not wish to make any sort of religious profession of faith are able to participate in a purely secular rite that will bring with it the same material benefits that their peers who are confirmed in church are receiving.

A similar experience is that of the church in some Eastern socialist and African countries where there is a solemn rite for the consecration of youth to the goals and ideals of the state. Often the young person is obliged to participate in the rite or else suffers serious social and educational discrimination. The church often finds itself offering confirmation first as the Christian substitute for this secular rite and then, because of a pastoral acquiescence to the social reality, as a Christian supplement. Children often find themselves consecrating themselves to the ideals of the state one Sunday and to Jesus Christ the next.

Two final questions must be posed when confirmation is used to sanctify a particular stage of the life cycle. The first bears on the unrepeatability of the rite. Most churches treat confirmation like baptism, as an unrepeatable event. This bears within it the seeds of a serious pastoral problem. Many children are confirmed just at the age they fall away from the church. In some churches 50-80% of young confirmands have stopped practising within the year of their confirmation. When they later return to the church and wish to make a public act of commitment to Christ, pastors are often at a loss as to a manner in which this can be expressed liturgically. Even in traditions that do not interpret confirmation sacramentally there is a general unwillingness to re-confirm those who wish to re-profess their allegiance to Jesus Christ. The one traditional means of "mature commitment" has been exhausted and the person returning to the church is left with a felt need that is unfulfilled.

The second question is that posed by child psychologists. What is accomplished by a rite of commitment that involves promises the child is not capable of making? Few children of 13-15 are able to conceive of, let alone profess, a life-long loyalty to anyone. Their understanding of the adult-oriented questions and promises that are asked and made are not those the adults posing them anticipate. What is the meaning of an adult oath to a teenager? How can one be expected to understand and keep that oath when one's word is not accepted as binding in any other social activity in which one participates? A quick look at the pastoral experience of marriage over the past two decades will quickly reveal that few people even in their twenties appreciate, or take seriously, a vow of life-long commitment. To elicit such a vow from a teenager is less than realistic and, in effect, reduces the seriousness with which any other religious vow is taken. Pastors continue to remind people of the seriousness of vows taken before God and then turn and ask the wrong people to make them.

Confirmation and catechesis

Just as relating confirmation with adolescence implies that baptism is for infants, so too confirmation as the culmination of an intense period of religious instruction implies that Christian education is for children and is something from which it is possible to graduate. In many churches confirmation has become totally subservient to an exalted view of catechesis. This is true in churches where confirmation has a sacramental status as well as in those where it does not. The earlier example of confirmation being withheld until adulthood is illustrative of this. In France it is not uncommon to use confirmation in a similar way to prolong the period of catechesis. Confirmation becomes one of those "events" in successive years (along with first communion and *profession de foi*) to assure that children continue to participate in the parish programme of catechesis. This poses several problems.

First, in churches that hold a sacramental view of confirmation, it subjects the reception of the sacraments to having completed a set course of religious instruction. This is a complete novelty in these traditions. To quote one Roman Catholic sacramental theologian: "Religious educators have invented an entirely new sacrament. They are making confirmation into something it has never been in our tradition." Despite the objections of sacramental theologians, confirmation is being treated as the sacrament of education.

In churches where confirmation has not been interpreted in a sacramental manner but in which it has long been associated with an intense period of religious instruction — be it six weeks or three years — the effect has been to conclude all religious instruction with confirmation. Religious education becomes a matter solely for the young. The popular view then becomes that once one is confirmed all that need be learned has been accomplished. This poses two acute problems. First it undermines the basic principle of religious education — that is, it is for adults and only derivatively for children. Religious education cannot and will not be taken seriously by adults as long as it is thought of being simply a course of instruction for the young similar to what they were given as children. That perhaps was once possible in societies that were pervaded by a Christian culture. It is certainly no longer possible today.

Second, the present practice of ending religious instruction with confirmation means that it ends just as it is beginning to become possible. Educators generally agree that the ability to conceptualize — to do what we usually mean by "thinking" — begins in early adolescence. Only with adolescence and adulthood is a person capable of constructing theory, philosophy or theology. The pre-adolescent is incapable of abstract thinking even though he or she may be taught abstract words. Not until somewhere between eleven and fifteen do formal operations, the capacity to think about thoughts (one's own or other people's) usually begin. Then a person can perform mental operations, form hypothesis, distinguish between what is real and what is possible, consider multiple possibilities, and formulate theories which interrelate many factors. [15]

The consequences of this to the present pattern of "confirmation-ends-catechesis" are staggering. For first it tells us that we have been teaching the wrong subjects. A pre-confirmation catechesis that places a heavy emphasis on doctrinal formulation is both inappropriate and irrelevant to the young people at whom it is aimed. They are simply not capable of dealing with such material.

The question that is raised for us is not "how can we make our children into Christians?" but "how can we be Christians with our children?" The task of influencing the religious development, or the task of Christian education, is not exclusively or even primarily about thinking. What we are discovering about faith development is making it clear that this is about belonging and participating — in family, in friendship groups, in special interest groups, in church as community of faith. [16] The question that we must then pose is whether or not confirmation at the end of catechesis helps or hinders this process. If confirmation is used as a barrier to full participation in the life of a Christian community, then it can only be seen as a hindrance to religious development. If the child cannot share in the eucharist before confirmation; if confirmation is a means of assuring that a certain achievement has been attained before one can participate fully in the life of the community — then it becomes a major barrier to a child's growth in faith.

Confirmation and the Church

There are three subjects that may at first seem unrelated but find in confirmation an integrating factor. These are: the Spirit, the eucharist and the bishop. In each case the question of confirmation poses important questions about how one understands the church.

The Spirit

It has become quite popular in a large spectrum of confirmation material to characterize confirmation as encounter with or engagement in the Holy Spirit. This should be the cause for considerable reflection. It must first be said quite clearly that biblical exegetes are quite unwilling to use any text from the Acts of the Apostles as a proof text for confirmation in the Apostolic church. [17] The instances of the gifting of the Spirit through the imposition of hands are atypical of the baptismal tradition received and practised in the church and the use of Acts as a proof text for confirmation was never employed in any confirmation rite of the Western church until after the Reformation (and naturally does not find a place in Eastern liturgies of baptism). Yet there is no doubt that those who received Christian baptism in the New Testament also received the Holy Spirit. It is not at all clear whether or not this was associated with any particular rite. What is clear, however, is that life in Christ was also life in the Spirit and that incorporation into the Body of Christ, the Spirit-formed community, without also sharing in the Holy Spirit was unthinkable. Thus to treat confirmation as an engagement in life in the Spirit is erroneous, if not dangerous.

If one thing can be learned from the Acts, and it is certainly confirmed in the charismatic movement in the churches today, it is that the Spirit cannot be restricted to particular liturgical events. Many churches today are experiencing the Spirit in a new and fresh way. The charismatic movement has had a profound effect on the life of many churches, yet it is difficult to see how this experience can be incorporated into the liturgical celebration of confirmation. Indeed the two are, in many ways, antithetical.

The eucharist

In a number of churches confirmation existed as a rite of admission to the eucharist. In some of these churches the rite was able to exist quite independently of either sacramental or maturity-commitment interpretations.[18] Over the past decade this rationale for confirmation has lost tremendous ground. The renewal of patterns of community life and the admission of young children to the eucharist by churches of almost all confessional families pose a particular question to this rationale for confirmation. What status does confirmation now confer? In the past it was that of communicant or full membership in the church. This is no longer the case. If baptism confers at least the right to receive the eucharist, as the continuing sign of membership in the body, churches whose rationale for confirmation was that it was, at least in part, a required rite to be received before communion need to examine their continuation of a rite that has lost its principal rationale.

During the examination it should be important to ask: "in exactly what way does confirmation relate the individual to the church?" For many churches confirmation has borne much of the weight that properly belongs to baptism. This can be understood and appreciated in any historical perspective when baptism was often administered indiscriminately, with no particular assurance that the infant baptised would grow up in the context of the community of faith. But today baptismal discipline is very different in many churches. It is no longer seen as being primarily for infants. The perspective in which incorporation into Christ and the church is seen makes the sharp distinction between the confirmed and the unconfirmed untenable. Again, this is particularly clear when one takes account of the increasingly common practice of admitting unconfirmed children to communion. They already receive all the church has to give, they cannot be fuller members of the body than they already are.

The bishop

In some churches confirmation can only be celebrated by the bishop. In some of these churches bishops have been the most resistant force to any change in their churches' traditional practice of confirmation. Why? Quotations from two bishops shed some light on the matter. The bishop of a large, urban, North American city commented: "Without confirmation I would have no right to visit a parish." Another European bishop remarked that "episcopal confirmation was important because it established a pastoral relationship between the bishop and the young". His diocese was so large that he could never visit each parish once during the course of his episcopate. On the other hand there are bishops who complain of being nothing more than a confirmation machine.

These comments reflect a crisis of *episcopé*. Oversight of the local church cannot be defined in terms of the right to come and confirm. Indeed, given the practice of many episcopal churches in which the bishop arrives shortly before the service and leaves shortly after it, it is difficult to see how bishops see this flying visit to a congregation as an occasion on which a pastoral relationship can be established with anyone, let alone a large group of young people who are often not prepared to let themselves be known by this strange visitor they may never have seen before in their church and may never see again for years.

Episcopal churches who reserve the rite of confirmation to bishops alone should ask themselves serious questions about their conception of *episcopé*. Having delegated the dominical sacraments of baptism and eucharist to other clergy, what rationale is there for not delegating confirmation too? Churches today are placing far greater demands on their bishops than they have for a long time. Communities are coming to expect more of an episcopal visitation than simply a celebrant at a confirmation. Is not perhaps the traditional practice of confirmation in these churches becoming an impediment to the bishop's exercising the type of pastoral ministry that is being asked of him by today's churches?

The Spirit, the eucharist and the bishop are three ways of interpreting the relationship between the individual and the whole body. All three are agents or signs of the unity of that body. In the past confirmation was an interpretative factor of that unity: it has been as gifting the Spirit, admitting to the eucharist, and establishing a particular communion between the individual and the bishop.

Today, however, the interpretative factor of confirmation is contested in each of these three. There are few who would maintain that confirmation is the unique gifting of the Spirit or that it is the determinative factor for admission to the eucharist. It is doubtful that it establishes a pastoral relationship with a bishop that was not begun at least in baptism and is not continued in every eucharist that is celebrated by the bishop's personal delegate in a particular Christian community. Confirmation has now become an impediment rather than an agent in interpreting the unitive agents of Spirit, eucharist and *episcopé*. One can only ask, can confirmation any longer be provided with a rationale for its independent existence?

Confirmation and pastoral practice

> I allow that confirmation be administered provided that it is known that God has said nothing about it, and knows nothing of it, and what the bishops say about it is false. (Martin Luther[19])

Having examined confirmation in terms of the life-cycle, catechesis and the unity of the church and in each case finding that it poses serious questions about current practice in various churches, something must be said of the positive qualities of confirmation. The first thing that must be said is that it has a tremendous resilience. Confirmation can be disowned by exegetes, disproved by liturgists, decried by theologians and denounced by educators, but it continues. This resilience cannot be dismissed totally as misdirected popular piety.

There is a very strong-felt need for some sort of rite in which there can be a mature profession of faith. This is sometimes diffused by using the paschal vigil or the baptism of others as a major occasion for all participating in the rite to renew their own baptismal vows. The regular celebration of, and participation in, the eucharist can also be used as an instrument of the renewal of commitment to Christ. Yet the demand for a special rite of commitment remains. The Orthodox are often willing to acknowledge that a rite of this type would be pastorally useful for them. The appearance of services for the profession of faith (as distinct from, and at a later age than, confirmation) in some Roman Catholic churches witnesses to this felt need as does the practice of some Roman bishops refusing to confirm until the candidates are in their final year of secondary school. There is almost universal agreement among Anglican theological commissions that have argued that confirmation cannot be justified apart from baptism. Yet the synods of the same countries insisting that some sort of rite for mature commitment be provided again points to the strong-felt need for a rite of maturity. All this cannot simply be ignored. What, then, is to be done?

A step in the right direction has been taken where the word confirmation has been dropped in favour of something like commitment. Confirmation cannot continue to bear the weight it has had in the past. To continue to use the word but to give it a new meaning only adds to the present confusion. The new meaning would inevitably be subsumed by the others by sheer weight of tradition. Experience has already shown this. Despite all the alternative interpretations that have been given to confirmation over past years (ordination of the laity, sacrament of ecclesial communion, rite of intensification etc.), the traditional interpretations are those which remain in general commerce, while the novelties fade away.

The secondary danger in giving confirmation new interpretations is that they almost invariably are qualities that are misattributed to confirmation. Both ordination of the laity and sacrament of ecclesial community are examples of this. The ordination of the laity is surely baptism; it is then that the individual comes to share in the royal priesthood. Can there be a sacrament of ecclesial communion greater or more specific than the eucharist? Much of what we would attribute to confirmation would be impossible if we stopped thinking that baptism was a purely infantile matter and took the eucharist seriously.

There is no reason that a rite of commitment could not sit comfortably alongside a renewed understanding of Christian initiation. Initiation into the body of Christ is by water and the Spirit. It is the rite by which one is endowed with all the privileges and responsibilities of the Christian community. It admits to the Supper. Later, at a time of religious maturity (completely independent of physical maturity or catechetical preparedness) *those who so desired* could make a public profession of their faith in Jesus Christ and a commitment to him. If they fell away and later returned to the church, or if they entered a new plane of religious experience or growth and felt they wished to renew this commitment they could do so freely.

But the rite would remain for *those who desired it*. It is impossible to programme religious growth. Our present experience with confirmation in the churches tells us at least that. It is quite possible to posit (in the West as well as in the Orthodox churches) a child who is baptized as an infant, comes each week with his or her parents to the eucharist and receives communion, participates in the community life of the congregation and its catechetical programmes, grows slowly into Christian maturity. Yet in all this experience there may never be a moment when one experiences one's commitment to Jesus Christ in such a radically different way one week from the next that it need be expressed in a particular rite of commitment. For the person that commitment may be adequately expressed in continued participation in the life of the faith community, the weekly eucharist or the general renewal of baptismal vows at public baptism or the Easter vigil. Such a person need not be made to feel that his or her commitment and status in the community is in any way wanting. Similarly, another person who has had the same experience as a child may feel a very strong need to make a personal public commitment in the twenties, or any other number of times, and for a variety of circumstances, throughout life. This too should be possible, encouraged, and given neither more nor less significance than the experience of the first person.

Neither of these experiences would be possible with any of the present teaching on, or practice of, confirmation. For one reason or another both experiences would be precluded by present practice. The first person would have been confirmed (feeling no particular need for it) somewhere between seven and fifteen, the second at the same time (thus leaving him unfulfilled later in life). For the first the experience was essentially pastorally coercive, for the second the pastor should not be surprised should he go out in search of someone who will baptise him, ignoring the previous baptism.[20] Both are possible if a repeatable rite of commitment should exist.

Conclusions

Confirmation as it has been traditionally practised by the Western churches has inherent and insoluble problems. This is as true for those who wish to give confirmation a sacramental status independent of baptism as it is for those who have seen it as a rite of maturity (administered to the wrong people) giving admission to the eucharist and full membership in the church. This is evident not only from the present crises of confirmation within all the churches who practise it under its diverse meanings but also from the present experience among the churches which can achieve essential agreement on the nature of baptism and the eucharist but no agreement whatsoever on confirmation.

Confirmation remains a rite in search of a theology and a rationale. When it finds either it is generally connected with factors that are imposed on the rite rather than inherent in it. The present renewal of both the study of Christian initiation and its pastoral practice continues to erode the traditional rationales for confirmation. Yet it is in the same study and practice that lie the seeds for the preservation of the positive aspects of confirmation. For it is this renewal that has caused both admission to the Christian community and the continued nurture of those who are its members to be taken with a refreshing seriousness. The new birth is not just for babies nor is Christian maturity the sole domain of adults. The presence of the Holy Spirit must be a fundamental characteristic of every Christian life. Religious education has been rediscovered to be for adults as well as children. Yet all of these discoveries undermine, rather than support, confirmation as it has been traditionally practised.

In the past, confirmation has been an instrument of division rather than unity. It divided communities themselves marking those who could or could not be fed at the Lord's Table, a division that has borne its arid fruit in our one-dimensional, exclusivist liturgies in which only the adult, the rational and the verbal find a place. It divided churches from each other by fencing the Lord's Table from those who had not been confirmed by a particular church or a particular minister. Divisions were engrained on the pretext of defending legitimate principles, but with the wrong tools. The fruit borne by confirmation has not been that which has been intended by any church.

Where confirmation continues to be practised, its liturgical celebration takes on a character that far outshadows the normal liturgical celebration of baptism and the eucharist. It is still common in some churches to baptise an adult privately and then confirm the person publicly a few hours or days later. This is, most would admit, an abuse, but it illustrates a dangerously skewed understanding of the relative importance of baptism that has developed through an unbalanced teaching on, and celebration of, confirmation.

The churches, as they learn to make their way through the era of post-Christendom, find themselves faced with an entirely new need that cannot necessarily be met with old tools. In the primitive church the normal candidates for admission to the church were adults. The single rite of baptism with eucharist bore the full weight of all that we could desire by way of initiation and expression of commitment. When children were admitted to the community with their parents, or as infants of Christian parents, they grew up entitled to, and receiving, all that the church had to give. There is no historical evidence for any specific rite of personal commitment. Later, in a society that was seen as coextensive with the church, society itself could bear the weight of any necessary commitment. The society as a whole provided the locus for Christian nurture; its goals were those of the church; there was no need for a rite of commitment apart from the normal civic and religious rituals that marked the life-cycle.

That is no longer the case. In a pluralist society the Christian must again and again say: "I am committed to this rather than that", or "I take my side here." In such a society, and in churches that continue to baptise infants as a matter of course, a rite of commitment can be both appreciated and understood. To use confirmation to meet this new need is to use an inadequate tool. The traditional rite simply cannot bear this new interpretation along with those of its past. What is needed must be new and recognizably different. It is only in taking that step that the churches can break free from the confirmation maze.

NOTES

1. Eusebius Gallicanus, "De Pentecosten", *CC* CI. p.337.
2. Faustus tells his faithful that "in baptism we are regenerated to life, after baptism we are confirmed to fight; in baptism we are washed, after baptism we are strengthened", *loc. cit.*
3. D.L. Douie & H. Farmer, eds., *Magna Vita Sancti Hugonis*, Edinburgh, 1962 Vol, I, pp.127-128.
4. Aidan Kavanaugh, *The Shape of Baptism*, (New York, 1978; J.D.C. Fischer, *Christian Initiation*, London, 1965; *Confirmation Then and Now*, London, 1978; G.W.H. Lampe, *The Seal of the Spirit*, London, 1952, 1968; 1965 Leonell Mitchell, *Baptismal Anointing* (London, 1966); Geoffrey Wainwright, *Christian Initiation* (London, 1969) all have placed a major role in the development of this point or would advocate these findings.
5. Aidan Kavanaugh, "Life-cycle Events and Civil Ritual", in James Schmeister, ed., *Initiation Theology*, Toronto, 1978 pp.21-22.
6. It is this premise that underlies the new *Ordo Initiationis Christianae Adultorum* of the Roman Catholic Church; the rites produced by the Episcopal Church in the United States, the Anglican Church of Canada, and the studies produced in the Anglican Provinces of Wales, South Africa and New Zealand, as well as the new North American *Lutheran Book of Worship*.
7. Louis Ligier, *La confirmation*, Paris, 1973, is perhaps the most extensive modern work on the question to take this point of view. A novelty in the question is the suggestion made by Pierre-Marie Gy at the 1979 Oxford Patristic Conference: confirmation can be received *ex voto*. This has been the traditional manner in which some churches have dealt with their anomalous situation in which both baptism and the eucharist were said to be generally necessary for salvation but infants and young children had stopped receiving communion. The reception of baptism engendered a desire to receive the eucharist which satisfied the requirement that it be received. Since its original use it has been extended to include the baptism "by desire" of those who wished to follow Christ but for some reason could not present themselves for baptism. To extend the concept to confirmation either puts confirmation on equal footing with baptism and the eucharist as the "sacraments of salvation and life", or else so dilutes the whole sacramental system that it collapses. The idea of *"ex voto"* is only possible in the context of a church that has lost the connection between sacrament and community so that sacraments have become salvific acts for the individual independent of the saving faith of the whole community.
8. There is a considerable division of opinion on these questions in both the Anglican and Roman Catholic traditions. This is reflected in a different way in the Lutheran tradition.
9. Paul Verghese, "Relation between Baptism, 'Confirmation' and the Eucharist in the Syrian Orthodox Church", *Studia Liturgica*, Vol. IV, No. 2, 1965, pp.81-93.
10. This is less common than it was a few decades ago and has virtually disappeared from scientific work on initiation. There are, however, still Western authors who try to keep the idea that chrismation = confirmation alive, c.f. Pierre-Marie Gy, "Pour une redécouverte du sacrament du confirmation", *France Catholique*, 15.4:79.

11. Cyrille Argenti, in his presentation at the Bad Segeberg consultation on children and the eucharist, made several comments that are helpful in resolving this impasse. The rigid numbering of the sacraments is not part of the Orthodox tradition, and when an Orthodox talks of baptism as the first sacrament and chrismation as the second, he does so in a very different sense than would a Western theologian. There is no problem for an Orthodox to talk of the oneness of baptism/chrismation as long as the reality expressed is the same. "Whether we call them two sacraments and celebrate one immediately after the other or whether we call it one sacrament but pray for the gift of the Holy Ghost at the end of the celebration of the sacrament, we do exactly the same thing." The reality that must be maintained is that the new birth is by water and the Spirit.

12. Sebastian Brock, "The Syrian Baptismal Anointings", *Studia Liturgica*, Vol. 12, No. 4, 1977, pp.177-183; *Holy Spirit in the Syrian Baptismal Tradition*, Poonah, 1979; Gabriele Winkler, "The History of the Syriac Prebaptismal Anointing in the Light of the Earliest Armenian Sources", *Symposium Syriacum*, Rome, 1978, pp.317-324; *Das armenische Initiationsritual, Entwicklungsgeschichtliche und liturgievergleichende Untersuchung der Quellen des 3-5 Jhs.*, Rome, 1980.

13. The same surveys revealed that up to 80 percent of those confirmed had stopped practising within a year of their confirmation. A similar situation exists in the Church of Sweden where 75 percent of those in their teens are still confirmed although the practice rate is 2-3 percent. Lars Eckerdahl, *Initiation — Discussions in Sweden*, typescript 1977.

14. Aidan Kavanaugh, "Life-cycle Events and Civil Ritual", in *Initiation Theology*, p.11.

15. Cf. David R. Marritt, "Studies on the Religious Development of Children", in *Education Newsletter*, Geneva, 1980, No. 1, pp.3-12.

16. *Ibid.*, p.11.

17. O.C. Edwards, "The Exegesis of Acts 8:4-25 and Its Implications for Confirmation and Glossalalia: Review Article on Haenchen's Acts Commentary", in *Anglican Theological Review*, December 1973, No. 100, pp.100-112.

18. Confirmation only came to be used in the Church of Sweden in the late nineteenth century and then only as a rite of admission to the eucharist. Lars Eckerdahl, *op. cit.*

19. *Von ehelichen leben* quoted in J.D.C. Fischer, *Christian Initiation: the Reformation Period*, London, 1970, p.172.

20. This has become an important pastoral concern at least in North America. Adults who have had a vivid experience of reconversion or renewal of faith often want to mark the event in some dramatic liturgical manner, often through baptism by immersion. Since they have usually been baptized as infants and also confirmed, their own churches are left without any significant liturgical act to offer. They then proceed to seek out someone who will re-baptize them (invariably in some church that does not participate in the ecumenical agreement on mutual recognition of baptism) where they are baptized. They then normally return to their own church, this felt-need fulfilled. Not only does this pose serious theological questions, but it demands a serious examination of the continued practice of indiscriminate baptism by some churches.

THE EUCHARISTIC MEMORIAL, SACRIFICE OF PRAISE AND SUPPLICATION

Max Thurian

When the tradition of the Church calls the eucharist a "sacrifice", it is not with the intention of making it the one act of religious worship, even the most remarkable and the most spiritual among others. The eucharist is the unique sacrament of the unique sacrifice of Christ; it is the sacrifice of praise and supplication of the Church, and it makes the believer a sacrifice acceptable to the Father by the power of the Spirit.

As was announced by the prophecy of Malachi, a prophecy frequently referred to by the fathers of the Church to designate the eucharist, "I have no pleasure in you,... and I will not accept an offering from your hand. For from the rising of the sun to its setting my name is great among the nations, and in every place incense is offered to my name, and a pure offering" (Mal. 1:10-11). In one of the earliest references (along with the Gospels) to the eucharist the *Didache*, we read: "And on the Lord's Day come together and break bread and give thanks, after confessing your transgressions, that your sacrifice may be pure. Let no one that hath a dispute with his fellow come together until they be reconciled, that your sacrifice may not be defiled. For this is that which was spoken by the Lord, 'In every place and time offer me a pure sacrifice; I am a great king, saith the Lord, and my name is wonderful among the gentiles.'"[1]

Justin, in the *Dialogue with Trypho*, quotes the same text from Malachi: "He then speaks of those gentiles, namely us, who in every place offer sacrifices to Him, i.e. the bread of the eucharist and also the cup of the eucharist, affirming... that we glorify His name...."[2] Still in the second century, Irenaeus of Lyons refers to this prophecy of Malachi about the pure sacrifice: "The oblation of the Church,

---

• Max Thurian is a Frère of Taizé, and Study Adviser of Faith and Order.

therefore, which the Lord gave instructions to be offered throughout the world, is accounted with God a pure sacrifice, and is acceptable to Him; not that he stands in need of a sacrifice from us, but that he who offers is himself glorified in what he does offer, if his gift is accepted.... And the Church alone offers this pure oblation to the Creator, offering to Him, with giving of thanks, (the things taken) from his creation".[3]

The eucharist — a new paschal meal

The eucharist cannot be understood unless it is placed in the atmosphere of the liturgical meal which the Jews celebrated, and still celebrate, each year at Passover: "I have earnestly desired to eat this passover with you before I suffer", Christ says to his disciples, "for I tell you that from now on I shall not drink of the fruit of the vine until the kingdom of God comes" (Lk. 22:15-16). When the temple sacrifices ceased, this paschal meal would be regarded as the sacrifice *par excellence*; it would be the great memorial of the deliverance of the people of God.

The New Testament has left us only the essentials of what Jesus said when celebrating the Last Supper with his disciples in the setting of the paschal meal. St Paul, who received the tradition of this celebration, recalls, as a good theologian, Jesus' command which gives the eucharist its whole meaning: "This is my body, which is for you. Do this as a memorial of me ... This cup is the new covenant in my blood. Whenever you drink it, do this as a memorial of me" (*eis ten emen anamnesin*, 1 Cor. 11:23-27; JB). This word "memorial" is central to the profound meaning of the eucharist. The memorial is not a mere subjective remembrance, but a liturgical action which actualizes the event of Christ's sacrifice and by which the Church presents to the Father this unique sacrifice as its offering of thanksgiving and intercession. So "do this as a memorial of me" really means, "do this so that my sacrifice may be present among you and that my Father may remember me on your behalf." This word "memorial" gave the Jewish paschal meal its whole meaning as an actualization of the deliverance of the people of God; it gives its whole meaning to the Christian eucharist, as an actualization of Christ's sacrifice, in the Church and before the Father.

We may gain a better understanding of the eucharist celebrated by Jesus in the setting of the Jewish paschal meal, if we take into consideration this liturgical meal of the people of God.

The prayers of the grace after meals *(birkat ha-mazon)* formed part of the paschal meal and can help us to grasp the meaning of the Last Supper and consequently of the eucharist. We give here the simple form of these prayers; they were amplified in the paschal liturgy, but the structure and meaning are the same. Jesus certainly used one of the forms of these prayers:

1. *Blessed art thou*, O Lord our God, King of the universe, who feedest the whole world with thy goodness, with grace, with lovingkindness and tender mercies ... Blessed art thou, O Lord, who givest food to all.

2. *We thank thee (Praise to thee)*, O Lord our God, because thou didst give as an heritage unto our fathers a desirable, good and ample land, ... thy covenant ... thy law ... life ... and food ... For all this, O Lord our God, we thank and bless thee ... continually and for ever ... Blessed art thou, O Lord, for the land and for the food.

3. *Have mercy*, O Lord our God, upon Israel thy people, upon Jerusalem thy city, upon Zion the abiding place of thy glory, ... upon the great and holy house that was called by thy name. Restore the rule of the family/house of David in its place and time.

(festal addition for Passover)

Our God and God of our fathers! May our remembrance rise and come and be accepted before thee, with the remembrance of our fathers, of Messiah, the son of David thy servant, of Jerusalem thy holy city, and of all thy people the house of Israel, bringing deliverance and well-being, grace, lovingkindness and mercy, life and peace on this day of the Feast of Unleavened Bread.

Remember us, O Lord our God, thereon for our well-being; be mindful of us for blessing, and save us unto life: by thy promise of salvation and mercy, spare us and be gracious unto us; have mercy on us and save us; for our eyes are bent upon thee, because thou art a gracious and merciful God and king.

And rebuild Jerusalem the holy city speedily in our days. Blessed art thou, O Lord, who in thy compassion rebuildest Jerusalem. Amen. *(Authorized Daily Prayer Book*, London, 2nd rev. ed., 1962, pp.378-380)

In these prayers we find the whole meaning that Jesus wished to give the Church's eucharist, while at the same time assuring it of his real presence by his Body and Blood as the risen Crucified, giving himself as food.

The two first prayers, beginning "Blessed art thou" and "We thank thee", relate to what biblical tradition called benediction or blessing and sacrifice of praise or thanksgiving. The first style of prayer consists in recalling the wonderful deeds which the Lord has done for his people, and in laying them before him. The second kind of prayer is an offering of praise and thanksgiving springing from the blessing in which the wonderful deeds and graces of God have been presented. This sacrifice of praise and thanksgiving is a sort of response to the wonderful works of God recalled in the blessing. The spiritual sacrifice gradually replaced in Israel the material sacrifices of the Temple. The Psalms are full of this idea of sacrifice of praise and thanksgiving. The whole of Psalm 99 (100) is a sacrifice of praise (cf. Ps. 26). Psalm 115 (116) forms part of the liturgy of the paschal meal; Jesus sang it with his disciples at the Holy Supper: "What shall I render to the Lord for all his bounty to me? I will lift up the cup of salvation and call on the name of the Lord... I will offer to the sacrifice of thanksgiving and call on the name of the Lord; I walk before the Lord in the land of the living."

As St Peter says, we have become a royal priesthood to "sing the praises of God who called you out of darkness into his wonderful light" (1 Pet. 2:9; JB). And the author of the Letter to the Hebrews describes our existence as Christians in this way: "Through him (Christ) then let us continually offer up a sacrifice of praise to God, that is, the fruit of lips that acknowledge his name. Do not neglect to do good and to share what you have, for such sacrifices are pleasing to God" (Heb. 13:15-16; cf. Ps. 50 (49):14, 23). Christian life is described here as a sacrifice of praise and a sacrifice of generosity, as a liturgy and a practical service which are one and the same, for the glory of God.

It is therefore in the spirit of benediction for the wonderful deeds of God and of a sacrifice of praise that Jesus celebrated the first eucharist in the course of the paschal meal. The Church has always understood it in this way, for the oldest liturgies place at the beginning of the eucharistic prayer a solemn benediction or blessing for the wonderful deeds of creation and redemption, which shows clearly that the eucharist is a sacrifice of praise and thanksgiving:

> Father all-powerful and everliving God, we do well always and everywhere to give you thanks; all things are of your making, all times and seasons obey your laws ... (Preface, Sundays of the Year V)

All the churches begin their eucharistic prayer in the style of benediction *(berakah)* and of sacrifice of praise *(todah)*.

The third prayer and its festive addition (memorial) is supplication and intercession: "Have mercy ... May our remembrance ..."

The eucharist likewise is a supplication and intercession founded on recalling Christ's sacrifice. It is because Jesus gave himself to the Father and to us in the sacrifice of the cross, because he intercedes for us before the Father, that we in virtue of that sacrifice and intercession can offer the eucharistic prayer of the Church as our supplication and intercession. That is what the Bible calls memorial: to recall before God what he has already done for his people so that he may grant us today all the benefits thereof. Memorial is the actualization of the work of God and at the same time the recalling in prayer to the Father of what he has done, in order that he may continue his work today.

The paschal meal is the memorial *(zikkaron) par excellence* in which the people of God actualize the historical deliverance, in a liturgy, and recalls to God what he once did, so that he may continue it today: "Our God, and God of our fathers!" says the Jewish paschal prayer, "May our remembrance (*zikkaron*, memorial) rise ... with the remembrance (*zikkaron*, memorial) of our fathers, of Messiah ... Remember us ..." (Authorized Prayer Book, p. 380). How many liturgical acts of the Old Testament are called "memorial"[4] in this way because they are a symbolic way of saying to God: "Remember us because of thy fidelity shown in former times by deliverance from slavery and by covenant with thy people!"

In the sacrifice of the oblation or in the offering of the shewbread, incense is burned which, Leviticus tells us, is a fragrance which rises as a memorial; that is to say, it recalls the person making the offering to God's remembrance (Lev. 2:1-3; 24:5-9). When the high priest enters the holy place, he wears a liturgical vestment adorned with twelve precious stones engraved with the names of the twelve tribes of Israel. "When he goes into the holy place", the biblical text tells us, "Aaron shall bear the names of the sons of Israel ... on his heart, to bring them to continual remembrance before the Lord" (Ex. 28:29). It is as it were a symbolic intercession recalling to God's remembrance the twelve tribes of Israel. Numerous examples could be given of memorial, all of which illumine our understanding of the eucharist.

It is not only an Old Testament conception, however. The Acts of the Apostles, for example, in the account of the conversion of Cornelius, reports these words of the angel of the Lord: "Cornelius, your prayers and alms have ascended as a memorial before God. And now send men to Joppa, and bring one Simon who is called Peter" (Acts 10:4-5, 31-32). Cornelius's prayers and alms have therefore been as it were a reminder to God, who has fulfilled his hope. So when at the Last Supper, in the course of the paschal meal, Christ uttered these, for Jews, highly significant words — "Do this as a memorial of me" (Lk. 22:19 JB) — the apostles undertood very clearly that Jesus was asking them to celebrate the eucharist in the manner of a sacrifice of supplication and intercession, in order to present to the Father the memorial of the sacrifice of the cross as a prayer full of promise for all humanity. That is why a great exegete could translate Christ's words at the Last Supper as: "Do this in order that the Father may remember me"[5] Using the terms of the Jewish paschal liturgy, we might gloss Jesus' words in this way: "Our Lord and God of our fathers, may the memorial of the Messiah, the Son of David thy servant, rise before thee, the memorial of his sacrifice ... Remember us!"

Thus the Jewish liturgy of the passover meal, in the course of which Jesus celebrated the Holy Supper, makes us understand that the eucharist is a blessing for the wonderful deeds of God, a sacrifice of praise and thanksgiving, a memorial; it is an actualization of the passion, resurrection and intercession of Christ, a memorial which rises before the Father as the Church's offering of prayer, recalling to God's remembrance all the needs of people: Remember, Lord, thy Church and all those for whom we present to thee the sacrifice.[6] As a very beautiful prayer of the Catholic liturgy expresses it: "Look with favour on your Church's offering and see the victim whose death has reconciled us to yourself" (Eucharistic prayer III).

These various elements of the prayer of the Jewish paschal meal gave its structure to the Christian eucharistic prayer. It begins with the blessing for the wonderful deeds of God and the sacrifice of praise to the Father (*berakah — todah*: preface — *sanctus*), continues with the memorial of the events of salvation in Christ presented to the Father in order that he may remember his people (anamnesis — sacrifical memorial), and ends with supplication and intercession to the Father for a new outpouring of the Spirit on the Church and to hear it in its prayers for all those whom it commemorates: "Remember, Lord... *(epiclesis — memento)*".

The eucharistic sacrifice

If we take into consideration what the Jewish liturgy of the paschal meal teaches us for a deeper understanding of the eucharist, we can outline the following explanation of why the eucharist may be described as a sacrifice:

1) It is a *sacrifice of praise and thanksgiving* recalling the wonderful deeds that God has done in the order of creation and in that of redemption;
2) It is the *sacrament of the unique sacrifice* of Christ: the sacramental presence of the sacrifice of the cross;
3) It is the *liturgical presentation* of that sacrifice of the Son by the Church to the Father in order that he may remember his people and grant it the blessings acquired by that unique sacrifice;
4) It is *participation in the intercession* of the Son before the Father for the application of salvation to all persons and the coming of the Kingdom.

1) The eucharist, sacrifice of praise and thanksgiving

If there is any subject on which all Christian tradition agrees, it is that the eucharist is a sacrifice of praise and thanksgiving. St Justin was already writing in the middle of the second century: "And the offering of fine flours, sirs", I said, "which was prescribed to be presented on behalf of those purified from leprosy, was a type of the bread of the eucharist, the celebration of which our Lord Jesus Christ prescribed, in remembrance of the suffering which he endured on behalf of those who are purified in soul from all iniquity, in order that we may at the same time thank God for having created the world, with all things therein, for the sake of man, and for delivering us from the evil in which we were (born)..."[7]

The eucharist is not only a sacrament relating to the liberation of humanity accomplished by Christ on the cross, but also a sacrifice of praise in thanksgiving for the work of creation. As St Irenaeus of Lyon, too, will say: "And the Church alone offers this pure oblation to the Creator offering to him, with giving of thanks (the things taken) from his creation."[8]

It is very important for us to see reconciled in the eucharist the order of creation and that of redemption. Too often out of puritanism, Christians are concerned only with their salvation and purification from their sins; they have made of the eucharist a pious, sad remembrance of Christ's passion, a means to cure us from sin.

The fathers of the Church remind us that in the eucharist there is also the presence of the whole of creation and of the world loved by God, and that in it we can offer the sacrifice of praise in thanksgiving for everything good and beautiful that God has made in the world and humanity. The Church today needs to recall this cosmic, ecological, positive and optimistic view of the eucharist, and to celebrate it in a liturgy which expresses heavenly joy on earth and expectation of the banquet in the kingdom of God.

I cannot resist quoting here a fine passage by Calvin, who is so often wrongly depicted in history as an austere and puritanical man. Here is what he writes on the Holy Supper as a sacrifice of praise:

"This kind of sacrifice is indispensable in the supper of the Lord, in which, while we commemorate and declare his death, and give thanks, we do no other than offer the sacrifice of praise. From this sacrifical employment, all Christians are called 'a royal priesthood'; because, as the apostle says, 'By Christ we offer the sacrifice of praise to God', that is, 'the fruit of our lips giving thanks to his name.' For we do not appear in the presence of God with our oblations without an intercessor: Christ is the Mediator, by whom we offer ourselves and all that we have to the Father. He is our High Priest, who having entered into the celestial sanctuary, opens the way of access to us. He is our altar, upon which we place our oblations, that whatever we venture to do, we may attempt in him. In a word, it is he that 'hath made us kings and priests unto God'."[9]

2) The eucharist, sacrament of the sacrifice

Without detracting in the slightest from the unique character of the cross, from the pardon, reconciliation, liberation accomplished by Christ, the eucharist is the sacrament of presence of the unique sacrifice of Christ, carrying out today for all people the application of salvation. The eucharist is the cross present in the Church, extending to all persons through space and time and in depth, the unique and perfect work of Christ. In the eucharist, the Church meets Christ, who conveys to each believer the fruits of the sacrifice of the cross and of the present intercession of the Saviour.

This sacramental presence of the sacrifice of the cross is accomplished by the power of the Holy Spirit and of the Word. No act of the Church is conceivable apart from the work of the Holy Spirit, and no sacramental liturgy can omit to mention it. The real presence of Christ and his sacrifice in the eucharist is a fruit of his Word full of promise: "This is my body.... This cup is the new Covenant in my blood..."; but these words are not a magic formula operating by its mere utterance. The Holy Spirit gives life to these words and makes them of actual effect in the sacrament celebrated by the Church. Without the Spirit acting in the eucharist, these words would remain a dead letter. A true celebration of the eucharistic sacrifice is a celebration in the Holy Spirit with the Word of Christ. That is to say, a eucharistic liturgy will include the words of institution of the holy Supper by Christ and an invocation of the Holy Spirit. Both accomplish the mystery of the living presence of Christ and of his sacrifice.

"The Spirit makes the crucified and risen Christ really present to us in the eucharistic meal, fulfilling the promise contained in the words of institution.... This is not to spiritualize the eucharistic presence of Christ but to affirm the indissoluble union between the Son and the Spirit. This union makes it clear that the eucharist is not a magical mechanical action but a prayer addressed to the Father, one which emphasizes the utter dependence of the Church on him. There is an intrinsic relationship between the words of institution, Christ's promise, and the *epiklesis*, the invocation of the Spirit, in the liturgy." [10]

Many Western Churches have now adopted in their eucharistic liturgies an epiclesis of the Holy Spirit. To illustrate this fact, I suggested the following epiclesis in the Lima liturgy, prepared for the Faith and Order Commission celebration on 15 January 1982:

O God, Lord of the universe,
you are holy and your glory is beyond measure.
Upon our eucharist send the life-giving Spirit,
who spoke by Moses and the prophets,
who overshadowed the Virgin Mary with grace,
who descended upon Jesus in the river Jordan
and upon the apostles on the day of Pentecost.
May the outpouring of this Spirit of Fire
transfigure this thanksgiving meal
that this bread and wine may become for us
the body and blood of Christ.
May this Creator Spirit accomplish the words of your beloved Son,
who in the night in which he was betrayed, took bread....[11]

It is therefore in virtue of the living word of Christ and by the power of the Holy Spirit that the eucharist becomes the sacrament or the presence of the unique sacrifice of Christ crucified and risen, our high priest and intercessor before the face of the Father.

3) The eucharist, presentation of the sacrifice

The eucharist is the liturgical presentation of the sacrifice of the Son, by the Church, to the Father. This liturgical presentation is the act of recalling to God the Father the unique sacrifice of his Son, eternally actual, and to beg him by this sacrifice to grant his people graces and blessings.

By celebrating the eucharist, the Church places on the holy table the signs of Christ's sacrifice, the sacrament of his Body and Blood, as Israel placed the "bread of the Presence" (Ex. 25:30; Lev. 2) on the golden table as a memorial before the Lord. The Church, in proclaiming Christ's sacrifice, accomplishes on the altar the presentation of the sacrifice of the Son before the Father, giving thanks to him and beseeching him to grant his grace. The Church thus participates, by this gesture of presentation of the cross, in the offering of the Lamb as immolated on the heavenly altar, in the intercession which the Son presents before the face of the Father.

The French Reformed theologians of the seventeenth century stressed this aspect of sacrificial memorial in the holy Supper. Thus Pastor Pierre du Moulin of Paris writes as follows: "There are particular causes why the Holy Supper may be called sacrifice: (1) This sacrament was instituted to proclaim the death of the Lord until he comes; thus the Holy Supper can be called sacrifice because it represents the sacrifice of the death of the Lord ... ; (2) It can be said that in the Holy Supper we offer Jesus Christ to God, inasmuch as we pray God to receive for us the sacrifice of his death; (3) the Holy Supper is an eucharistic sacrifice, that is to say, a sacrifice of thanksgiving for God's blessings ..." [12]

Another 17th century theologian, Jacques Basnage (1653-1723), sums up this idea of the presentation to the Father of the unique sacrifice of the Son as the Church's intercession, in a formula which is perhaps too trenchant, but which has the merit of clarity: "There is no new sacrifice performed (in the eucharist), but a commemoration of the sacrifice of the Son of God which, represented to his Father by the symbols of bread and wine, obliges him to allow himself to be moved and to grant us the fruits of the true sacrifice which is that of the cross. [13]

4) The eucharist, participation in the intercession of the risen Christ

When the Church celebrates the eucharist, it puts itself again in intimate relation to its Lord and gives an ever-renewed form to his unique and eternal intercession.

The eucharist is one of the essential forms of the life of Christ as priest and intercessor in the Church. The Church has to allow to pass into its liturgy the unique and eternal intercession of Christ crucified and risen. He lived that intercession historically once and for all on the cross, and he continues to live it eternally in glory, and sacramentally in his Body which is the Church. The Church shows forth and applies the redemptive intercession of the Son of God through the eucharist which renders visible and actualizes his passion and resurrection.

In a very fine text, Luther has shown how in the eucharist, Christ's intercession and the Church's offering are closely united: "We do not offer Christ, Christ offers us (to God). In this way it is permissible and even useful to call the ceremony a sacrifice, not in itself, but because we offer ourselves in sacrifice with Christ. In other words, we lean on Christ with a firm faith in his covenant and we present ourselves before God with our prayer, our praise and our sacrifice only in the name of Christ, and through his intermediary ... in the assurance that he is our Priest in heaven before the face of God. Christ welcomes us, presents us (to God), our prayer and our praise; he also offers himself in heaven for us ... He offers himself for us in heaven, and offers us with him." [14]

The liturgy of the Reformed Church of Scotland has a very beautiful formula expressing this union with Christ's intercession: "Wherefore, having in remembrance the work and passion of our Saviour Christ, and pleading His eternal sacrifice, we Thy servants do set forth this memorial, which He hath commanded us to make; and we most humbly beseech Thee to send down Thy Holy Spirit to sanctify both us and these Thine own gifts of bread and wine which we set before Thee, that the bread which we break may be the Communion of the body of Christ, and the cup of blessing which we bless the Communion of the blood of Christ; that we, receiving them, may by faith be made partakers of His body and blood, with all His benefits, to our spiritual nourishment and growth in grace, and to the glory of Thy most holy name." [15] This presentation of the memorial in communion with Christ's intercession, itself founded on the sacrifice of the cross, is a very exact expression of the eucharistic sacrifice, all the more so as this memorial unfolds later as a sacrifice of thanksgiving and an intercession closely linked with communion: "And here we offer and present unto Thee ourselves, our souls and bodies, to be a reasonable, holy, and living sacrifice; and we beseech Thee mercifully to accept this our sacrifice of praise and thanksgiving, as, in fellowship with all the faithful in heaven and on earth, we pray Thee to fulfill in us, and in all men, the purpose of Thy redeeming love ..." [16]

The eucharistic sacrifice implores the application of salvation to all women and men: the accomplishment of the sanctification of the faithful, until Christ returns, and the gift of liberation to those who do not yet know him.

For although Christ has done everything for the salvation of all persons, and although objective redemption and reconciliation have been accomplished in fact on the cross, it remains for the Church, the Body of Christ, to be the instrument for the application to each and all the graces of salvation. By the eucharist as sacrifice of intercession, the Church unites with Christ's intercession founded on his sacrifice of the cross, and intercedes with the Father in favour of all persons, for the forgiveness of their sins, for their liberation and happiness, and implores the glorious manifestation of the kingdom.

In communion with Christ's intercession and with his sacrifice on the cross, by setting before the Father the memorial of that sacrifice as praise and supplication, the Church offers itself, each of the faithful offers himself or herself, in an act of adoration and consecration. As Luther wrote: " ... we present ourselves before God with our prayer, our praise and our sacrifice, only in the name of Christ and by his intermediary ... He offers himself in heaven, and offers us with him." [17] And Calvin has this admirable image: Jesus Christ in the heavenly sanctuary "is our altar, upon which we place our oblations, that whatever we venture to do, we may attempt in him" [18]

Of itself, the Church cannot offer or present anything to God except its utter poverty, but in Christ it can offer a true sacrifice of thanksgiving and intercession, for it can present to the Father the sacrifice of the cross by uniting itself as Body of Christ: that is its true praise, its efficacious prayer, its possible sacrifice, because it is the very sacrifice of Christ presented by himself.

The eucharist as an offering of the creation

Reading the Fathers and the liturgies of the ancient Church, one is struck by the presence of the creation in the eucharist and in the liturgy generally. St Irenaeus of Lyons shows us that in the eucharist there is first of all an oblation of the first-fruits of God's own creatures. [19] The bread and wine come from the creation and are offered to the Creator in thanksgiving for his material benefits so that he may consecrate them by his Word and make of them the Body and Blood of Christ, the only perfect sacrifice. The offertory is an important moment in the eucharistic celebration: it shows that the Church has preserved the oblation of the first-fruits of the earth and that this oblation forms the link between the order of creation and the order of redemption, which will be manifested in the sacrificial memorial. Those theologians and liturgists who minimize the offertory and place all the emphasis on the sacrificial memorial of Christ, separate creation and redemption, detach the eucharist from the world of creation and humanity in order to make it simply a means of spiritual grace. There is a danger there which may affect the fullness of the eucharistic mystery.

The new offertory prayers of the Catholic liturgy are very rich in meaning. Bread is fruit of the earth, wine fruit of the vine; both are work of human hands; we offer them to the God of all creation so that they may become the bread of Life and the wine of the eternal kingdom, the Body and Blood of Christ. The liturgy here points to a double movement: the wheat and vine have been worked by people to become bread and wine; we offer them to the Creator in order that by his Spirit he may act on them to make them the Body and Blood of Christ. This double passage of the creation is signified by the offertory and the consecration. [20]

St Hippolytus of Rome, at the beginning of the third century, also speaks much of the oblation of the first-fruits of creation. Bread and wine are offered, but also milk and honey, water, oil, olives, fruits, flowers ... [21] The liturgy proclaims both the wonderful deeds of creation and those of redemption.

We ought fully to recover this sense of the oblation of creation in the eucharist, so as to make it quite clear that the liturgy is not cut off from humankind but comprises our complete nature: we can offer both the gifts of creation and the supreme gift of the Body and Blood of Christ.

The Church's offertory, in which it brings to the altar the material and spiritual possessions of the faithful, is as it were an impulse to make offering which involves a crisis. When the Church has gathered everything together to present it to God, it realizes its utter poverty; all it can do is to put this utter poverty into the hands of Christ who, taking it up into his own sacrifice presented in intercession, makes of it a true praise, an efficacious prayer, a valid sacrifice, "through him, with him and in him".

"The Church, gratefully recalling God's mighty acts of redemption beseeches him to give the benefits of these acts to every human being. In thanksgiving and intercession, the Church is united with the Son, its great High Priest and Intercessor (Rom 8:34; Heb 7:25). The eucharist is the sacrament of the unique sacrifice of Christ, who ever lives to make intercession for us. It is the memorial of all that God has done for the salvation of the world. What it was God's will to accomplish in the incarnation, life, death, resurrection and ascension of Christ, he does not repeat. These events are unique and can neither be repeated nor prolonged. In the memorial of the eucharist, however, the Church offers its intercession in communion with Christ, our great High Priest."[22]

NOTES

1. *Didache*, 14: *The Teaching of the Apostles*, ed. H. de Romestin, London, 1885, p.85.
2. *Dialogue with Trypho*, 41; The Ante-Nicene Fathers, Vol. 1, Grand Rapids, 1975, p.215.
3. *Adversus Haereses*, 4, 18, 1 and 4; The Ante-Nicene Fathers, Vol. 1, Grand Rapids, 1975, pp.484-5.
4. The Hebrew words *zikkaron* and *azkarah* are rendered in Greek by *anamnesis* or *mnemosunon*. See my book *The Eucharistic Memorial*, 1960, Vol. I.
5. J.Jeremias, *The Eucharistic Words of Jesus*, London, 1955, p.161ff.
6. See my book, *The Eucharistic Memorial*, 1960, Vol. II.
7. Dialogue with Trypho, 41; *op. cit.*, p.215.
8. *Adversus Haereses*, 4, 18, 4; *op. cit.*, p.485.
9. *Institutes of the Christian Religion*, IV, XVIII, 17; transl. John Allen, London, 1938, Vol. 2, p.530.
10. Lima text, Eucharist No. 14 and commentary.
11. *The Eucharist Liturgy of Lima*. See p.242.
12. *Le bouclier de la foi*, 1635, p.269ff.
13. *Histoire de l'Eglise*, 1699, p.995.
14. 1520 Weimar Ausgabe VI, 369; Sermon on the New Testament.
15. *Book of Common Order of the Church of Scotland*, 1962, p.119.
16. *Ibid.*, p.120.
17. 1520 Weimar Ausgabe VI, 369.
18. See Note 9 supra.
19. *Adversus Haereses*, 4, 17-18.
20. We have taken these words from *The Eucharistic Liturgy of Lima*.
21. *The Apostolic Tradition*, 5-6, 23, 28; ed. G.Dix, London, 1937 and 1967.
22. Lima text, Eucharist No. 8.

THE EUCHARIST, GIFT OF GOD

J.M.R. Tillard

Max Thurian has dealt with the idea of Memorial (*anamnesis, zik-karon*), which constitutes the focal point where all the main tradi-tional lines of the eucharistic mystery meet; what I propose to do in this study is to look at these lines themselves. There is no difference between Max Thurian's view of Memorial and my own; our two studies are complementary.

I. The Eucharist: gift of God to the Church

The dominant line of the Faith and Order document is undoubtedly its emphasis on the eucharist as the gift of God. It is no accident that the document begins with the affirmation: "The Church receives the eucharist as a gift from the Lord" (II,1). But this gift is rigorously con-tinuous with the fundamental gift of the work of God which culminates in Jesus Christ. Moreover, the heart of the eucharist is the *anamnesis*, the Memorial, "the Church's effective proclamation of God's mighty acts and promises" (II,7). This Memorial is no empty sign, no word without objective content: "Christ himself with all that he has ac-complished for us and for all creation... is present in this *anamnesis*, granting us communion with himself. The eucharist is also the foretaste of his parousia and of the final kingdom" (II,6). This presence, moreover, though unique, is nevertheless real: "Jesus said over the bread and wine of the eucharist: 'This is my body... this is my blood....'" What Christ declared is true and this truth is fulfilled every time the eucharist is celebrated. The Church confesses Christ's real living and active presence in the eucharist" (II,13).

• J.M.R. Tillard is Professor of Dogmatics in the Dominican College of Ottawa.

It is because the eucharist is gift, or, more precisely, because the eucharist offers access to the Gift of which it is also the Memorial — that it implies and invokes a presence. Thus, after centuries of controversy, we link up once again with the dominant line of the living Tradition of the Church. To cite just three great witnesses in support:

Ignatius of Antioch, at the threshold of the patristic period, says of the Judaizing docetists:

> They abstain from the eucharist and from prayer, because they confess not the eucharist to be the flesh of our Saviour Jesus Christ, which suffered for our sins, and which the Father, of His goodness, raised up again. Those, therefore, who speak against this gift of God, incur death.[1]

Deep in the Middle Ages, the catholic liturgy of Corpus Christi, associated with the rise of a devotion to the Lord present in the eucharistic host, revolves as it were around the well-known antiphon which matches the teaching of Thomas Aquinas:

> O sacred banquet in which Christ is eaten, the Memory of his Passion is recalled, the spirit is filled with grace, the pledge of the coming glory is given to us.[2]

And in 1541, in his *Short Treatise on the Lord's Supper*, John Calvin explains:

> If God cannot deceive or lie, it follows that he performs all that it signifies. We must then really receive in the Supper the body and blood of Jesus Christ, since the Lord there represents to us the communion of both. For otherwise what would it mean that we eat the bread and drink the wine as a sign that his flesh is our food and his blood our drink, if he gave only bread and wine and left the spiritual reality behind? Would it not be under false colours that he had instituted this mystery? We have then to confess that if the representation which God grants in the Supper is veracious, the internal substance of the sacrament is joined with the visible signs; and as the bread is distributed by hand, so the body of Christ is communicated to us, so that we are made partakers of it. If there were nothing more, we have good reason to be satisfied when we realize that Jesus Christ gives us in the Supper the real substance of his body and his blood, so that we may possess him fully, and, possessing him, have part in all his blessings.[3]

Strictly speaking, therefore, what is involved is not the gift of a presence but a presence which accomplishes the gift of God. The document makes this very clear: "The eucharist is essentially the sacrament of the gift which God makes to us in Christ through the power of the Holy Spirit. Every Christian receives this gift of salvation through communion in the body and blood of Christ" (II,2). The nuance, it seems to me, is essential. By failing to grasp it, ecclesial groups in the past have distorted the main underlying purpose of the sacrament of the Lord. Because it is in this way the sacrament of the gift of God, the eucharist is necessarily found at the intersection of the powerful currents which form, so to speak, the channels of the gift of God for the traditions transmitted by Scripture and then for the early centuries in the course of which the Church develops its doctrine. The Lima document recalls these essential currents with a logic which, while it might perhaps have benefited by being more closely connected with that of the church fathers, nevertheless does not distort anything. I shall present these currents here in a sequence which, though not following the structure of the document, does nevertheless respect its insights.

1. The Eucharist: response of the Spirit to the prayer of the Church
     Since the essential purpose of the eucharist is to grant a share in the gift of God and to lead the Church towards this gift, it is only in the power of the Holy Spirit that the eucharist can be accomplished. The very fact that it is a Memorial, moreover, associates it inseparably with the work of the other Paraclete, which the Johannine gospel presents as essential: "He will bring to your remembrance all that I have said to you" (Jn 14:26); "He will take what is mine and declare it to you" (Jn 16:14-16). Being inseparable from the resurrection of Christ and from Pentecost, which is so to speak the obverse of the resurrection, the eucharist cannot be other than an event of the Spirit.[4]
     The Lima document rightly emphasizes this while at the same time refraining from any precipitate settlement of the debate between East and West; in other words, it is careful to connect the role of the Spirit with that of the words of the Lord Jesus. Hence the following neat formulation:

> The Spirit makes the crucified and risen Christ really present to us in the eucharistic meal, fulfilling the promise contained in the words of institution. The presence of Christ is clearly the centre of the eucharist, and the promise contained in the words of institution is therefore fundamental to the celebration. Yet it is the Father who is the primary origin and final fulfilment of the eucharistic event. The incarnate Son of God by and in whom it is accomplished is its living centre. The Holy Spirit is the

immeasurable strength of love which makes it possible and continues to make it effective. The bond between the eucharistic celebration and the mystery of the Triune God reveals the role of the Holy Spirit as that of the One who makes the historical word of Jesus present and alive. Being assured by Jesus' promise in the words of institution that it will be answered, the Church prays the Father for the gift of the Holy Spirit in order that the eucharistic event may be a reality: the real presence of the crucified and risen Christ giving his life for all humanity (II,14).

In short, "it is in virtue of the living word of Christ and by the power of the Holy Spirit that the bread and wine become the sacramental signs of Christ's body and blood" (II, 15).

By restoring the Holy Spirit to its essential place, not only for the liturgical adoration but also in the entire eucharistic celebration and what makes it the event of grace (II,16-18), the text makes possible an enrichment of the Western traditions. In this way they are once again connected with a traditional line from which they had to some extent departed but which was faithfully maintained in the East. For it is astonishing to see how the main Lutheran, Anglican, and Reformed liturgies and their derivatives have been constructed around a vision which at this point focuses to such an extent on obedience to the "command of the Lord" — and therefore on the repetition of the words of the Supper — that they have forgotten the function of the Spirit.[5] Although the Roman canon itself contains a definite form of *epiclesis*, it showed more circumspection at this point. The invocation of the Spirit was implicit here; the canonist tradition (presupposed particularly in the *De defectibus in celebratione Missae occurrentibus* printed at the front of the Missal) ignored the function of the *epiclesis*.[6]

From the discussions with the East on this question, down to the decisions of the Council of Florence,[7] moreover, it is abundantly evident how unwilling the official representatives of the Roman Church were to entertain the requests of its sister churches. The approval by the Faith and Order Commission — and this with absolute unanimity! — of a doctrinal statement on the eucharist which once more restores the function of the Holy Spirit to its leading role is indubitable evidence of the fecundity of the ecumenical movement. Thanks to the contribution of the East, therefore, the Western churches and the churches deriving from them (in Africa especially) are beginning to break free from the rigid Christomonist shell in which they had gradually become encased. They are becoming receptive to the totality of the trinitarian mystery. What is more, by doing so they are becoming more in accord with the balance attested in Holy Scripture itself.[8]

It might perhaps have been useful if the document had given a fuller explanation of the extremely important statement that "the Church, as the community of the new covenant, confidently invokes the Spirit, in order that it may be sanctified and renewed, led into all justice, truth and unity, and empowered to fulfill its mission in the world" (II,7). For the main Tradition, in fact, the prayer that the bread and the wine be transformed is wholly included in, and subordinated to, the prayer that life be converted thanks to the sacramentally accomplished Gift of God. In the very ancient *anaphora* of Addai and Mari,

> the coming of the Spirit is not yet invoked in order to consecrate the sacrifice (even although it is in the immediate proximity of the first sacrificial formulas that it is invoked); nor is it invoked in order to transform the elements, but rather in order that our celebration of the eucharist may produce its fruits in us: the consummation of the Church in unity, in order through the Son, in (or with) the Spirit, to glorify the Father for ever.[9]

Moreover, the *anaphora* of Hippolytus' *Apostolic Tradition* (about the beginning of the 3rd century) concludes (after the recitation of the words of institution) in the following *epiclesis*:

> And we beseech thee that thou wouldst send thy Holy Spirit upon the oblation of thy holy Church; and that thou wouldst grant it to all the saints who partake, making them one, for fulfilment of the Holy Spirit and for the confirmation of their faith in truth; that we may praise and glorify thee through thy Son (servant) Jesus Christ, through whom be glory and honour to thee, to the Father and to the Son with the Holy Spirit in thy Holy Church, both now and for ever.[10]

Through the sacramental body and blood of the Lord, the purpose of the Spirit of the resurrection is *to transform, to change*, the daily life of the men and women who are nourished at the Holy Table into a life as living members of the body of Christ.[11] If "God himself acts" (*sc.* in the eucharist), "giving life to the body of Christ and renewing each member" (*sc.* of this body) (II,2), it is only by his Holy Spirit that he does so.

2. The Eucharist: gift of the "Arrhes" of the Kingdom of God

Because thanks to the bread and the cup touched by the Spirit, the ecclesial community receives at the Lord's Table the Body and Blood of the Lord, in sacramental form it "receives" in this way "the life of the new creation and the assurance of the Lord's return" (II,17) and consequently "a foretaste of the Kingdom of God" (II,18). For the latter is "a new reality which transforms Christians into the image of Christ and therefore makes them his effective witnesses" (II,26).

That "the eucharist opens up the vision of the divine rule which has been promised as the final renewal of creation" (II,22) is shown by the signs employed in its institution and celebration. For it is impossible, in fact, to focus attention myopically on the consecrated bread and wine alone (as the Western tradition was constantly tempted to do). It is essential to set them within the context of the Lord's Supper. The Gospel narratives attach great importance to the meals of Jesus. [12] And this throws light on the significance of the Last Supper. In fact

> the meals which Jesus is recorded as sharing during his earthly ministry proclaim and enact the nearness of the Kingdom, of which the feeding of the multitude is a sign. In his last meal, the fellowship of the Kingdom was connected with the prospect of Jesus' sufferings. After his resurrection, the Lord made his presence known to his disciples in the breaking of the bread. Thus the eucharist continues these meals of Jesus during his earthly life and after his resurrection, always as signs of the Kingdom. Christians see the eucharist prefigured in the Passover memorial of Israel's deliverance from the land of bondage and in the meal of the covenant on Mount Sinai (Exod. 24) (I,I).

But the eucharistic meal is not only rooted in the basic symbolism of the meals of the people of God on its journey and the meals of the first Christian community gathered around its Risen Lord, it also reminds us of the prophetic image of the eschatological banquet. It is not simply the announcement of that banquet but the mysterious "anticipation of the Supper of the Lamb" (I,1). Every time it is celebrated, there is not only a meeting with the Lord in his "sacramental meal", "as the continuing people of God, until his return" (I,1), but we are also nourished with hope. According to the interpretation proposed by J.Jeremias, [13] the words "until he come" (*achri hou an elthé*) in 1 Cor.11:26 denote far more than waiting for the final moment of history; they imply an active reaching out towards it, a sighing, a prayer, a *marana tha*.

It is by the forgiveness of sins that this Kingdom first penetrates into our world. Thus "in accordance with Christ's promise, each baptized member of the body of Christ receives in the eucharist the assurance of the forgiveness of sins (Mt.26:28) and the pledge of eternal life (Jn 6:51-58)" (II,2). If it were not a sacrament of pardon, the eucharist would not be a sacrament of hope.[14] Perhaps the Lima document could have dwelt a little more on this point, recalling more the way in which the evangelists link Jesus' meals with sinners with the assurance of God's pardoning presence in the mysterious guest who eats and drinks with them. The remission of sins, moreover, is specifically mentioned in Matthew's account of the Supper. If the eucharist is indeed the memorial of the sacrifice "accomplished once and for all on the cross and still operative on behalf of humankind" (II,5), how could it possibly be otherwise?

But to pardon sin is not simply to overlook it. By its very nature, forgiveness issues in a very tangible reality, namely, in reconciliation (along the lines of Jn 11:52 and Eph.2:13-19), in *koinonia*, with its two dimensions of communion with the Father and communion between brothers and sisters in and through Christ and his Spirit. This is frequently recalled in the Lima document: "In the eucharistic meal, in the eating and drinking of the bread and wine, Christ grants communion with himself" (II,2); "granting us communion with himself" (II,6); "the bread and wine become the sacramental signs of Christ's body and blood; they remain so for the purpose of communion" (II,15); "in the celebration of the eucharist, Christ gathers, teaches and nourishes the Church" (III,29). But in two very important paragraphs, the Faith and Order document concentrates on this aspect in particular: one of special importance for the very nature of the Church as a eucharistic community, the other for the profound nature of the Church's mission in the world.

One of the major rediscoveries of contemporary ecclesiology is the radical connection between the identity of the Church and the community's participation in the Lord's Supper. With a clarity which would have seemed impossible even fifteen years ago, the Faith and Order text, right from the start, adopts this standpoint. This renews the connection not only with the fathers of the Eastern Church but also with some of the main statements of Augustine[15], familiar to the Latin Middle Ages and to the early Reformers:

> The eucharistic communion with Christ present, who nourishes the life of the Church, is at the same time communion within the body of Christ which is the Church. The sharing in one bread and the common cup in a

given place demonstrates and effects the oneness of the sharers with Christ and with their fellow sharers in all times and places. It is in the eucharist that the community of God's people is fully manifested. Eucharistic celebrations always have to do with the whole Church, and the whole Church is involved in each local eucharistic celebration (II,19).

If, in accordance with the old tag *eucharistia fabricat ecclesiam*, the eucharist is thus the sacrament of the Church, this is simply because all believers, by the sacramental body of Christ (his *corpus mysticum*, his body-in-the-mystery), enter into participation in the same, unique, indivisible Body of the Lord. This had been stated earlier by Augustine in an extremely condensed form:

You are the Body of Christ and its members; it is your own mystery which lies there on the Lord's Table. It is your own mystery which you receive. It is to what you are that you respond "Amen"... Be what you see, receive what you are... On his Table he has instituted the sacrament of our peace and of our unity.[16]

Thomas Aquinas takes this up again:

the *res* (ultimate reality) of this sacrament is the unity of the mystical body without which there is no salvation.[17]

At the time of the Reformation, the *Scots Confession* of the 1560 did not think it was on the wrong tack in affirming:

So that we confess and undoubtedly believe that the faithful, in the right use of the Lord's table, do so eat the body and drink the blood of the Lord Jesus, that he remaineth in them and they in him, yea, that they are so made flesh of his flesh and bone of his bones'.[18]

Is this not based very literally on the letters of Paul?

The Church of God "is manifested" — owns itself in face of the world, is reinforced in its very nature — every time Christian men and women, who have become living members of Christ by their baptism, gather around the Lord's Table, eat the same bread which is the sacramental body of Christ, share the same cup and are transformed into what they receive. It is then, in its assembly, that the Church experiences what it truly is. More than that, to the extent to which a local church can *recognize* in the eucharist of another Christian assembly the very reality of its own life, it knows it is in real communion with this other church, however different its rites, traditions and expressions of the common faith may be.

This communion, rooted in this participation in the very mystery of God's reconciliation and love, finds expression first of all, of course, in the quality of relationships within the Christian community itself. There, above all, "the eucharistic celebration demands reconciliation and sharing among all those regarded as brothers and sisters in the one family of God" (II,20), following the example of the first generation of Christians.[19] And, clearly, "all kinds of injustice, racism, separation and lack of freedom are radically challenged when we share in the body and blood of Christ" (II,20), for "through the eucharist the all-renewing grace of God penetrates and restores human personality and dignity" (II,20). The document notes that the liturgical rites underline this "solidarity in the eucharistic communion of the body of Christ" and this "responsible care of Christians for one another" (mutual forgiveness of sins, the sign of peace, intercession for all, the taking of the elements to the sick or the celebration of the eucharist with them, etc.). The celebration of the supreme act of Christ the Servant is meant to transform the community into a servant community; there is a direct connection between the eucharistic table and the assuaging of human need and distress, and this bond "testifies to the redeeming presence of Christ in the World" (II,21).

But the eucharistic grace of communion, coming as it does from the memorial of the Sacrifice offered once and for all for the salvation of the whole world, and being given in the power of the Spirit of the new times inaugurated by the resurrection of Christ, overflows the frontiers of the celebrating community and even of the Church. Implicit in this grace is care for the world, the commitment of the will to the transformation of this world into the world which God wills, and therefore to the disappearance of injustice, war, hatred, exploitation and the sources of these evils. In a paragraph which was still being revised right up to the last moment, the Lima document states this plainly:

> The eucharist involves the believer in the central event of the world's history. As participants in the eucharist, therefore, we prove inconsistent if we are not actively participating in this ongoing restoration of the world's situation and the human condition. The eucharist shows us that our behaviour is inconsistent in face of the reconciling presence of God in human history: we are placed under continual judgment by the persistence

of unjust relationships of all kinds in our society, the manifold divisions on account of human pride, material interest and power politics and, above all, the obstinacy of unjustifiable confessional oppositions within the body of Christ (II,20).

Until the day when Christ "delivers the kingdom to God the Father after destroying every rule and every authority and power" (1 Cor.15:24), the members of the ecclesial body of the Lord, nourished by the bread and wine at his Holy Table, must be actively committed to changing the world, to the coming of "appropriate relationships in social, economic and political life" (II,20).

3. The Eucharist: the implantation of the community in the Gospel claim

Only if it is lived *in Christ* is the responsibility of the Church in its mission within the structures of the world authentically fulfilled. For this responsibility is an evangelical claim explicable only by the possession of the first-fruits (*arrhes*) of the new creation inaugurated by the resurrection of the Lord Jesus Christ, and slowly infiltrating human history's tortuous windings. The eucharist, a meal which anticipates the great eschatological banquet,

> brings... a new reality which transforms Christians into the image of Christ and therefore makes them his effective witnesses... The eucharistic community is nourished and strengthened for confessing by word and action the Lord Jesus Christ who gave his life for the salvation of the world. As it becomes one people, sharing the meal of the one Lord, the eucharistic assembly must be concerned for gathering also those who are at present beyond its visible limits, because Christ invited to his feast all for whom he died (II,26).

For the Christian, therefore, the longing for the transformation of the world is inseparable from the lordship of Christ. The responsibility of Christians in the renewal of the world is simply another form of the radical claim engraved in them by baptism and renewed by the eucharist: "to live for God, in Jesus Christ" (Rom. 6:10-11), so to act that God's plan for the world may be accomplished, that the event of Cross and Resurrection may shine in all its radiance.

This is why, when the memorial is celebrated, the Christian assembly is open towards the world. Using a bold formulation — placed at the head of a paragraph which unfortunately fails to set it off in the way it deserves — the Lima document goes so far as to affirm that "the very celebration of the eucharist is an instance of the Church's participation in God's mission to the world" (II,25).

There are, so to speak, two elements in this participation. The first is an element of joyful laudatory "recognition" that the new creation is, in a sense, *already* present:

> Signs of this renewal are present in the world wherever the grace of God is manifest and human beings work for justice, love and peace. The eucharist is the feast at which the Church gives thanks to God for these signs and joyfully celebrates and anticipates the coming of the Kingdom of Christ (1 Cor.11:26; Mt. 26:29).
>
> The world, to which renewal is promised, is present in the whole eucharistic celebration. The world is present in the thanksgiving to the Father, where the Church speaks on behalf of the whole creation (II,22-23).

The other element, on the contrary, is a cry to God, an ardent appeal to him that what is *not yet* may come soon:

> The world is present ... in the memorial of Christ, where the Church, united with its great High Priest and Intercessor, prays for the world; in the prayer for the gift of the Holy Spirit, where the Church asks for sanctification and new creation (II,23).

In the power of the Spirit of the Risen Christ, Christians are to become the agents of this "new creation". For this is how the prayer of *epiclesis* is to be fulfilled, a prayer which, as we have already said, is not primarily concerned with the bread and the cup but an invocation that the faithful may be transformed into authentic members of Christ:

> reconciled in the eucharist, the members of the body of Christ are called to be servants of reconciliation amongst men and women and witnesses of the joy of resurrection (II,24).

Their solidarity not only with the marginalized but with all who are in any way crushed by human distress originates in the eucharist, therefore. Does the Lord's Supper not remind us of the meals of Jesus with the tax-collectors, sinners, outcasts and rejected (II,24)?

These are important paragraphs, especially if they are seen in the context of the work of Faith and Order. For some time now, the Faith and Order Commission has been deeply aware of the connection between the confession of Christ as Lord and involvement in the struggle against poverty and its causes. This disquiet was, so to speak, crystallized in the Bangalore statement *A Common Account of Hope*. The urgent need to study this question with the seriousness it deserves and in the light of the Faith and Order mandate became clear. Rightly understood, therefore, these statements we have been commenting on demonstrate, on the one hand, that since the very beginning, if Justin's testimony is anything to go by, the struggle against poverty and commitment to the cause of the poor spring from *communion* in the death and resurrection of Christ the Servant, of which the eucharist is the Memorial, and, on the other hand, that this struggle and commitment only correspond to their genuinely Christian orientation in the degree to which they are an expression of the spiritual worship offered in the eucharist to God in *communion* with Christ:

> In Christ we offer ourselves as a living and holy sacrifice in our daily lives (Rom.12:1; 1 Peter 2:5): this spiritual worship, acceptable to God, is nourished in the eucharist, in which we are sanctified and reconciled in love, in order to be servants of reconciliation in the world (II,10).

II. The Eucharist: gift received in thanksgiving

A gift of God in the Spirit, the eucharist is also praise and thanksgiving to God. This is the derivation of its name, eucharist. We know from Ignatius, Justin and the *Didache* that this is an ancient name. A study of the works of Philo[20] shows the connection between this term and the "sacrificial" traditions of the Old Testament; it seems to be derived from "the sacrifical liturgy of the Temple". More precisely still, it goes back to the Old Testament *todah*, which we know means a laudatory confession of God, a proclamation of the wonders of the divine grace, a glorification of the power at work in salvation[21]. As the Lima document says, "the eucharist is a proclamation and a celebration of the work of God" (II,3).

The Lima text would certainly have been improved had it paid more attention to the distinction between blessing (*berakah, eulogia*) and thanksgiving. To translate *eucharistein* as 'to bless', without qualifications, is impossible, as serious studies have shown. The term *eucharistia* in its verbal connotation refers basically to confession, to proclamation in the form of praise.[22] The importance of this for the essential connection between the celebration of the Memorial of the

Lord and the living faith is obvious. In the strictest sense of the term, the eucharist — as understood by Ignatius and Justin — is a sacrament of faith: it proclaims the heart of the faith (cf. 1 Cor. 11:26); it communicates what the words proclaim, since by it "every Christian receives this gift of salvation through communion in the body and blood of Christ" (II,2). It is far more, therefore, than "the benediction (*berakah*) by which the Church expresses its thankfulness to God for all his benefits" (II,3). "To confess" is incomparably more than "to bless". To say without qualification that the *berakah* is the primary origin (III,27) is inexact.

That said, it must be acknowledged that the Faith and Order document describes very accurately the content of the eucharistic thanksgiving:

> the eucharist is the great thanksgiving to the Father for everything which he accomplished in creation, redemption and sanctification, for everything which he accomplishes now in the Church and in the world in spite of the sins of human beings, for everything that he will accomplish in bringing his Kingdom to fulfilment (II,3).

By the prayer of the person who presides, the community gathers together what may be called the response of faith, expresses "the whole Christian outlook", the evangelical attitude "before God". It confesses God as he really is. Since, moreover, according to his revelation, he has revealed who he is only by his intervention on behalf of humankind, this confession of God is impregnated with praise, gratitude, wonder, hope. This initiative of God who, by the Holy Spirit, enables us to participate in the "sacrifice accomplished once and for all on the cross and still operative on behalf of all humankind" (II,5), and even offers us *hic et nunc* a foretaste of the Kingdom of God (II,18), finds its response in the word in which the Church mingles indissolubly faith and intercession, thanksgiving and hope, admission of poverty and recognition of infinite mercy.

"The eucharist", therefore, "is the great sacrifice of praise by which the Church speaks on behalf of the whole creation" (II,4). To develop this point here would be to trespass on the theme dealt with by Max Thurian. What we can emphasize, however, is that this sacrifice of praise is itself communion in the Risen Lord's own praise and thanksgiving. At the Memorial table, it is only *in Christ* that the Church addresses itself to the Father.

***

One further remark in conclusion. The Faith and Order Commission is sending the Lima document to the churches at a time when the need to link up again with an ecclesiology of communion is being rediscovered in some theological circles. The hope of renewal in this document goes much further than the field of ritual and liturgy. In the view of the writer, it constitutes the basis without which every attempt to re-establish the *koinonia* which God wills would be nothing but an expense of energy and liberality doomed to failure.

NOTES

1. To the Smyrnaens, ch. VII, *Ante-Nicene Fathers,* Vol. I, p.89.
2. For Thomas Aquinas, every sacrament is at one and the same time reminder of the past event, implantation *hic et nunc* in the grace of that event, sowing of the seed of the life to come. See *Summa theologica*, IIIa, 60,3. The eucharist is all that but in a pre-eminent sense. See *ibid.*, 73,4. The "presence" is understood in terms of the movement from the Easter event to the entry into the final kingdom.
3. The Library of Christian Classics, Westminster Press, Philadelphia, Vol. XXII, *Calvin: Theological Treatises*, p.148.
4. I may be permitted to refer to my own article "L'eucharistie et le Saint Esprit" (in NRT 91, 1968, pp.363-387) and my contribution to the collective work *L'eucharistie* (J. Zizioulas, J.M.R. Tillard, J.J. von Allmen), Paris, 1970. A bibliography will be found in both these articles. Father Congar deals with this problem in his *Je crois en l'Esprit Saint*, Vol. III, *Le fleuve de vie*, Paris, 1980.
5. See Louis Bouyer, *Eucharistie*, Desclée, 1966, pp.367-414.
6. See *ibid.*, pp.232-238.
7. Texts in *DS* 1321.
8. See Y. Congar, *Je crois en l'Esprit Saint*, Vol. III, which provides a summary of current studies. See also the fine book by James D.C. Dunn, *Jesus and the Spirit*, London, 1975.
9. Louis Bouyer, *op. cit.*, pp.183-184.
10. *Documents of the Christian Church*, ed. Bettenson, World's Classics, London, OUP, 1943, p.107.
11. See my contribution to Zizioulas, Tillard, von Allmen, *L'eucharistie.*
12. There is a vast literature on this point. See O. Cullmann, *Early Christian Worship*, tr. Todd & Torrance, SCM Press, London, 1953, pp 12-26; J. Danielou, "Les repas de la Bible et leur signification", in *MD*, 18, 1949, pp.7-33. The study of the biblical meals has been enriched by the more recent studies by C. Perrot, "Le Repas du Seigneur" in *MD*, 123, 1975, pp.29-46, H. Cazelles, "Eucharistie, bénédiction et sacrifice dans l'Ancien Testament", in *ibid.*, pp.7-28.
13. J. Jeremias, *The Eucharistic Words of Jesus*, London, 1966, p.253.

14. On this point, see J.M.R. Tillard, *L'Eucharistie Paque de l'Eglise*, Collection *Unam Sanctam*, No. 44, Paris, 1964; *idem*, "Pénitence et eucharistie", in *MD*, 50, 1967, pp.103-131; *idem*, "Le pain et la coupe de la réconciliation", in *Concilium*, 61, 1971, pp.35-48.

15. See the excellent book by H. de Lubac, *Corpus mysticum. L'eucharistie et l'Eglise au Moyen Age*, collection *Theologie* 3, Paris, 1944.

16. *Sermo* 272, *PL* 38, 1246-1248.

17. *Summa theologica*, IIIa, 73,3.

18. Article 21 of the Scots Confession. See Niesel (ed.), *Bekenntnisschriften und Kirchenordnungen der nach Gottes Wort reformierten Kirche*, 1938, p.108.

19. Cf. Justin, *Apol*, I, 67.

20. See J. Laporte, *La doctrine eucharistique chez Philon d'Alexandrie*, Paris, 1972.

21. On the *todah*, see in particular H. Cazelles, "L'Anaphore et L'Ancien Testament", in B. Botte, J. Codier et al., *Eucharisties d'Orient et d'Occident*, collection *Lex Orandi*, 46, Paris, 1970, pp.11-21.

22. See the studies by R. Ledogar, *Aknowledgement, Praise-Verbs in the Early Greek Anaphora.*, Rome, 1968, pp.101-106; Thomas Julian Talley, "De la Berakah à l'eucharistie, une question à réexaminer", in *MD*, 125, 1976, pp.11-39.

CONVERGENCE ON THE ORDAINED MINISTRY

EMMANUEL LANNE

In the light of comments from the churches on its first draft of a statement on the ministry, the Faith and Order Commission now presents an entirely revised version. It will be helpful to show how far, on fundamental points, the Roman Catholic teaching finds itself adequately reflected in this document. In fact, the new statement reaches a striking convergence on this difficult question of the conception of the ordained ministry in the different Christian traditions.

From the Roman Catholic standpoint, the questions which arise concerning the ministry may be grouped under three headings: (1) the distinction between the ordained ministry and the other ministries within the ecclesial community; (2) the threefold form of the ordained ministry: episcopate, presbyterate, diaconate; (3) the relationship of the ordained ministry to the priesthood.

These three traditional *loci*, which were among those on which the Roman Catholic tradition opposed the Reformation of the sixteenth century, have been joined for some time now by a fourth: the question of the admission of women to the ordained ministry on the same footing as men. On this point, the new document on the ministry was able to make only a single recommendation: that of "openness to each other" (§54). The exegetical, doctrinal and pastoral questions arising from the admission or non-admission of women to ordination were not tackled by the document. This is undoubtedly a real limitation in this new text, which is specifically intended to make it possible for the churches to reach a truly common concept of the ministry. This in no way detracts, however, from the objective value of the doctrinal convergence it has succeeded in registering on the three

---

• Emmanuel Lanne is a Benedictine monk of the Chevetogne (Belgium) community.

traditional *loci* of the controversy of the past. Only a few years ago, the obstacles they presented seemed insurmountable. The advances achieved since then, evidenced in this document, should make us confident that a solution will eventually be found for the question of the ministry of women which at present has reached an impasse. For the moment, it is the advances made in the direction of a converging view of the ordained ministry which should hold our attention.

I. The ordained ministry and the other ministries

An initial surprise awaits the reader of this document on the ministry. It begins in fact with a long preamble describing "the calling of the whole people of God". Only in the closing paragraph of this first section §6) is the question of the ordained ministry broached. In this way the document clearly intends to affirm that the ordained ministry has meaning only in relation to the Church. For it is the Church which is the primary object of the divine calling. The ordained ministry is for the Church. It finds its *raison d'etre* in the Church.

This standpoint, though simple and obvious, has not always been perceived and respected as clearly as this in all the Christian traditions or in every period. In the Roman Catholic Church, the Second Vatican Council vigorously restored it to its rightful place by the important statement on "the Church", the Constitution *Lumen Gentium*. The chapter of the Constitution dealing with "the hierarchy", i.e. the ordained ministry (bishops, priests and deacons) was preceded by two chapters dealing respectively with the "mystery of the Church" in the plan of God, and then with the people of God. A like intention governs the arrangement of the Faith and Order document on the ordained ministry. In no sense, therefore, can the ordained ministry be regarded as a "caste" located outside the people of God. Their mutual dependence is brought out in §11.

It is nonetheless necessary to make clear the specific nature of the ordained ministry as distinct from the other gifts, charisma and ministries by which the life of the Church is invigorated. The document does this in §8 by pointing out that "within a multiplicity of gifts" in the Church there are those who are "responsible for pointing to its fundamental dependence on Jesus Christ" and "thereby provide... a focus of its unity".

The next paragraph (§9) points out that "the Church has never existed without persons who have a specific authority and responsibility" and refers to Jesus' choice and commissioning of disciples as witnesses of the Kingdom, and then to the promise made to the Twelve, their role and that of the apostles (§§ 9 and 10). While distinguishing between what is specific and unrepeatable in this role of the apostles, the document goes on to say: "Christ, who chose and sent the apostles, continues by the Holy Spirit, to choose and call persons with a view to the ordained ministry" (§10).

It is well known that Roman Catholic doctrine insists on the effective link between the college of the Twelve and the apostles, on the one hand, and the hierarchy of ordained ministries in the church (and particularly the college of bishops), on the other. This doctrine of apostolic succession in the ministry was more fully set forth in the Constitution on the Church at the Second Vatican Council (*Lumen Gentium* §18 ff). It had already been formally taught by the Council of Trent (Session XXIII, DS 1764 ff.) and reaffirmed by the First Vatican Council as basis of the doctrine of the papal primacy (DS 3050). All that the Second Vatican Council did was to state more fully the implications of this doctrine for the episcopate. Nevertheless, while the bishops are, as the Second Vatican Council solemnly teaches (*Lumen Gentium* §20), successors of the apostles, this does not refer to the unique and unrepeatable function of the apostles as witnesses of the risen Christ but to their role as pastors and teachers.

This "apostolic succession" of the bishops in their pastoral and teaching functions is regarded by the Roman Catholic Church as one of the main clarifications of what the Niceno-Constantinopolitan Creed means when it affirms "apostolicity" as one of the constitutive properties of the Church along with its unity, holiness and catholicity (cf. *Lumen Gentium* §8 and *passim*). The property of apostolicity embraces other aspects, such as the "apostolic preaching", the "apostolic scriptures" and the "apostolic tradition" (cf. the Second Vatican Council's Constitution on the Divine Revelation, *Dei Verbum* §8 etc. and *Lumen Gentium* §20). This apostolic property of the Church also embraces, in more recent parlance, the activities of all church members, especially the laity, in the work of Christian evangelism and witness. They are said to exercise an "apostolate" or an apostolic activity (cf. *Lumen Gentium* §27 etc. and the Decree on the Apostolate of the Laity, *Apostolicam actuositatem* §1 et seq.). When therefore the Faith and Order document (§30) connects the Church's "apostolicity" as confessed in the Creed to the continuity of the whole life of the Church with the apostles and their preaching, the standpoint seems at first sight to be the opposite of that of the Roman Catholic Church. In reality, however, it is very close to it. The perspective *appears* to be the opposite because the Roman Catholic teaching connects the various forms of the Church's apostolic life to the form it takes in the succesion of the ministry received from the apostles, whereas the Faith and Order document first affirms the permanence of the whole apostolic tradition and only then goes on to list among the characteristics of this permanence the following: the witness to the apostolic faith, the proclamation and reinterpretation of the Gospel, the celebration of baptism and the eucharist, the transmission of ministerial responsibilities (that is to say, what we understand by apostolic succession), fellowship in prayer, love, joy and suffering, etc. Succession in the ministry from the apostles onwards is only mentioned, therefore, as one of the elements in this apostolic nature of the Church, whereas in Roman Catholic doctrine it is first and fundamental.

But this apparent reversal of standpoints should not mislead us. The convergence of standpoints is greater than it seems. I have already pointed out the way in which Vatican II's Constitution on the Church, by dealing with the hierarchical ministry only after having spent two chapters setting forth the mystery of the Church and its vocation as the people of God, reversed the perspective which had previously prevailed. Pointing in the same direction is the fact that this same document on the Church begins its first chapter with several paragraphs describing the divine plan of salvation in terms of sendings or "missions" (*Lumen Gentium* §§2-4). Another Second Vatican Council document, the Decree on the Church's Missionary Activity, has the same structure which it amplifies and enriches (*Ad Gentes* §§1-5). What these documents say about the mission of the Church, therefore, tends to connect up again with what is said in the passages of the Faith and Order document we are examining. Even if the two standpoints do not coincide, it is nevertheless right to emphasize this convergence. The commentary in §30, moreover, is quite acceptable in this respect.

It is along these lines, too, that the tactful phrase used to open §36 will be understood. When the document asserts that "under the particular historical circumstances of the growing Church in the early centuries, the succession of bishops became *one of the ways...* in which the apostolic tradition of the Church was expressed" (my italics), it does not wish to imply that there were ways of succession in the ministry other than that of episcopal succession. It offers no verdict on this obscure and disputed question which is explained in a careful and excellent manner in the commentary. All that is said is that this succession of bishops is not the only form in which the apostolic tradition finds expression. Other forms are the transmission of the Gospel and the life of the Christian community. It will be noticed in this connection how closely the deep underlying purpose of this document is similar to that of the Roman Catholic Church. Only within the framework of the living tradition, which embraces the whole life of the Church through the centuries, does the uninterrupted chain of episcopal succession acquire its true significance. In terms of its own intrinsic point of view, this Faith and Order document seems, therefore, to bring out with sufficient clarity the uniqueness and necessity of the "ordained ministry" transmitted since the apostles within the life of the Church and the diverse gifts in which this life is embodied.

This uniqueness of the ordained ministry is sanctioned in the Roman Catholic tradition by the doctrine of the "sacrament of order". It was formulated by the Council of Trent (Session XXIII, and canon 3, DS1773): "No one should doubt that order is truly and properly one of the seven sacraments of the Church".[1] Scripture support for this is found by the Council in 2 Tim. 1:6-7 and 4:14, as well as in the apostolic tradition and the unanimous consensus of the church fathers. It is argued that "by holy ordination, accomplished by words and outward signs, a grace is conferred".[2]

The Faith and Order document does not say that ordination to the ministry is a sacrament. Yet in the paragraphs dealing with ordination, its meaning and its form, we find the essential elements on the basis of which the Roman Catholic tradition recognized the ordained ministry as a sacrament. Let us indicate some of these: "The laying on of hands is the *sign of the gift of the Spirit*, rendering visible the fact that the ministry was instituted in the revelation accomplished in Christ, and reminding the Church to look to him as the source of its commission" (§39: See also the commentary on this §). Further on, this is stated more explicitly and, from the Roman Catholic standpoint, in a more adequate manner: "The act of ordination by the laying on of hands of those appointed to do so is at one and the same time: invocation of the Holy Spirit (*epiklesis*); sacramental sign; acknowledgement of gifts and commitment" (§41), a statement which is then developed in the three paragraphs which follow

(§§42-44). The document explains the second element in the act of ordination, "sacramental sign", as follows: "Ordination is a sign performed in faith that the spiritual relationship signified is present in, with and through the words spoken, the gestures made and the forms employed" (§43).

One last point should be made in respect of the sacramental character of ordination. Roman Catholic doctrine affirms that ordination confers a "character" on the person receiving it. The Council of Trent declared that this character can be neither effaced nor removed (Session XXIII, DS 1767; cf. canon 4, DS 1774). Vatican II's Constitution on the Church and the same Council's Decree on the Ministry and Life of Priests retain this doctrine but without insisting on the "indelibility" of this character (*Lumen Gentium* §21; *Presbyterorum Ordinis* §2). The Faith and Order document, while not proposing any doctrine of the character conferred by ordination, does make the following welcome statement: "In recognition of the God-given charism of ministry, ordination to any one of the particular ordained ministries is never repeated" (§48). The ground given — recognition of the charism of the ministry given by God — converges with the Roman Catholic perspective.

II. The threefold form of the ordained ministry

The Roman Catholic Church has always held that the ordained ministry, in the strict sense, included three "degrees", that of bishop, that of priest or presbyter, and that of deacon. For centuries, however, the third of these "degrees" or "orders" — the diaconate — has had only a symbolic, transitional role and it was impossible to assign it any clearly defined profile. The Second Vatican Council restored the dignity of the diaconate (cf. *Lumen Gentium* §29) and it is now exercised in many places as a full-time ministry by men who devote their best endeavours to it as Christians. From the theological standpoint, however, it is still difficult to give a precise definition of this ministry.

Somewhat similarly, while the unanimous Catholic tradition has placed the episcopate at the summit of the ministries and linked it directly with the apostles, its precise nature has sometimes been obscured by theologians who interpreted the difference between it and the presbyterate exclusively in terms of more extensive "powers" exercised for the spiritual benefit of the people of God. Rare but well attested cases of presbyters having received the authority to ordain other presbyters helped to blur the radical distinction which exists between the episcopate and the presbyterate. Here, too, it was the Second Vatican Council in particular which redressed the balance by restoring the episcopate to the summit and as the source of the other ecclesial ministries. Nevertheless, it is easy to understand that, in periods of considerable uncertainty, ecclesiologically and pastorally, such as the sixteenth century, it came to be thought, on the one hand, that there was only one fundamental (ordained) ministry and, on the other hand, that this ministry was exercised by the ministers in charge of the local congregations, rather than by bishops lacking any real relationships with the flock committed to their care or by deacons of whom there were very few at the parish level. Pushed by circumstances, this was the choice made by several of the main Reformers. This also explains the theological orientation of many daughter churches of Protestantism which did not regard the episcopate as an essential function belonging to the *esse* of the Church but at most only to its *bene esse*.

The Council of Trent came out in favour of the threefold form of ministry (Session XXIII, DS1765, and canons 6 and 7, DS1776-1777), but in a not altogether satisfactory way, so that Vatican II was able to give a much more precise picture. From a Roman Catholic standpoint, therefore, it is in the light of these historical facts that chapter III of the Faith and Order document, entitled "The Form of the Ordained Ministry", must be considered. Among the paragraphs in this section to which special attention will be paid is §23, establishing the uniqueness of the ministry of *episkope*. "Every church", it says, "needs this ministry of unity in some form in order to be the Church of God, the one body of Christ, a sign of the unity of all in the Kingdom."

What is said in §29 about the functions of bishops also corresponds in large measure to what those churches who have deliberately preserved the apostolic succession recognize in them. But, on the basis of the threefold pattern of the ministry, §24 rightly raises questions not only for churches which have not preserved it but also for those which have. We have already spoken of the fluctuations in Roman Catholic teaching on this matter down to very recent times. One would have to be very shortsighted indeed not to see that certain of our practices and the principles underlying them continue to present a problem. It is not easy to explain the growth in numbers of bishops not exercising strictly episcopal functions in any regular manner, the bishops of the Curia for example. Nor the *de facto* place occupied by priests who are not bishops in the ordinary government of the Church, as for example the "major superiors" of religious orders; nor, finally, the distinction which exists in canon law between the functions carried out by a deacon and those exercised by a member of a religious order who is entrusted with pastoral duties.

The substance of this chapter of the Faith and Order document should make it possible, therefore, for all the churches to enrich still further their conception and practice of the ministry and to draw closer to a common conception.

III. Relationship of the ordained ministry to the priesthood

Reference was made earlier to the sacramental nature of the ordained ministry, differentiating it within the church as a whole from other gifts, charisms and ministries. Since the patristic period, however, the ministry of the bishop and the presbyter was recognized in the tradition of both East and West as a form of Christian priesthood distinct from that in which every Christian shares in virtue of baptism. It is customary to speak today of ministers as "priests", whether they are presbyters or bishops. Support for this way of understanding the ordained ministry was given by the Council of Trent which, in the session to which reference has already been made more than once, speaks explicitly of the ministry as a "priesthood" and relates it directly to the celebration of the eucharist understood as a "sacrifice" (Session XXIII, DS1764-1765, and canons 1 and 2, DS 1771 and 1772). Even though this way of presenting the ministry finds considerable support in the ancient texts, one can easily see how it exacerbated conflicts in the polemical setting of the sixteenth century and subsequently, and could lead people to think that substantially different and even opposing realities were meant by the Catholic and Reformed ministries.

The Second Vatican Council developed a much broader view of ministry within the ecclesial community. It affirmed that the unique priesthood of Christ was the basis both of the priesthood of all Christians and of that of the ministers. At the same time, however, it reaffirmed that the common priesthood of the faithful and the ministerial priesthood (or "hierarchical priesthood") differ not only in their degree but also in their nature. This difference has its basis in the role assigned to the celebrant of the eucharist both in his relationship to Christ and in his relationship to the community.

The Faith and Order document is very discreet about this thorny question of the connection between the ordained ministry and the priesthood. It affirms that while "ordained ministers are related, as are all Christians, both to the priesthood of Christ and to the priesthood of the Church", "they may appropriately be called priests". The reason given is that "they fulfill a particular priestly service by strengthening and building up the royal and prophetic priesthood of the faithful". The means whereby they do this are: word and sacraments, prayers of intercession, and pastoral guidance (§17). This is a larger area than the "eucharistic sacrifice" and the "remission of sins" mentioned in the Tridentine text but the direction is clearly the same.

This impression is confirmed when this section is seen in the light of statements scattered through the document. For example, speaking of the three main functions of ordained ministers, the document identifies the first as follows: "Ordained ministers are representatives of Jesus Christ to the community, and proclaim his message of reconciliation" (§11). It then stresses that "it is especially in the eucharistic celebration that the ordained ministry is the visible focus of the deep and all-embracing communion between Christ and the members of his body" (§14). With regard to the threefold ministry, it notes that "in the earliest instances, where threefold ministry is mentioned, the reference is to the local eucharistic community" (§20). "The bishop was the leader of the community. He was ordained and installed to proclaim the Word and preside over the celebration of the eucharist" (*ibid.*).

If these pointers are combined with others already mentioned earlier in respect of the threefold ministry and if all this is combined with the teaching in the document on the eucharist, which it is not our task here to examine, it must be recognized that, on this very difficult question of the "ministerial priesthood", a convergence is beginning to emerge which would have been inconceivable even a few years ago. The paragraph on the priesthood must not be taken to say more than its few lines contain, of course, but the fact remains that the vision of the whole document, in which the *episkopé* is central and the eucharistic celebration given a fundamental role, points us in the direction of a satisfactory solution.

Conclusion

This document on the ministry seems to us to have taken steps which, from a Roman Catholic standpoint, are decisive. If the churches accept it and make it the basis of unions between themselves, considerable progress will have been achieved on the road towards unity. On the other hand, as we have already had occasion to point out incidentally, it is not only from the churches stemming from the Reformation of the sixteenth century that an effort is required to readjust and deepen the doctrine and practice of the ministries. The churches of the Catholic tradition must also learn from, and face up to the questions raised by the traditions deriving from the Reformation. A number of the achievements of the Second Vatican Council were assisted by the fresh light afforded by the other Christian traditions. The advance represented by this ecumenical document on the ministry should make the further development of these convergences possible in a decisive way.

NOTES

1. Denz. *Enchiridion Symbolorum*, ed. 31 1960, p. 337.
2. *Ibid.*, p. 336f.

RECONCILIATION IN MINISTRY

GEOFFREY WAINWRIGHT

The importance of the question concerning ministerial order can be mistaken by no one who has taken part in unity negotiations between churches, on the one hand, which have a threefold ministry of bishop, presbyter and deacon and which claim an episcopal succession from the apostles, and churches, on the other hand, which shape their ministry differently or make no such claim.

Certainly, some sub-theological factors, of a psychological and sociological kind, may contribute to apparent difficulties: in this case each party may feel that the other is threatening its communal identity, vocational integrity or professional livelihood. But genuinely theological matters are at stake in so far as the structure of an ecclesial community, the significance it attributes to its ordained ministers, and the functions which such ministers fulfill, all serve (1) to express the community's life before God, within itself, and towards the world, (2) to locate the particular community with regard to the wider Christian community throughout time and space, and (3) to demonstrate the community's response to the crises of Christian history and to the opportunities offered by a variety of surrounding cultures.

I will lay my cards on the table by declaring that I am an ordained minister of the British Methodist Church, which has a single rank of ordained ministry, namely presbyter, and which makes no claim to episcopal succession. I write also, however, as someone who judges that an ordained ministry, which is in principle adaptable in structure, should at this point in history become adapted, where this is not

---

• Geoffrey Wainwright is Professor of Liturgy at Union Theological Seminary (New York).

already the case, to the long-traditional structure of bishop, presbyter and deacon — precisely for the sake of church unity, which will itself enhance the testimony borne by the church to the gospel of reconciliation which it celebrates before God and proclaims before the nations. I agree with paragraph 25 of the document on *Ministry* that all churches should share in the task of fully developing the potential of the threefold pattern for the most effective witness of the church in the world.

My purpose here is to explicate the document on *Ministry* in such a way that its advocacy of "the traditional pattern" may find less resistance among churches without such a ministry, while assuring the "traditional" churches that it is indeed the historic ministry upon which theological convergence is focusing, even though the understanding and exercise of it may be enhanced and even "corrected" by the experience of communities which have hitherto been differently ordered.

On the basis of the document I want to examine four questions:
— first, how the Christian community stands, and orders its life, before God;
— second, how the continuity and unity of the universal church is expressed;
— third, how the church accomplishes its mission and service in the world;
— fourth, whether what I will call a "lex orandi" method may not be employed in the reconciliation of the mutually separated Christian communities and their ministries.

I. How the Christian community stands, and orders its life, before God

In Jesus Christ our Lord and great High Priest, the church stands before God as a "royal priesthood", a "kingdom of priests" (1 Pet. 2:9; Rev. 1:6; 5:10). We offer "spiritual sacrifices" (1 Pet. 2:5), a "sacrifice of praise" (Heb. 13:15). All the churches agree on that. In a special sense, however, "many churches use the word "priest" to denote certain ordained ministers" (*Ministry* §7.d). On the whole, the greatest theological significance is attached to such usage by churches which have a threefold ministry and which claim episcopal succession from the apostles. Paragraph 17 attempts to reconcile differences on this matter. In this connexion, it is important to note that the special usage of the word "priest" attaches precisely to those ordained ministers who preside at the eucharist, namely the bishop and the presbyter. Now the eucharist is the pre-eminent liturgical form of our spiritual oblation; it is the sacrifice of praise *par excellence* As such, it is made by the whole people in Christ. The eucharistic prayer is offered, from first to last, by the entire community: "Let us give thanks to the Lord our God... through Jesus Christ our Lord... Amen." To call "priests" those who preside in the liturgical assembly and speak its prayers may therefore be regarded as *appropriate*, in rather a strong sense of the term. As a matter of historical fact, it is likely that, from the earliest days of the church, regular presidency of the worshipping assembly helped to reinforce the leading role of the minister in the whole life of the congregation, just as leadership in the general life of the congregation will have made such persons the "natural" presidents of the worshipping assembly. The function of "the priest", in the ministerial sense, is not to deny the priesthood of the whole people in Christ but rather to help it to expression.

Special charisms have been present in the church from the beginning (cf. §§5,33), and they serve to remind the congregation that everything it has is in fact received as a gift from God through Christ in the Holy Spirit (cf. §§39, 42-47). To recognize the dependence of the church on God is to recognize the rule of a Lord who rules precisely by giving himself for our salvation. As gifts from God to the congregation, persons endowed with charisms are the ministers of God's rule within the church, provided they rule according to the gospel: "You know that the rules of the gentiles lord it over them.... It shall not be so among you; but whoever would be first among you must be your slave; even as the Son of Man came not to be served but to serve, and to give his life as a ransom for many" (Matt. 20:25-28; cf. Luke 22:25-27). This servant role is exercised by persons who in a real sense *spend their lives* in preaching the gospel, teaching the faith, dispensing the sacraments, caring for the flock, discerning, distributing and coordinating the gifts of all the members for the edification of the entire body in love.

From early times the institutional form of this rule in the Church was concentrated in bishops and presbyters. The document on *Ministry* does not take sides on the historically and theologically controversial question: does the presbyterate descend from the episcopate through the delegation of some episcopal functions to it, or does the episcopate arise from the presbyterate through the function of presiding over it? In my view, it is in any case preferable to abandon the idea of movements upwards or downwards in this matter. On a horizontal plane, the bishop surrounded by the presbyters may rather be seen as "a focus of unity" (§8) in the Church (cf. §§20-27, 29-30). If, in churches with a "historic" ministry, the collegial character of this ministerial rule has tended to grow weak, and the communal setting has tended to become a rather passive context for ministerial action, then it may be that one of the main contributions brought by the more "protestant" churches will be their experience with "regular representative synodal gatherings" (§§26-27).

II. How the continuity and unity of the universal Church is expressed

While it is the Lord and the Spirit who are the divine sources of the church's continuity and unity, the human manifestation of that continuity and unity is the apostolic tradition. Paragraph 34 describes the apostolic tradition thus: "Apostolic tradition in the Church means continuity in the permanent characteristics of the church of the apostles: witness to the apostolic faith, proclamation and fresh interpretation of the gospel, celebration of baptism and the eucharist, the transmission of ministerial responsibilities, communion in prayer, love, joy and suffering, service to the sick and the needy, unity among the local churches and sharing the gifts which the Lord has given to each." The plain and sorry fact is that the historic and persisting divisions among the Christian people have at the least renderd the church's continuity and unity problematic, if not indeed non-existent. Because "the ordained ministry has a particular task of preserving and actualizing the apostolic faith" (§35), relationships between mutually separated communities often centre on the question of reciprocal recognition of their ordained ministers. In this connexion, the document on *Ministry* appears to me to make at least four important points for relations between churches which claim a historic episcopate and those which do not.

First, the document uses only very sparingly and rather indirectly the juridical language of validity (cf. §§38 and 39 comm.). Yet one can be sure that this question still haunts conversations between "catholics" and "protestants". The most cogent argument which "catholics" advance for the importance of "validity" is the pastoral-theological argument that valid orders provide an objective assurance to the whole community that, from God's side, grace is being offered it through the service of its ministers. Now, if our document is right in stating that "in churches which practise the succession through the episcopate, it is increasingly recognized that a continuity in apostolic faith, worship and mission has been preserved in churches which have not retained the form of the historic episcopate" (§37), then we are approaching a situation in which the factual presence of what "validity" meant to safeguard is being acknowledged even where validity in the technical sense is absent. The reality rightly takes precedence over what proves to be only *one* of the means intended to achieve it. On the other hand, our document offers no encouragement to laxity in the transmission of the ministry: "The orderly transmission of the ordained ministry is... a powerful expression of the continuity of the Church through history.... Where churches see little importance in orderly transmission, they should ask themselves whether they have not to change their conception of continuity in the apostolic traditon" (§35).

Second, the document follows current biblical scholarship in declaring that "the New Testament does not describe a single pattern of ministry which might serve as a blueprint or continuing norm for all future ministry in the Church. In the New Testament there appears rather a variety of forms which existed at different places and times" (§19). The conclusion is drawn that "the churches need to avoid attributing their particular forms of the ordained ministry directly to the will and institution of Jesus Christ" (§11 comm.). Episcopalians, presbyterians, congregationalists and pentecostalists are thereby freed from dominical or scriptural pressure to make exclusive claims for their structures of government.

Third, the document recognizes that there have been "developments" and "crises" in the complex history of ministerial structures and forms (§§19-21). Crises may lead to positive developments, while some developments may become so problematic as to lead to crises. Thus the settlement into a threefold pattern of ordained ministry (§19) with an emphasis on episcopal succession (§36) was at least in part a response by the church to the crisis of self-definition in face of heretical currents (the definition of a scriptural canon and the fixation of creeds belong to the same response). Yet even a church with a threefold ministry and the episcopal succession could fall into decay, and some later departures from the predominant pattern are to be seen as positive responses to crises. Thus the medieval Waldensians replaced the "father" by the "uncle", the *barba*; most of the sixteenth-century Reformers sooner or later adopted new ministerial structures which they believed closer to the New Testament or which they believed to be within the Church's competence to effect; the Methodists in eighteenth-century England, under the imperative of evangelization, evolved their own ministerial structures which finally separated them from the Anglican Church. The document on *Ministry* states that "in the history of the Church there have been times when the truth of the gospel could only be preserved through prophetic and charismatic leaders. Often new impulses could find their way into the life of the church only in unusual ways. At times reforms required a special ministry" (§39). Where the rest of the church has *not* been "attentive to the challenge of such special ministries", one may reckon that a break in succession, a change in structure, and even a rupture of communion, have been regrettable necessities. Once the particular crisis is past, however, reconciliation itself becomes an evangelical obligation upon all parties.

Fourth, the document proposes that "the threefold ministry of bishop, presbyter and deacon may serve today as an expression of the unity we seek and also as a means for achieving it" (§22). In this connexion it is noted that "the threefold ministry became the generally accepted pattern in the Church of the early centuries and is still retained today by many churches". In particular, the episcopal succession was understood, from the days of the ancient church, as "serving, symbolizing and guarding the continuity of the apostolic faith and communion" (§36; cf. §34 comm.). The non-espiscopal churches are now invited to "appreciate the episcopal succession as a sign, though not a guarantee, of the continuity and unity of the Church" (§38). I suggest that it may be right to view the episcopal succession as a kind of sacrament which does not always produce its full fruits but is nevertheless not thereby rendered ineffective. Certainly the episcopal churches have a better record of unity than much of fissiparous Protestantism. It would, however, make it easier for non-episcopal churches to recover an episcopal ministry and succession, if such a move were part of a process whereby churches claiming a historical episcopal succession were able to become reconciled among themselves and so remove the difficulty of conflicting episcopates and even rival bishops in a single place (cf. §38).

III. How the church accomplishes its mission and service in the world

The document begins with the purpose of God for the whole of humanity, moves on to describe the place and function of the church within God's purpose, and only then deals with the ordained ministry. This sequence must be taken as indicating that the ordained ministry subserves the church in its totality, while the church itself is part of God's larger purpose for the world, which will be consummated in God's Kingdom. Here is a corrective for that narcissism which, for the sub-theological reasons mentioned in my introduction, tends to invade discussions of the ordained ministry.

Paragraph 12 declares that ordained ministers "serve to build up the community in Christ and to strengthen its witness". Since "these tasks are not exercised by the ordained ministry in an exclusive" but rather "in a representative way" (§13 comm.), the underlying thought appears to be what the Consultation on Church Union in the U.S.A. expresses thus: "Their ordination marks them as persons who represent to the Church its own identity and mission in Jesus Christ." Or as the British Methodist *Statement on Ordination* of 1974 puts it: "As a perpetual reminder of this calling (of the whole people of God to be the body of Christ) and as a means of being obedient to it, the Church sets apart men and women, specially called, in ordination. In their office the calling of the whole people of God is focused and represented, and it is their responsibility as representative persons to lead the people to share with them in that calling. In this sense they are the sign of the presence and ministry of Christ in the Church, and through the Church to the world." The notion of the ordained ministry as a focalizing and enabling "representation" is good, and helps to break through the badly-formulated alternative of a difference in *kind* or in *degree* between the ordained and the rest. Precisely as *representatives* of Christ and his church the ordained ministers are *distinct*, but *what* they represent is not *other* than the character and mission of the whole church, and this itself is nothing other than participation, by the grace of the Holy Spirit, in the ministry of Christ the Saviour and Head of the church.

I suggest that this perspective helps also in the consideration of the diaconate: "Deacons represent to the Church its calling as a servant in the world.... They exercise a ministry of love within the community (§31). Attempts to renew the diaconate, in which the document on *Ministry* is much interested, will remain confused unless they concentrate on care for the needy within the household of faith and indeed among humanity at large (cf. Gal. 6:10). The liturgical side of this diaconal ministry consists chiefly in the leading of intercessions and (a practice already recorded by Justin Martyr) in the distribution of communion elements to the absent.

The church is called "to proclaim and prefigure the Kingdom of God": it "announces the gospel to the world"; all members of the church are called "to confess their faith and to give account of their hope", "to identify with the joys and sufferings of all people as they seek to witness in caring love", "to struggle with the oppressed towards that freedom and dignity promised with the coming of the Kingdom" (§4). And "in order to fulfill this mission faithfully, they will seek relevant forms of witness and service in each situation." Without contradicting the judging and renewing content of the gospel with regard to the world, certain features of the ordained ministry may and should be adapted to the "varying political, social and cultural context" (*ibid.*). Taking account of "contextual needs" (§22) is an appropriate heading under which to consider such variables as the size and composition of dioceses and parishes (cf. §§20-21),the payment and upkeep of ordained ministers (§46), their training for ministry (§49), the possibility of married and celibate ministries (§45), and perhaps even the controversial question as to whether the ordained ministry may and should include women from among the baptized (cf. §18). The practical forms of exercising the ordained ministry have been very variable, historically and geographically; the much greater fixity of its sacramental structures has contributed a valuable stability. The universal adoption of the threefold structure should not diminish but rather protect the variety of operational styles.

God's purpose is his eschatological kingdom as the church proclaims and prefigures that kingdom and brings to the world a foretaste of its joy and glory (cf. §4), so the ordained ministry carries a certain orientation towards the future. The suggestive words here are "vigilance" (§14 comm.) and "responsibility" (§§29, 30, 37). "Authority has the character of "responsibility before God" (§15). Like Ezekiel's "watchman", the ordained ministers are accountable to God; and many traditional ordination prayers ask that the ministers may at the last judgment receive the reward of their stewardship.

IV. Whether a "lex orandi" method may help in the reconciliation of mutually separated Christian communities and their ministries

From an examination of their liturgies H.J. Schulz has concluded that there exists sufficient agreement in trinitarian belief and in the doctrine of Church, sacraments and ministry for the Catholic and

Orthodox churches to consider themselves "united in faith" and so free *on that score* to be reconciled in eucharistic communion.[1] Some years earlier, the Lutheran theologian and pioneer in Faith and Order, Edmund Schlink, had written: "If one compares in the different churches the canonical and dogmatic statements on the ministries, the apostolic succession, and the relation of bishop to presbyter, one finds immense differences; and an ecumenical dialogue which limits itself to a comparison of these statements will remain stuck in fruitless confrontation. These differences, however, appear in another light and can be largely eliminated, if one considers the service which is actually carried out through those ministries and relates it to the service committed to the apostles. Only if they are translated back into the elementary functions of church life, can canonical rules be compared in fruitful dialogue. For those elementary functions have their centre in the worshipping community."[2] I have myself used this theological method extensively in my book *Doxology.*[3]

If the churches will examine what is done and said in their worship assemblies, particularly at the eucharist, and in their services of ordination, my guess is that in many, many cases they will find that, despite differences in liturgical style, their "ways of worship" (the *lex orandi*) already confirm what is expressed in theological mode in the Faith and Order texts on *Eucharist* and on *Ministry* (particularly §§10, 13-14, 15, 17, 39-44 of the latter).[4] Where substantial differences occur, the churches may feel invited to revise their practices in light of the approach towards doctrinal agreement — a kind of ecumenical *lex credendi* — which is being made in the Faith and Order texts (cf. *Eucharist*, §§27-33; *Ministry*, §§37-38, 51-59). To recognize and promote convergence in liturgical practice could become the most effective factor in the process towards the mutual reconciliation of churches and ministries.

When the time for such reconciliation is ripe, the mutual recognition of churches and their ministries will require both juridical decisions and liturgical acts (*Ministry*, §55). Granted the absolutely fundamental importance of how the church appears *coram deo*, the greater emphasis should fall upon the acts in the worship setting, where the promise of God's grace is sure. I judge it would be appropriate for there to take place the mutual (not merely the common) confession of sin and declaration of pardon (cf. §2), followed by the common celebration of the eucharist and reception of communion. If churches are to accept new structures of ministry and their ministries enter into the episcopal succession, it would also be fitting that the first ordinations take place during the service of reconciliation.

* * *

In order to avoid the suspicion that I have been proposing simply a Protestant reading of the document on *Ministry*, let me end by quoting a passage from Avery Dulles which harmonizes remarkably with the Faith and Order text at a number of very important points, and which demonstrates that the convergence is taking place from Catholic starting-points too. With appeal to his fellow Jesuit Karl Rahner and to the Benedictine Cipriano Vagaggini, Dulles writes as follows:

> The church, in its fundamental reality as sacramentally representing Christ, has a plenitude of apostolic authority that is prior to, and hence independent of, its own canonical regulations. By virtue of this 'pre-canonical' power *the Church can structure its own pastoral office in certain specific ways.* It is not absolutely essential that the Church call its highest office-holders by the title of bishop or that they be inducted into office by having other bishops impose hands on them. These canonical regulations, which currently have the force of law within the Roman Catholic Church, are not necessarily binding on all churches for all time. The question as to the conditions under which the Catholic or Orthodox churches can partially or fully recognize the pastoral ministries in churches that lack the "historic episcopate" is far too complicated to be treated in this essay. Much of the current literature maintains that the Church is not faced with a simple alternative between validity and invalidity. Any church or ecclesial community, to the extent that it participates in the reality of the Church of Christ, has a capacity to confer spiritual power on its own pastors, even though these pastors be not ordained by bishops. This is not to claim, however, that all church polities are equally good or that all genuine Christian ministers have the same measure of ministerial power. According to a growing body of ecumenical opinion, the episcopal form of polity is to be esteemed as an efficacious sign of continuity and solidarity in the apostolic ministry.[5]

NOTES

1. H.J. Schulz, *Oekumenische Glaubenseinheit aus eucharistischer Uberlieferung*, Paderborn, Bonifacius, 1976.
2. E. Schlink, "Die Struktur der dogmatischen Aussage als okumenische Problem", in *Kerygma und Dogma*, 3, 1957, pp.251-306. English translation in *The Coming Christ and the Coming Church*, Edinburgh, Oliver & Boyd, 1967.
3. G. Wainwright, *Doxology* New York, Oxford, 1980.
4. See W. Vos and G. Wainwright, *Ordination Rites Past and Present*, Rotterdam, Liturgical Ecumenical Center, 1980.
5. A. Dulles, "Successio apostolorum, successio prophetarum, successio doctorum", in *Concilium*, No. 148, October 1981, pp.61-67. He refers to K. Rahner, "Vorfragen zu einem ökumenischen Amtsverständnis", *Quaestiones Disputatae 65*, Freiburg, Herder, 1974, and to C. Vagaggini, "Possibilità e limiti del riconoscimento dei ministeri non cattolici", in *Ministères et célébration de l'eucharistie*, *Studia Anselmiana*, 61, Rome, Editrice Anselmiana, 1973.

RECEPTION, TRADITION, COMMUNION

ANTON HOUTEPEN

Introduction

For the second time within seven years, the World Council of Churches, through its Faith and Order commission, "recommends that each church be asked to make an official response at a level carrying authority, taking positions and presenting comments on the matters in the Baptism-Eucharist-Ministry documents as one step *within a process of reception*"[1] This recommendation is made with both the member churches of the World Council and the Roman Catholic Church in mind; as well as other interested non-member churches. In the preface to the Lima texts on Baptism, Eucharist and Ministry, which were unanimously approved for transmission to the churches by the Faith and Order Commission in its plenary meeting, 3-15 January 1982, it is said: "The Faith and Order Commission invites all churches to prepare an official response to these texts *at the highest appropriate level of authority*, whether it be a council, synod, conference, assembly or other body. In support of this process of reception, the commission would be pleased to know as precisely as possible

— the extent to which your church can recognize in this text the faith of the Church through the ages;

— the consequences your church can draw from this text for its relations and dialogues with other churches, particularly with those churches which also recognize the text as an expression of the apostolic faith;

• Anton Houtepen is a theologian at the Inter-university Institute for Missiology and Ecumenics, Utrecht.

— the guidance your church can take from this text for its liturgical, educational, ethical and spiritual life and witness;

— the suggestions your church can make for the ongoing work of Faith and Order as it relates the material of this text on Baptism, Eucharist and Minstry to its long-range research project 'Towards the Common Expression of the Apostolic Faith Today'."[2]

These four questions together with the request for an authoritative response mark a decisive new phase in the ecumenical movement. From 1948 onwards many resolutions, statements, proposals and reports have been received by the World Council and recommended to the churches "for their study and appropriate action". According to the Rules of the World Council this is the only recommendation that may be in order.[3] This ruling is consistent with the Toronto Statement on the Ecclesiological Significance of the World Council of Churches, where it is said, that" ...membership in the Council does not in any sense mean that the churches belong to a body which can take decisions for them". Each church retains the constitutional right to ratify or reject utterances or actions of the Council. The authority of the Council consists only "in the weight which it carries with the churches by its own wisdom" (William Temple).[4]

Yet the Nairobi Assembly felt that a new type of ecumenical commitment through decisions of the churches themselves was urgently needed: "We ask the churches to undertake a common effort to *receive*, re-appropriate and confess *together*, as contemporary occasion requires, the Christian truth and faith, delivered through the Apostles and handed down through the centuries. Such common action, arising from free and inclusive discussion under the commonly acknowledged authority of God's Word, must aim both to clarify and to embody the unity and the diversity which are proper to the church's life and mission."[5] And with regard to the Faith and Order texts on Baptism, Eucharist and Ministry in their version from Accra 1974, it stated: "...the essential need is for actions by the churches which strengthen the development of true conciliar fellowship. We ask the churches for such actions: deliberate steps towards a fuller fellowship with other churches. As an example of one such decision, we ask the churches to consider the three agreed statements on 'Baptism, the Eucharist and a Mutually Recognized Ministry'.... In responding, the churches should not only examine whether the agreed statements reflect their present teaching and practice, but indicate the ways in which they are prepared to contribute to the common advance towards unity."[6] Perhaps the churches were not yet ready at that time to respond to such questions. Among the replies of churches, universities, groups and individuals only 20% referred directly to the Nairobi questions about possible implications for further unity.[7] In spite of this the Crêt-Bérard report, having carefully analyzed the churches' replies, declared hopefully: "What is new here is a significant beginning in theological response by the member churches *themselves*. A transition is under way: from documents agreed upon by theologians to agreement among member churches. From now on, it is said, the churches should be helped by the Faith and Order Commission to participate in the "consensus process". This calls for "a new kind of reception": "The churches need to *appropriate* critically the agreements reached in ecumenical encounter and discussion". This means "receiving afresh our own tradition while at the same time transcending its limitations," so "that we are able to recognize the common faith of the whole church in the ecumenical consensus achieved."[8]

After several years of correspondence and revision, the Lima text on Baptism, Eucharist and Ministry, according to the preface "aims to become a faithful and sufficient reflection of the common Christian Tradition on essential elements of Christian communion".[9]

Of course Faith and Order cannot and may not "examine" the churches, nor "impose agreement." It cannot "proclaim consensus".[10] The texts reflect convergence, based on the theological agreement of the Faith and Order Commission members who are perhaps representative for but not the representatives of their churches.

The texts are not yet the expressions of real ecclesiastical consensus, not yet the result of an authoritative "determinatio fidei" event, as conciliar statements might be. We cannot therefore speak of "official reception", though we are able to speak of "a process of reception", in which "the churches are respectfully invited to enable the widest possible involvement of the people of God at all levels of church life in the spiritual process of receiving these texts". Such invitation is not totally new within multilateral and bilateral dialogue processes. Comparable initiatives were the discussions about the World Council of Churchs' basis in 1948 and 1961, the reception process of the Leuenberg Concordia of Lutheran, Reformed and United Churches in Europe during the years 1971-1981[11], and the beginning of the reception process of the Anglican-Roman Catholic Documents. Never before, however, was such a large-scale reception process set in motion.

Several questions arise in the context of this bold initiative of Faith and Order: about criteria for "official reception," about the nature of consensus and the role of authoritative teaching and, finally, about the goal and the model of unity behind the whole idea of trying to reach consensus on Baptism, Eucharist and Ministry. We shall try to elucidate the impact of those questions for the ecumenical movement according to the Roman Catholic understanding of the goal of that movement under the three headings of the title of this article: reception, tradition, communion. Without taking into account the rich theological content of these three keywords of Christian fellowship and identity, all ecumenical conversations are in danger of becoming endless variations on the same theme: the ritual encounter of ecumenical experts, a permanent alibi for lasting division. Many church members are complaining about the lack of ecumenical advance in a time of growing consensus and of deepening awareness of joint Christian responsibility for justice, peace and survival. Theologians get frustrated if their statements of consensus seem to have no impact on the life and the relations of the divided churches. [12] Third World theologians turn to other themes of Christian life and thinking and are tired of dealing with the wearisome history of the conflicts of European or Western Christianity. In terms of reception, one might say, they do not want to "receive" the conflicts of the past and do not bother about their solution within the framework of the language-games in which they originated. [13] It would be a false conclusion, though, to regard the actual issue of baptism, eucharist and ministry as an outdated area of debate. It is not about such parts of theology that could easily be changed into other theological currency like liberation, hope or solidarity. It deals with the fundamental structures of our faith and hope, with the heart of the church's tradition and confession and with the "cement" of unity and communion.

There is a second reason to value the Baptism, Eucharist, Ministry debate as most relevant for the ecumenical movement as a whole. It is the first multilateral dialogue on the international level which has been brought to such a considerable convergence. Even churches which do not celebrate sacraments, like the Society of the Friends, or do celebrate them but in quite a different form and with different understanding, like the Kimbanguist Church, have participated.

They did not oppose the growing convergence between the traditions that do practise a sacramental life. And the latter were not deaf to the historical and actual reasons that hinder other disciples of Christ from adopting the sacramental practice of the majority of the churches, like the fear for ritualism or the lack of adoration in Spirit and Truth. Both sacramental and non-sacramental traditions have found each other on the basis of obedience to the apostolic witnesses that oppose any ritualistic reduction of the effective signs of the "memoria Christi", but are equally sure in affirming these signs as the cement of their unity which may not be abandoned.[14]

Now, indeed, the time of testing has come. Do these statements, within the one ecumenical movement, stand the test of reception so that they may become part of the common Christian tradition and may lead to communion between the churches?

a. Reception: a continuing process of appropriation

"Reception" seems to be a rather new theme of study within ecumenical theology. In handbooks, dictionaries and compendia we find only a few references. The term as such has too wide a meaning to be caught in easy definitions. Together with terms like "accipere," "suscipere", "firmare", "confirmare", "comprobare" and their Greek equivalents like "bebaioun", "sphragizein", "(apo)dechesthai", "(apo)lambanein", "recipere/receptio" was at home in canonical discussions and regulations regarding the authority or authentication of councils and synods,[15] the validation of legislative action,[16] the validity or validation of baptism, eucharist and ordination within heretic communities[17] and, rather recently, in the theoretical context of a philosophy of law, with regard to the introduction of Roman or German law into Canon Law or Civil Law.[18] The first three of these canonical meanings gained new theological importance within the ecumenical movement. First in the context of Vatican II and the hopes it raised for the restoration of unity.[19] Then in the atmosphere of Uppsala and its call for a genuinely universal council.[20] Finally in reflections about the nature of the consensus-process within multilateral and bilateral dialogues of the last decade, most of all stimulated by the Faith and Order initiative to share the documents on Baptism, Eucharist and Ministry with the churches and to ask for official comments.[21]

The idea of the "reception" of councils as a necessary aspect of their authentication, being the prolongation of the conciliar process for those who were absent, mutual communication between local synods and wider conciliar gatherings or the final confirmation of the authenticity and ecumenicity of one council by a subsequent one or by the Roman see, proved to be fruitful for ecumenical ec-clesiology. It brought back an awareness of the necessity of council where this was lacking. It stressed the role of the people of God and of the "consensus fidelium" for the true paradosis of the Gospel. It made the churches aware of their "ecumenism in time" by pointing to the fact that the churches find themselves, within the ecumenical movement, in a process of continuing reception or re-reception of the councils. [22]

Within Roman Catholic ecclesiology the Orthodox idea of con-ciliarity and sobornost was restored. The famous phrase of Vatican I, which says that papal definitions *ex cathedra* are irreformable *ex sese et non ex consensu ecclesiae* is now understood better in the light of Vatican II's new emphasis on the necessity of appropriation and consultation of the people of God: not to confirm conciliar or papal decisions juridically, but to assure that they are in line with the apostolic Tradition. [23] Even the First Vatican Council had never denied that it is the function of the Church's teaching ministry to "declare" what has been accepted and received, not to invent new doctrines of faith. [24] As H. Sieben has demonstrated in the conciliar theory of the Ancient Church, reception has a circular form: in the synchronic or horizontal assent of the churches which receive a coun-cil as authentic or ecumenical, they confirm the fact that they con-sider it as a sufficient expression of a diachronic or vertical consensus and as consonant with the apostolic tradition. Reception means the recognition of a *consensio antiquitatis et universitatis*. [25]

This does not mean that there is only repetition of the past. Recep-tion means a continuing process of reinterpretation or appropriation of the Gospel in new circumstances. [26] Such idea of "reception," be-ing a dynamic reality in the life of the churches, functions also in the field of legislative action. The validity of legislation does not totally depend on consensus or on the will of the people, but without such consensus no law can finally be kept. This principle is recognized even in Roman Canon Law. In recent Roman Catholic Church history there are many examples of legislation which did not "work" because it was not received by the faithful. [27] What is true for legisla-tion, is much more true for authoritative teaching: no determination of faith (*determinatio fidei*) can serve its goal — the assurance of the truth of the Gospel — without communication of faith (*communicatio fidei*). In the end, the synchronic principle of catholicity and orthopraxis — which means the hearing tradition (*ecclesia discens*) of the church taken seriously as the field where the Spirit of God is speaking to the churches — must heed the diachronic principle — which means the continuity of the deposit of faith, to be guaranteed by the ministerial teaching authority of the church (*ecclesia docens*) — for becoming static, tautologous, self-defensive.

Within the ecumenical movement of our times it is the communication of faith of all the hearing traditions, in dialogue with the common Christian paradosis of the Gospel, which is the "receptor" of the Spirit, guiding us into all Truth. The analogy with the reception processes and methods of the Ancient Church and its Councils is therefore a legitimate one, even if it is, juridically speaking, not the same event. Within the text on Baptism, Eucharist and Ministry itself this circular process of reception, of listening to one another and of listening to the common heritage has been crystallized: pedo-baptists and believer-baptists corrected one another; churches of the West learned from churches of the East to restore the epicletic character of the eucharist; Catholics and Protestants learned from the Jews what it means to celebrate the Memorial of Christ as *zikkaron-anamnesis*; episcopal churches had to learn together with non-episcopal churches, what "episcopé" really means both in the Ancient Church and today, and did forward proposals for a threefold ministry in line with the intentions of the Ancient Church and, hopefully, corresponding with the renewal of ministry which is needed for our times.

It is now the kairos for the churches to look at the results of their own endeavour to communicate with each other.

The second locus of the use of the term reception in canonical language is perhaps even more close to the actual reception process. It refers to the recognition or reconciliation of sacraments and ministry within separated communities.[28] As long as the intention is there to do what the church always has done (*intentio faciendi quod facit ecclesia*) sacraments and ministry in separated communities may be recognized according to old traditions. In such cases there might be large differences of theological opinion and even heresies which hinder full communion or demand excommunication. Nevertheless it would be possible to have valid and true sacraments and ministries, and to "receive" them as such. In the atmosphere of Vatican II's new approach to other churches as sister churches and as authentic instruments of salvation, its clear doctrine about baptism as the basic sacrament of unity,[29] official mutual recognition of baptism was followed by many studies on the conditions of valid ministries and authentic sacraments within non-Catholic churches. The bilateral dialogues between the Roman Catholic Church and the churches of the Reformation focus on such "reception". The most significant text of the Decree "De Oecumenismo" is, in this respect, the following:

> ...all who have been justified by faith in baptism are members of Christ's Body, and have a right to be called Christian, and so are with solid reasons *accepted* as brothers in Christ by the children of the Catholic Church.[30]

This is not only true for the individual members of such churches, but also for the churches themselves which "have been by no means deprived of significance and importance in the mystery of salvation. For the Holy Spirit has not refrained from using them as means of salvation which derive their efficacy from the very fullness of grace and truth entrusted to the Church".[31] And "Catholics must gladly acknowledge and esteem the truly Christian endowments from our common heritage which are to be found among our separated brethren. It is right and salutary to recognize the riches of Christ and virtuous works in the lives of others who are bearing witness to Christ, sometimes even to the shedding of their blood. For God is always wonderful in his works and worthy of all praise. Nor should we forget that anything wrought by the grace of the Holy Spirit in the hearts of our separated brethren can be help to our own edification. Whatever is truly Christian is never contrary to what genuinely belongs to the faith; indeed, it can always bring a deeper realization of the mystery of Christ and the Church"[32] We meet here two times the expression "agnoscere". The Spirit-bound reality of salvation is given to the Church and the churches; it may only be recognized and received. It is not to be constituted by agreement, but to be found in prayer, love, dialogue and renewal, on the basis of the same "intention of faith".[33]

The whole concept of "intentio fidei" could be misunderstood, if we read it as a rather subjective category. In English and American idiom, "intention" seems to express a rather non-committing good will to do something. In the theological tradition, coming from Albert the Great and Thomas Aquinas, "intentio fidei" means an objective reality, visible in external expressions and signs, to do what the church always has done *facere quod fecit ecclesia*. As long as there is such an "expressed will" to stay faithful to the apostolicity of the church — expressed in the same sacramental signs, ministerial succession, the same "marks of the church" — any separated community must be regarded as belonging, in one way or the other, to the one, apostolic and catholic church.

Of course such common intention of faith must also be articulated in theological agreement, as a prerequisite for mutual trust, as an echo of the actual "consentire" of Christians in many situations of life: in mixed marriage, in missionary situations, in common education, in joint service and joint pastoral care. Such theological agreement and practical convergence should be "received", i.e. digested and endorsed by the people of God and its authoritative teachers. It is in this last sense that we are confronted now with a big gap between theological understanding and offical church positions handed down in conciliar decisions and formulations, in catechisms and rules of conduct, in church structures and many non-doctrinal consequences of separate development.

This complicates the dialogue process, because we have to find a common language which is nevertheless recognized as a faithful expression of the confessional positions. And even if a variety of interpretations is legitimate *within* a tradition, such variety produces a fear of ambiguity in common so-called "consensus texts".

Therefore, more theological consensus is needed to restore unity than to preserve unity. Within the community of faith a wide diversity of interpretation is legitimate on the basis of the same authentic intention of faith. But in the search for communion between separated or dis-united communities such variety of interpretation is often understood as ambiguity which has to be clarified. It might turn out to be the paradox of reception, understood as the recognition of each other's intention of faith, that it serves as an alibi for mutual trust and recognition: a consensus is asked for as long as it is not formulated; and when it is formulated, other factors preclude the restoration of the communion. From the Roman Catholic use of reception/*recipere* in this second sense — the acknowledgment of the gifts of the Spirit within other communities — we may learn, that the "intention of faith" is an objective reality, not completely dependent on theological formulation or liturgical practice. As long as there is a sufficient reflection of the common apostolic tradition and the expressed will to be faithful to the common heritage, churches which want to be in communion, should no longer be regarded as disunited. We are now in a position, given theological formulation on our intention of faith with regard to baptism, eucharist and ministry, to invite the churches to restore communion by "receiving" one another's sacraments and ministries.[34]

It will be clear from such canonical approach of the "reception process", that it is not so easy to jump over to Faith and Order's actual consensus process. Faith and Order is not in the position of a council nor can it speak authoritatively on the ecclesial nature and the authenticity of the sacraments of the member churches. What is equal to the process of conciliar reception is a kind of circular structure: within the ecumenical movement we find a first form of mutual reception on the basis of a minimum confession of faith and a kind of negative or silent consensus on each other's ecclesial status according to the Toronto Statement of the World Council of Churches in 1950 or, on the basis of the *Decree Unitatis Redintegratio* of Vatican II. The bilateral dialogues are, in addition to that, a more than symbolic sign of mutual recognition as "sister churches" or even the instrument for the restoration of effective communion as was the case in the Leuenberg Agreement or of the Bonn Agreement between the Anglican Communion and the Old Catholic Churches. But what we can learn most of all from the analogies we mentioned is this: "ecumenical reception" is much more than the acceptance of or the agreement with theological formulations; it really means acknowledgement ("agnoscere") of each other's structures of communion. "Reception", therefore, is really correlated to "tradition" and "communion". It is not first of all a canonical, but a theological category.

b. Reception and tradition

Reception in its original biblical sense (*lambanein/apolambanein, dechesthai/apodechesthai*)[35] is one of the main characteristics of faith itself. We believe that we receive our existence as creatures from God, our salvation as redemption through Jesus Christ, new life as "anointed ones" in the Holy Spirit. We will meet a new creation and a time of grace through the Gospel of God (Mk 1:15; Rom. 1:1). We receive the body and blood of Christ through the bread and cup of the eucharist. We receive the mission to be disciples and ministers, prophets and teachers, messengers and guides of the community through the laying on of hands in the Spirit within the apostolic tradition. We, too, receive our unity as a gift from God, reconciliation, brotherhood, communion through God's initiative of grace and through the appeal of the Spirit.

Through the reception of this whole Gospel of the Kingdom, we receive afresh that part of Israel's tradition which goes back to the Promises of God to Abraham, Moses and David, which was renewed by the prophets and which is the permanent call of the Lord (ekklèsia) among all nations to be the Israel of God.[36] Such reception-receptiveness does not mean the acceptance of doctrines *about* creation, redemption, grace and mission, nor is it a mere interception of incidental activities of God. It is really a time-embracing and life-long reception process: a constant hearing, learning and thanking attitude of life — obedience of faith — which is carried on and guaranteed — always anew by a continuing hearing tradition. This started in Israel (Deut. 6:4-7), culminated in Jesus Christ, the obedient Servant of the Lord, Abba, and continues within the hearing tradition of God's ekklèsia, i. e. those who are called by God within history to hear Him by receiving Jesus Christ (John 1:14) and by listening to what the Spirit tells the churches. Within that hearing and receiving tradition, we *are* received by God through Jesus in the Spirit. It is in this Spirit, to remembrance (anamnesis, memoria) of Jesus Christ and to the glory of God the Father, that we celebrate the sacraments of our communion — baptism and the eucharist — and continue to be sent as servants and guides in God's mission. Together with the word of God in the scriptures and the rule of faith of the Ancient Church, together with the discipline of the discipleship of Jesus, these structures of communion make possible our Christian identity. Within the process of human longing and despair, success and failure, glory and sin, joy and suffering, birth and death, God himself reveals and discloses to us his way, the way of the kingdom.

And within this ongoing process of revelation, we receive among many scriptures *the* Scriptures, among many prophets *the* prophets, among many creeds *the* Creeds of the Church, among many sacramental signs, *the* sacraments of the Lord. True doxology and orthodoxy, holiness and orthopraxis are built up, guided by the Spirit of God through the voices of authoritative teachers and prophets: martyrs, monks, confessors, virgins, widows, bishops, presbyters, deacons. Through multiform ways of communication — correspondence, visitations, regulations, church order, liturgical forms — such "communication of faith" goes on. This is tradition in the form of reception and each fresh reception means the continuation of this tradition within the church as a hearing, learning community.[37]

This is the real reason why we speak of a reception process: because we have to deal now with the heart of our receiving faith. The content which has to be received has a definite influence on the status of our debate within the ecumenical movement. It should be limited to those elements of our communion which matter for the true paradosis of the Gospel and we had to wait for that common insight before the churches could start at all a reception process as is required now. Not because we receive perfect theological texts, but because we are part of the same receiving community of faith, that lives from the tradition of the elements of our communion, we may say now: it will be impossible not to receive these texts and to be in unity with those who receive them, unless we are convinced, that the texts are not consonant with our common Christian tradition and do not reflect our common "intentio fidei".

Of course such an emphasis on the common tradition from which we live does not preclude the criticism on the wording or the formulation of the text. It is possible to "receive" the text as an expression of the common tradition and to forward amendments for its improvement. Any textual result of the ecumenical dialogue should be considered as the draft of an agreement which declares consensus about former points of division. As such it is only a proleptic consensus. But at this special "kairos-moment" within the ecumenical history, we have reached such a considerable degree of agreement about such essential elements of our common tradition, that we really need solemn declarations of intent from the side of the participating churches themselves about the actual status of the unity debate. That is precisely, what the four questions of the Lima preface ask for.

For the Roman Catholic Church these questions have a special meaning. After Vatican II, she made herself one of the main bearers of the one ecumenical movement. At the Second Vatican Council itself she stressed the importance of the one and common tradition about faith, sacraments and ministry. "Every renewal of the Church is essentially grounded in an increase of fidelity to her own calling. Undoubtedly this is the basis of the movement towards unity."[38] In looking back for the authentic tradition, a "hierarchy of truths" functions.[39] For the restoration of unity it is therefore of the utmost importance to be aware that "the inheritance handed down by the apostles was *received* with differences of form and manner, so that from the earliest times of the Church, it was explained variously in different places, owing to diversities of genius and conditions of life". Such differences have led to divisions through lack of charity and mutual understanding, says *Unitatis Redintegratio*.[40] Now we see the reverse process through the dialogue of love and common relecture of the one Tradition" ...from time to time one tradition has come nearer to a full appreciation of some aspects of a mystery of revelation than the other, or has expressed it to better advantage. In such cases, these various theological expressions are to be considered often as mutually complementary rather than conflicting."[41]

What Vatican II said on the churches of Eastern Christianity, could this now, after many years of theological dialogue, be said also of the other churches, who would be prepared to receive the Faith and Order drafts for agreement? It would mean to welcome those into the position of "sister churches", carrying through history the same "intention of faith", being parts of the same tradition, of whom Vatican II declares: "All this heritage of spirituality and liturgy, of discipline and theology, in its various traditions, this holy Synod declares to belong to the full catholic and apostolic character of the Church."[42] Such declaration would be the fulfilment of that other guiding principle of catholic ecumenism, solemnly proclaimed by the Vatican Council in 1964: "....this sacred Council solemnly repeats the declaration of previous councils and Roman Pontiffs, that for the restoration or the maintenance of unity and communion, it is necessary 'to impose no burden beyond what is essential' (Acts 15:28)."[43]

Of course such far-reaching "reception" of "ecclesial communities" as sister churches could only be carried through by authoritative acts of recognition and reconciliation. Without fundamental changes in the sacramental and ministerial praxis of many churches, it would be, probably, impossible for the Roman Catholic Church to do so. But such changes are foreseen in the Lima-document, not only for the practice of the Reformation churches but also for other traditions. Is it too optimistic to hope for their realization for the sake of unity?

c. Reception, tradition, communion

If "reception" does not apply to texts alone, but to the living reality of faith itself; if by "receiving" a dogmatic statement of another church or of the ecumenical dialogue, churches recognize those other churches as faithful to the apostolic tradition; then "reception" not only expresses a rational "consensus" or "mutual understanding"; it also is the beginning of "acceptance" and of "homology": common confession, which is an essential condition for communion and unity. Ecumenical reception is not the signature under a contract, but a kiss of peace among sister churches.

It is important, at this point, to overcome any "all-or-nothing" idea of "communion" and unity, and to learn what it means to speak about "growing communion". Within the Roman Catholic ecumenical vocabulary, coined by Vatican II and the Bishops of Rome since then, terms like *communio fere plena*, *communio nondum completa* have found their definite place. They make possible a catholic understanding of the existing ("subsistit") unity of the Church, which was never completely lost in spite of the many divisions, and a catholic understanding of the ecumenical movement as a movement towards unity by stages. To receive the Lima text on Baptism, Eucharist and Ministry would mean a decisive step towards such growing communion. It would mean different things for the various relations to other churches, but for all of them it would mean a considerable step towards fuller communion.

The idea of communion (koinonia), presupposes a special understanding of the goal of the ecumenical movement. Anyone who is familiar with the history of Faith and Order knows the keywords of the search for unity, each of them being the echo of a gradually developed common understanding of the goal of unity: organic union (based on the Chicago and Lambeth Quadrilaterals); corporate reunion (based on the idea of the undivided church of the early centuries or on the return to a "mother-tradition" of one specific true church); cooperative action (on the basis of the God-given spiritual unity which was — by God's grace and the work of his Spirit — never totally lost); union through federation (from the viewpoint of those who want to stress the values and richnesses of the various confessional traditions); intercommunion (as the highest possible degree of mutual hospitality, trust and recognition before full communion); reconciled diversity (as a gradual recognition of the broken reality of the one church of Christ, which is nevertheless called to a sisterhood of churches, to common witness and reconciling service in the world); conciliar fellowship (according to the model of Acts 15: a communion capable of holding representative councils whenever required); and, finally, communion, koinonia (anchored on participation in Christ and the Spirit, made visible through the faithful paradosis and remembrance of Jesus Christ by a common confession of faith, by shared sacraments of baptism and eucharist, by a mutually recognized ministry and common discipleship of Jesus Christ).

The founders of the Faith and Order movement and later the architects of the World Council of Churches deliberately refrained from authorizing any particular concept of unity as a *conditio sine qua non* for the dialogue.[44] But the New Delhi and Nairobi Assemblies received gradually refined "definitions" of the goal of unity, as follows:

The Faith and Order Commission is committed to keep before the churches this vision and goal (of Nairobi). It is its constitutional task to contribute to the creation of conditions which will make it possible for the churches to enter into full communion. They will then recognize each other's ministries; they will share the bread and the cup of their Lord; they will acknowledge each other as belonging to the body of Christ in all places and at all times; they will proclaim together the Gospel to the world; they will serve the needs of humankind in mutual trust and dedication; and for these ends they will plan and take decisions together in assemblies constituted by authorized representatives whenever this is required.[45]

Such vision does not compete with the merits of other concepts of unity like "conciliar fellowship" or "unity in reconciled diversity", but tries to present a way to unity which can give real hope to ordinary members of the people of God and which makes clear that the vision is, in spite of all difficulties, both desirable and achievable according to the will of God.

For that same reason, because "communion" is a living reality of grace amidst the daily life of Christians, the reception process with regard to baptism, eucharist and ministry, needs "the widest possible involvement of the people of God" and not only — though this is equally important — "at the highest appropriate level of authority". Unity in faith, sacraments, ministry and common life in Christ are not mere "conditions", "characteristics" or "requirements" for full communion. They are the essential "elements" of the one Christian koinonia, the living "structures" and ramifications of the one "life in Christ" and "in the Spirit", of the one participatory life of the people of God, living "from God" and "for God".

In dealing with the 'reception' of the proleptic consensus texts on baptism, eucharist and ministry, the whole people of God should therefore pray and work together with those who guide, assemble and build up the church through their ministerial service. Universities and parishes, theologians and catechists, poets and musicians should be invited in all the churches to become familiar with the content of the Lima text. Local councils of churches should treat them carefully as orientation for their ecumenical programmes. Synods, bishops' conferences, ecumenical commissions should study them thoroughly. This must be the spirit of the reception process in the years ahead, because it was also the spirit behind the consensus process, wonderfully summarized at Faith and Order's Bangalore meeting:

> The one faith is confessed and lived in the community of the faithful who have been called through the preaching of the Gospel and gather around the Lord in the Spirit. We enter into this community through baptism which is our participation in the death and resurrection of Jesus Christ. We are incorporated into the eucharistic community in which, the Word is proclaimed and the sacraments duly celebrated. The one faith is the full responsibility of each member of the community, not, however, separately one from another, but in communion. The presence of the Lord in the midst of His people expresses itself in a variety of charisms and services, which equip them for their mission among men. Such charisms and services are the instruments of the Holy Spirit in the building up of the church, enabling its community to persevere in the apostolic teaching, in fraternal communion, in the breaking of bread and in prayer (cf. Acts 2:42). The one(s) who preside(s) over the community has the particular responsibility of being, in the Holy Spirit, the servant of the Unity of the Church by the proclamation of the Word in the eucharistic community. His (their) service aims at reinforcing the communication in the community, with a vision of fuller communion.[46]

Is it too big a hope to ask for such a "reception for communion" in the years ahead?

NOTES

1. Minutes, Central Committee, Dresden 1981, p.64.
2. Preface to the Lima text on "Baptism, Eucharist, Ministry".
3. Rules of the WCC, Art. XIV, par. 6, sub (a), *Breaking Barriers: Nairobi 1975*, p.339.
4. The church, the churches and the World Council of Churches, Minutes, Central Committee, Toronto 1950, Geneva, 1950, p.85. See also Rules of the WCC, art. IX on public statements: "While such statements may have great significance and influence as the expression of the judgment or concern of so widely representative a Christian body, yet their authority will consist only in the weight which they carry by their own truth and wisdom, and the publishing of such statements shall not be held to imply that the World Council as such has, or can have, any constitutional authority over the constituent churches or right to speak for them" (*Breaking Barriers*, p.333).
5. Nairobi Assembly, Report of Section II, *Breaking Barriers*, p.66.
6. *Ibid.*, p.68-69. What Nairobi asked was surprisingly more than the preface to the Accra edition of the texts had demanded, viz. to send in comments and to initiate a discussion in each church about possible implications: see *Faith and Order Paper* No. 73, p.7.
7. See L. Hoedemaker, "Churches on the Way to Consensus: a Survey of the Replies to the Agreed Statements 'One Baptism, One Eucharist, and a Mutually Recognized Ministry'," *Faith and Order Paper* No. 77/3, Geneva, 1977 (mimeographed), p.75ff.
8. Towards an Ecumenical Consensus on Baptism, the Eucharist and Ministry: a Response to the Churches, *Faith and Order Paper* 84, Geneva, 1977,pp. 3 and 5.
9. Preface to the Lima text on BEM. Cf. Standing Commission, Taizé, *Faith and Order Paper* 98, Geneva, 1979, p.29: "The leading question must be quite clear: e.g. 'Does your church find these texts a sufficient reflection of the common apostolic tradition to be used as a continuing point of reference in its life and witness?'"
10. Standing Commission, Annecy, 1981, *Faith and Order Paper* 106, p.12. Cf. Standing Commission Taizé, 1979, *Faith and Order Paper* 98, p.28: "The World Council of Churches cannot, constitutionally, agree for the churches; each church must find its own way of being reconciled with other churches. But we see these texts as anticipating and serving the wider and more living unity in faith."
11. For the discussions on the basis, see: W. Theurer, *Die trinitarische Basis des ORK*, Frankfurt, 1967; for the reception of the Leuenberg Agreement, see "Konkordie und Kirchengemeinschaft (*Oekumenische Perspektiven* 10), Frankfurt, 1982. A more negative example would be the story of the first Faith and Order consensus text of Edinburgh 1937, the "Declaration on Divine Grace", which was unanimously accepted but never really digested or received.
12. See P. Lengsfeld und H.G. Stobbe (ed.), *Theologischer Konsens und Kirchenspaltung*, Stuttgart/Berlin/Koln/Mainz, 1981.
13. See H.R. Weber, "Out of All Continents and Nations", in H. Fey, *The Ecumenical Advance*, London, 1970, pp.65ff., who quotes D. T. Niles saying: "The older churches were discussing the reasons and circumstances which had led to their earlier divorce: the younger churches were only just getting married and did not wish to be asked their opinion on the subjects which had led to the quarrels between the older churches" (quoted from the Amsterdam Assembly Reports, Vol. V, p.62).

14. Among the replies of churches and groups to the Accra texts, there were several questions about the theological doctrine on the sacraments. We do not find an explicit dealing with the idea of sacraments as such in the Lima text, but the sacramental nature and understanding of baptism, eucharist and ministry is clearly presupposed in the text. A very fine treatment of the ecumenical problem of the sacraments is the Document of the Groupe des Dombes, *L'Esprit Saint, l'Eglise et les Sacraments*, Taizé, 1979.

15. See H. Sieben, *Die Konzilsidee der Alten Kirche*, Paderborn/Munchen/ Wien/Zurich, 1979, pp.53-55, 178-181, 333-339, 340-343, 515; W. Kuppers, "Reception, Prolegomena to a Systematic Study", in *Councils and the Ecumenical Movement*, pp.76-98.

16. H. Muller, *Rezeption und Konsens in der Kirche: eine Anfrage an die Kanonistik*, Oesterreichisches Archiv fur Kirchenrecht, 27, 1976, 3-21.

17. See Denzinger-Schönmetzer 478 and 705. Cf. DS 356. Cf. A Lumpe, Zu "recipere" als gültig annehmen, anerkennen im Sprachgebrauch des römischen und kanonischen Rechts, *Annuarium Historiae Conciliorum* 7, 1975, 118-135.

18. F. Wieacker, *Privatrechtsgeschichte der Neuzeit unter besonderer Berücksichtigung der deutschen Rechtsentwicklung*, Göttingen, 1967, pp.97-248; W. Wilhelm, *Bemerkungen zur Rezeption auslandischen Rechts: Ius commune*, Vol. V, Frankfurt, 1975, pp.122-137. Such reception seems to be part of a much larger phenomenon: the general cultural exchange of ideas. In that sense the ecumenical movement as such is a continuing process of giving and receiving "in six continents".

19. See B. Botte a.o., *Le Concile et les Conciles*, Chevetogne/Paris, 1960; H.J. Margull (ed.), *Die okumenische Konzile der Christenheit*, Stuttgart 1961; *Councils and the Ecumenical Movement* (World Council of Churches Studies No. 5), Geneva, 1968; A. Grillmeier, Konzil und Rezeption. Methodische Bemerkungen zu einem Thema der okumenischen Diskussion, *Theologie und Philosophie*, 45, 1970, pp.321-352.

20. L. Vischer, "A Genuinely Universal Council...", *The Ecumenical Review*, 22, 1970 pp.97-108; The Significance of the Council of Chalcedon (Bristol 1967-Louvain 1971), *The Ecumenical Review*, 22, 1970, No. 3; K. Krikorian, La réception des conciles, *Istina*, 18, 1973, pp.378-402; J.B. Bauer, "The Reception of the Councils", *Wissenschaft und Weisheit*, 2, 1974, pp.94-102.

21. G. Gassmann, Rezeption im okumenischen Kontext, *Okumenische Rundschau*, 26, 1977, pp.314-321; F. Wolfinger, "Die Rezeption theologischer Einsichten und ihre theologische und okumenische Bedeutung: von der Einsicht zur Verwirklichung, *Catholica*, 31, 1977, pp.202-232; W. Hryniewicz, "Die ekklesiale Rezeption in der Sicht der orthodoxen theologie", *Theologie und Glaube*, 65, 1975, pp.250-265; F. Wolfinger, "Rezeption — ein Zentralbegriff der okumenischen Diskussion oder des Glaubensvollzugs. Ein Vergleich zweier Veroffentlichungen", *Okumenische Rundschau*, 27, 1978, pp.14-21; K. Schmidt-Clausen, "Die Rezeption okumenischen Bewegung", *Okumenische Rundschau*, 27, 1978, pp.1-13. Further *Faith and Order Paper*, 84 (Cret-Bérard Report) and 107 (The Three Reports of the Forum on Bilateral Conversations).

22. *Faith and Order Paper*, Louvain 1971, p.29: "Reception represents the process by which the local churches accept the decision of a Council and thereby recognize its authority. This process is a multiplex one and may last for centuries. Even after the formal conclusion of such a process and the canonical reception of a Council's doctrinal formula usually through a new Council, the process of reception

continues in the same way or other as long as the churches are involved in self-examination on the basis of the question whether a particular Council has been received and appropriated properly and with justification. In this sense we can say that in the ecumenical movement the churches find themselves in a process of continuing reception or reception of the Councils".

See also *Councils and the Ecumenical Movement*, o.c., p. 16: "The criteria for the reception of a council, especially of its dogmatic decisions was whether it was legally held or especially whether it conformed to the norm to which it knew itself to be subject, namely to hold fast the ancient apostolic tradition against new heresies. Although non-theological factors were no less at work in reception than in the conciliar process, reception is to be understood at its core as a spiritual process, even where it seems to be an act of constitutional obedience. Proof is precisely the long process of critical appropriation which both preceded the formal reception and followed it. Reception as a spiritual event corresponds to the council's claim to be the voice of the Holy Spirit. This presupposes that the same spirit of God who leads to all truth by witnessing to Jesus, the incarnate word of God, is at work both in the council and the church as a whole."

In East and West, however, the criteria for reception were different. In the famous Letter of Pope Gelasius I we read: "...synodum male gesta (est) contra Scripturas, contra doctrinam patrum, contra ecclesiasticas regulas, quam tota merito Ecclesia non recepit et praecipue sedes apostolica non probavit" and "... per bene gestam synodum, id est secundum Scripturas sanctas, secundum traditionem patrum, secundum ecclesiasticas regulas pro fide catholica et communione prolatam, quam cuncta recepit Ecclesia, quam maxime sedes apostolica comprobavit" (Gelasius I, Ep. 26,6 CSEL 35, 380, 2ff.).

In the East are the five patriarchs (the Pentarchy) who have to affirm. In the course of time even in the West these criteria were not always unanimously received. Sieben, o.c. pp.324-343, points to the Libri Carolini, where the two principles of the classical conciliar theory — horizontal/synchronic and vertical/diachronic consensus — are modified and put under the critique of rational arguments of an exegetical nature and under the norm of majority. It is, then, no longer the voice of the Pentarchy, but the individual local churches which decide together by majority vote. This is the beginning of modern "democratic" consensus-thinking: one of the main causes of the conflict between papalism and conciliarism.

23. H. Fries, "Ex sese, non ex consensu ecclesiae", in *Volk Gottes, Festgabe fur Josef Hofer*, Freiburg/Basel/Wien, 1967, pp.480-502; U. Horst, "Das Votum Joseph Cardonis uber die Unfehlbarkeit des Papstes aus dem Jahre 1869", in *Unterwegs zur Einheit, Festschrift fur H. Stirnimann*, Freiburg, 1980, pp.663-684; G. Thils, *L'Infaillibilité pontificale*, Gembloux, 1969, p.175: "... l'acquiescement préalable, concomitant ou subséquent de l'Eglise peut être considéré comme une condition *habituelle* et relativement nécessaire des jugements infaillibles du pape. Cette façon de voir ne contredit pas les décrets de Vatican I et II. En fait, toutes les Eglises chrétiennes sont très sensibles à resserrer au maximum l'union organique entre l'ensemble du peuple chrétien et ses pasteurs." Cf. Y. Congar, "La 'réception' comme réalité ecclésiologique", *Revue des sciences philosophiques et théologiques*, 56, 1972, pp.369-403; *id., L'ecclésiologie du Haut Moyen-Age*, Paris, 1968, pp.380-382; M. Garijo, "Der Begriff 'Rezeption' und sein Ort im Kern der katholischen Theologie", in P. Lengsfeld and H. Stobbe (eds), *Konsens and Kirchenspaltung*, o.c., pp.97-114.

24. See DS 3000, 3006, 3020, 3069-3070 and Mansi 53, 168AB.
25. Sieben. o.c., pp.515-516.
26. *Faith and Order Paper*, Louvain 1971, p.137: "Established on what it has received and receives, pressing on towards the full achievement of the salvation for which it hopes, the church is called to realize its catholicity day by day. Not only must it be 'open' in proclaiming that it is without respect of persons, races, classes or culture, but also 'habitable' by all, the 'home' of all because it realizes in its structures and in its existence the whole variety of the gifts of the Spirit, the whole diversity of mankind redeemed by Christ. It is sent to all the nations, to the very ends of the earth; it is called to be present to all the situations of man at each hour of history and to make itself all things to all men in the name of the Lord. It has received, insofar as it is catholic, power to express all the elements of the gospel message and ceaselessly seeks to grasp in faith and to proclaim in its message and make fruitful in its life the infinite richness of the mystery of Christ."
27. H. Muller, o.c., points to the example of the apostolic constitution "Veterum Sapientia" of Pope John XXIII dd. 22 February 1962. Cf. Verbindliches Lehren der Kirche heute (*Beiheft zur okumenischen Rundschau* 33), Frankfurt, 1978, pp.120-208.
28. Cf. note 17. Especially in the Lutheran-Roman Catholic Dialogue in the USA on Eucharist and Ministry, this aspect of "reception" was studied. See: *Lutherans and Catholics in Dialogue*, Vol. IV, Washington, 1970, articles by H.J. McSorley and G. Tavard; cf. G. Tavard, "The Recognition of Ministry", *Journal of Ecumenical Studies*, 11, 1974 pp.65-83; K. Rahner, Vorfragen zu einem okumenischen Amstsverstandnis (*Quaestiones Disputatae* 65), Freiburg/Basel/Wien, 1974, pp.40ff.
29. *Unitatis Redintegratio* No. 3 and 22; *Lumen Gentium*, No. 8 and 15.
30. UR 3.
31. *Ibid.*, UR 3.
32. UR 4.
33. Cf. Second Forum on Bilateral Conversations, *Faith and Order Paper* 107, p.19.
34. Cf. W. Hryniewicz, "Okumenische Reception and konfessionelle Identitat"; *Una Sancta* 36, 1981 pp.116-131; H. Meyer, Wer ist sich mit wem woruber einig?, in: P. Lengsfeld and H. Stobbe, *Theologischer Konsens und Kirchenspaltung*, pp.15-30; P. Lengsfeld, "Oekumenische Spiritualitat als Voraussetzung von Rezeption", *Ibid*, pp.126-134.
35. See the contribution of U. Kühn in this volume for a more elaborate treatment of the meaning of those terms.
36. The BEM text is full of such "receptive" language: Baptism par. 8,12,13,14; Eucharist, No. 1,2,21,30,32; Ministry No. 5,7,14,16,20,27,40.
37. See: *Kirche als Lerngemeinschaft*, Berlin, 1981.
38. UR 6.
39. UR 11.
40. UR 14.
41. UR 17.
42. UR 17.
43. UR 18.
44. Cf. Lausanne conference 1927: "It (this conference) is emphatically *not* attempting to define the conditions of future reunion", Preamble, Faith and Order. Proceedings of the World Conference Lausanne, New York, 1928, p.459; Toronto

1950: "Membership in the World Council does not imply the acceptance of a specific doctrine concerning the nature of church unity", The Church, The Churches and the World Council of Churches, No. 7, Minutes, Central Committee, Toronto, p.85; "It is essential that the right of every church to hold and develop its own particular attitude to the problem of church unity should be fully recognized and respected", Executive Meeting, Odessa, 1964.

45. *Sharing in Hope*, Bangalore, 1978
46. *Ibid.*, pp. 245-246.

THE FRIENDS UNITED MEETING, THE SALVATION ARMY AND THE DOCUMENT ON BAPTISM, EUCHARIST AND MINISTRY

The Friends United Meeting

The Friends United meeting proposed an addition to the BEM-texts as follows:

"Because the Friends United Meeting is not identifiable as a eucharistic Fellowship employing rites which uses material signs, but do have a sacramental life through the living Presence of Christ which is shared in common with Christian bodies who are identifiable as eucharistic Fellowships, they are accepted into the oneness of the Church. Although this document is addressed primarily to those communions who use material signs, the Friends United Meeting accepts them as significant expressions of oneness in Christ".

The Salvation Army

A summary of its traditional position authorized by the present international leader, General Jarl Wahlstrom.

The Salvation Army as a founder-member of the World Council of Churches has found a happy acceptance of and within the terms of the constitutional basis of membership. This fully accords with the Army's simple understanding of the right of entry into the Church Universal itself — those who are "incorporate in Christ Jesus" (Eph. 1:1 NEB). Repeated assurances of Council leaders and fellow-members have given the Army reason to believe that its non-eucharistic position is understood and respected and that its place within the fellowship of the Council remains assured notwithstanding the more recent expansion of "Functions and Purposes". It is the Salvationist's belief that the grace of the one God and Father of all, the presence of the only Saviour and the outworking of the one Spirit in the life of each believer — the gift of God mediated directly to each faithful heart — joins the disciple to his living Head and at the same time to his brother in the Lord (Rom. 12:5).

Regarding the particular sacraments under discussion the Salvation Army is by no means critical of those who, observing these rites, truly experience the redeeming work of Christ and the abiding cleansing and inspiration of the Holy Spirit. With such there is complete fellowship as the salvationist witnesses to his belief and experience regarding the work of the Holy Spirit leading him to "Full Salvation", the blessing of Holiness or Sanctification, and the indwelling living presence of Christ Himself.

The Salvation Army cannot be termed completely "non-sacramental" as its "outward signs of inward grace" are sacred indeed: the act of penitence and confession often made at a "Mercy Seat", the acceptance of biblical teaching in harmony with mainstream evangelical faith, and the scriptural discipline of a Soldier of Christ involved in the public declaration and enrolment ceremony for Salvation Army Soldiership (church membership plus). Nor is the teaching of Holiness, the seeking of that blessing and the subsequent living of a life that is wholly sacramental, any less significant to the salvationist than participation in a communion service and its subsequent relation to daily living.

Regarding its ministry the Salvation Army claims that its trained and Commissioned Officers, following their Lord by virtue of the same calling as the original twelve, denying themselves as he required and dedicated in personal covenant for his service, in God's name ordained as "Servants of Christ and Preachers of his Gospel" by the hand of the General or his repesentative, may rightly be accepted by the ordained of any other denomination.

In short, the Salvation Army has no difficulty in accepting the sincerity of those whose understanding of God's Word leads them to forms of worship differing from its own, and humbly accepts the kind judgment of those who declare their belief that it continues to prove its case and bear its testimony by the evidence of its character and service. It is the salvationist's prayerful desire to perpetuate the meaningful sentiment expresed by its former General, Albert Orsborn:

> My life must be Christ's broken bread,
> My love his outpoured wine....
> That other souls, refreshed and fed,
> May share his life through mine.

RECEPTION — AN IMPERATIVE AND AN OPPORTUNITY

ULRICH KUHN

The convergence documents on Baptism, Eucharist and Ministry, produced by the Faith and Order Commission in a process which has taken no less than fifty-five years,[1] have now been presented to the churches. But how will the churches, which, so to speak, "commissioned" these documents and delegated theologians to help to draft them, deal with the results now available to us? What conclusions will they be ready to draw from them? Are they really interested at all in these findings? These are increasingly urgent questions, not just in respect of the Faith and Order documents in question but also in view of the findings of a whole interrelated complex of bilateral conversations; in other words, at a stage in the ecumenical movement when, as has rightly been said, the results of discussion are being transposed into the living fellowship of the churches.[2] The problem of *reception* has thus emerged as a key problem of the ecumenical movement.[3] This problem goes beyond the various dialogue groups and commissions and confronts the churches themselves as a whole with questions to be answered and decisions to be taken. Involving as it does the official transmission of jointly produced ecumenical documents to all the churches, it is a process which sets the churches quite a new problem, one of considerable significance in the history of the Church.

The preface to "Baptism, Eucharist and Ministry" speaks of an "ecumenical reception process" including, as a decisive step, the request to the churches for an "official response to this document on the highest relevant level of authority". These words have been very

---

• Ulrich Kuhn is a pastor and professor in Leipzig Theological Seminary.

carefully chosen. The reference to a "reception *process*" implies from the start a complex procedure which is not to be limited to a formal juridical act of consent on the part of an authoritative church court.[4] The preface refers explicitly to theological study, as well as to worship and witness, as forms and steps in the whole process of reception. It is certainly the case that special emphasis is placed on the request for an "official response" from the churches. But this response itself is not described as "official reception", as it had been in an earlier draft of the preface. At the same time, this also means that the possibility of a critical response is more seriously and more explicitly allowed for. It is nevertheless assumed too, that even a critical response would certainly represent a stage in the "reception process", one which would then lead, of course, to further reflections on what is affirmed in the documents themselves.

1. Differing structural conditions in the churches

The request to the churches in the preface to "Baptism, Eucharist and Ministry" is addressed to churches with very diverse structures, particularly with regard to questions about their authority to make doctrinal decisions. For example, whereas the governing function of the bishops and the pope in the Roman Catholic Church is combined with a strong official doctrinal authority which is defined in precise legal terms, so that the question there is whether and to what extent the decisions of the magisterium need to be buttressed by a non-official reception by the people of God,[5] in the case of many Reformation churches the exact opposite is the case. It is, of course, true that those who are entrusted with the ministry of *episkopé* in the Church are assigned a function of controlling doctrine by reference to the criterion of Holy Scripture (and, in certain cases, especially in the Lutheran churches, by reference also to the recognized confessional statements).[6] But there is no suggestion here of any competence to make doctrinal decisions in the sense of developing the standard doctrine of the particular church.[7] During the process whereby the Leuenberg Agreement came to be adopted, this sometimes led to radical questioning based on appeals to the church constitution, even though synods and church courts in practice exercised a *de facto* authority in this respect which it was not obvious in theory that they really possessed. As a result of this, however, many

Lutheran churches have been careful to insist that their doctrinal position has not been affected by this decision. In some respects this is a quite unsatisfactory state of affairs, leading in some cases, especially in Lutheran churches, to a much too static view of the nature of official doctrine. In face of the challenges of ecumenical developments, fresh thinking is urgently needed on the possibilities and structures of "authoritative teaching" in the Church.[8] On the other hand, this deficiency also allows for the possibility of insisting on the responsibility of the whole people of God in the development of church doctrine.[9] This enhances the importance of the way in which the preface broadens the concept of reception to include much more than eventual official decisions by church courts. In approach, this is also in harmony with the document on "Ministry" which explicitly sets the function of the ministry firmly within the function of the whole people of God.[10]

2. History of the idea of reception

If the history of the idea of reception is examined with these problems in mind, it becomes clear how appropriate, precisely from this standpoint, the broad concept of reception in the statement on "Baptism, Eucharist and Ministry" is.

(a) What is denoted by the Latin words "receptio" or "recipere" has its counterpart in the New Testament in the Greek words "lambanein" and "dechesthai" and their derivatives.[11] "Lambanein" has a more markedly passive sound ("receive") than "dechesthai" ("accept"). For example, the word is "accepted" (Mk. 4:20), and so too, Jesus' message (Acts 2:41); the gospel is "received" (1 Cor. 15:1), and so too, God's Spirit (1 Cor. 2:12). Jesus himself, and therefore God, is "accepted", and this, be it noted, by the very fact of accepting those sent by Jesus, i.e. his disciples and messengers (Mt. 10:40 *dechesthai*; Jn. 13:20 - *lambanein*). Those who belong to Christ, however, are those who have first been "accepted" by Christ and are in consequence called upon to "accept" one another (Rom. 15:7 - in each case "proslambano" RSV "welcome"). Clearly, all these expressions denote a vital spiritual process which in its various aspects is absolutely constitutive for the life of Christians and the Church. Important, too, is the fact that acceptance of Christ is coupled with mutual acceptance and welcome among Christians themselves.

The idea of reception is also found in the New Testament in those passages where Paul speaks of the process of tradition. He introduces the recital of the accounts of the institution of the Lord's Supper (1 Cor. 11:23) by making use of the technical rabbinic terms denoting the process of *traditio-receptio* ("paradidonai" — "paralambanein"). Reception of the tradition includes here the interpretation of what is received, whereby the message of God contained in the tradition comes to be applied with special force to the contemporary moment.[12] In actual fact, such an interpretative reception and transmission of the tradition is also found in the gospel transmission and already in the Old Testament too. The formation of the New Testament canon must also, therefore, be regarded as a reception process in which the scriptures, already "received" by their use in the Christian communities and whose content was already held to be apostolic, came to be confirmed and adopted as authoritative for the Church.[13]

A specifically ecclesial reception process is found in the New Testament in the Acts of the Apostles, where a conciliar process is reported in idealized terms. The decree of the apostolic council in Jerusalem was transmitted by messengers to the church in Antioch and the church there "rejoiced at the exhortation" it contained (Acts 15:30f.). The validity of the so-called "apostle's decree" was in this way confirmed by reception.

However much the processes may differ in detail, the real reception process discernible in them must surely be viewed in context. At the deepest level, what is involved even in the acceptance of tradition and the glad reception of a conciliar decree is the reception of the good news of the Gospel and, indeed, of the Lord himself, and this is always an event in the Holy Spirit.

(b) Compared with the breadth of the idea of reception found in the New Testament, a certain narrowness is already discernible in the tendency in scholarly research in the last twenty years to speak of "reception" only in two main connections.[14] In the first place, attention has been concentrated mainly on reception processes, in the pre-Constantinian period especially, in which decisions made by local or regional synods were made known to other churches by means of synodal letters, and accepted by these churches.[15] Underlying this was the realization that a particular church is only authentically the Church if it lives in fellowship with the other churches. The other reception process on which attention has been focused is that whereby decisions made by the imperial councils since Constantine were received. These councils, to which the bishops of the entire world church were summoned, spoke for the whole Church. What is decisive, however, for the validity of their decisions for the Church in later times, is the reception process which begins after the council. This process takes the form of a thoroughly critical discussion of the conciliar decisions. Such discussion may prepare the way for the explicit and formal reception of earlier conciliar decrees at a later council, but it could also lead to the rejection of conciliar decrees. The reception process for conciliar decisions, moreover, included the unending process of interpreting these decisions in theology, proclamation and the devotional life.

In these reception processes in the ancient Church, the role of formal juridical acts is therefore a relatively subordinate one, one of confirmation and completion, rather. Taken as a whole, reception is a spiritual and theological process whereby decisions taken in the Church are accepted. But the only adequate way of understanding the reception that takes place in this way is to reinsert it in the wider framework of the spiritual event of transmission and acceptance, which in the light of the New Testament we have learned to regard as fundamental for the life of Christians and the Church.

(c) The notion of ecclesial reception plays hardly any role in the theological outlook of the Reformation churches,[16] even in the discussion of the councils or synods.[17] The emphasis of the Reformers was more on the limited validity of conciliar decisions, which only have authority to the extent that they accord with the witness of Holy Scripture. This, of course, highlights a vital criterion for the acceptance of church decisions, as well as reflecting the truth that even councils have no absolute infallibility.[18] In actual fact, however, reception processes are conspicuous even in the story of the Reformation. The confessions of the Reformed churches, for example, accept while at the same time interpreting doctrinal decisions of the ancient Church.[19]

The authority of the Reformation confessions itself rests on a reception process at different levels. Their validity in the Reformation churches does not derive from their validation by a magisterium clothed with authority. They have authority because they express the "divine truth once recognized and confessed" in the beginning of the Reformation.[20] The reception process continued even after the end of the period of the formulation of confessions in the sixteenth century.

It is true that, at first, no further writings were adopted as a doctrinal basis. But the number of officially recognized confessions varies in the different Reformation churches,[21] and, above all, different interpretations constantly modify the sense in which the confessions claim authority.[22] The only case of church reception of a new doctrinal formulation in the twentieth century is that of the *Barmen Theological Declaration*, although widely different views are taken of the authority of this confession. The most recent example of a *formal* reception process in the Reformation churches of Europe is the acceptance of the Leuenberg Agreement. This acceptance was achieved after thorough theological examination of each church's own tradition in the light of Holy Scripture and, above all, only after taking into account the further development of the ecclesial and theological identity of each church, a process which posed the question already referred to, namely, the competence of Protestant church courts to make doctrinal decisions. Precisely because of this particular difficulty, these two recent cases of reception could be extremely important for the future, while the reception of the *Leuenberg Agreement* is also at the same time an example of the reception of an ecumenical document, a subject to which we shall need to return for a closer examination.

Once again, however, none of these reception processes in the history of the Reformation churches is to be viewed in isolation. Here, too, of course, there are many other reception processes which do not entail formal commitments (e.g. forms of piety, hymns and writings, theological ideas and systems), not to mention the fact that for the Reformation churches, too, the fundamental process whereby Christ and our brothers and sisters are accepted is meant to be the law of life.

3. Reception in the context of the ecumenical movement

In the ecumenical context of the twentieth century, the question of reception arises in a new way compared with the processes so far considered.[23] Broadly speaking, the new element is that the churches involved in a reception processes are churches separated from each other in various ways. We have already mentioned one structural problem this presents: the different churches are very diversely structured for dealing formally with reception and doctrinal processes. Obviously a minimum of agreement is essential here if processes of ecumenical reception are to be achieved at all. Also, and above all, in one respect the documents whose acceptance is now a question for the churches differ fundamentally in both form and content from the documents involved in the reception process in earlier church history. The documents whose reception or validity is in question here are not simply decisions, traditions, statements of one church (our own), as was the case in the reception processes in the New Testament and in the conciliar practice of the ancient Church, and even in the later process of reception in separated churches. Nor have we here simply an example of so-called "exogenous" reception involving the reception of the decisions of other churches, as happened between different churches in the pre-Constantinian period.[24] On the contrary, what is involved in the reception of the findings of ecumenical discussions is the acceptance of documents and insights which have been arrived at with the official participation of representatives of one's own church in real responsible exchange with representatives of other churches hitherto separated from one's own church.

These texts themselves, therefore, are the fruit of a process of encounter between theologians of different church traditions. It can even be said that the reception process now before us already presupposes a long and many-sided history of reception without which the texts now up for reception would never have seen the light of day.[25] This long process consisted, in fact, of the initial discovery by the separated churches that they were ready to reflect together on possible steps towards unity and to provide the necessary resources, human and financial, for this purpose; then the lively exchange which developed in which, by listening to others and understanding them more fully in the light of the authoritative Scriptures acknowledged by all, questions were put to one's own tradition, spiritual and theological insights were exchanged and, finally, at length, the joint affirmations now before us emerged. The process which led up to the reception phase on which we now enter was, therefore, one of mutual acceptance by different partners,[26] recognition of the other as a fellow-Christian and, inseparable from this, a re-reading of Holy Scripture and of one's own church tradition.

This listening and discussing was accompanied, moreover, by closer contacts between the churches and their members at various levels. The practical result of such contacts was a marked alteration in relationships between the churches and among Christians, a real modification of the identity of each.[27] After their entry into the ecumenical movement, the churches became *de facto* different from what they were before, though of course in differing degrees. To some extent this is reflected in the jointly authorized dialogue findings which include not only the documents of the Faith and Order Commission but also the many reports of bilateral conversations. And the fact that the content of these texts is not simply a reproduction of *one* church tradition but is more than that and different from that, is also not unconnected with this change which has come about in the life of the churches.

The new and unique element in the reception process now before us, therefore, is that it is an important stage in a process in which churches which are separated from one another are being changed in their relations to one another by their common endeavour. It is also a process which in turn challenges us and encourages us to a further breach of the frontiers of our own tradition, to change in relationship to one another and in this way to move towards the fullness of Christ. For the Lutheran churches, for instance, this can be shown by the following examples from the documents. The Faith and Order statement on baptism invites the Lutheran churches, to a greater extent than previously, to understand holy baptism as an action based on faith and therefore to concede a relative justification for the churches which practise believer's baptism. The Faith and Order statement on the Eucharist invites the Lutheran churches to understand Holy Communion not one-sidedly in terms of the forgiveness of sins but as a eucharistic act of the Church, and this as a basic, essential interpretation of the Lord's Supper. The statement on the Ministry invites the Lutheran churches to a new theological and spiritual view of the office of bishop, one which goes beyond their previous doctrinal tradition. A similar list of invitations could be drawn up for the other churches to whom these reports have now been transmitted. For some churches, doubtless, the pressing invitation to examine from fresh angles the question of the validity and possible recognition of the ministries of other churches, and thus at the recognition of these churches as churches in the full sense, will be of special ecumenical importance. All these theological invitations are inseparable from the invitation to changes or further developments in practice, in worship, doctrine, proclamation, church fellowship. Change always involves an

element of threat and, in fact, what the churches are invited to enter
into by the statements on Baptism, Eucharist and Ministry — more
perhaps than by many of the findings of the bilateral dialogues — is a
"dangerous learning process".[28] But this learning process basically
means no more than a committed confirmation and acceptance of
the process which the churches entered into when they entered the
ecumenical movement and in which they have in fact been engaged
for some time and already have come a long way.

Only if the forthcoming reception process is seen in this broader
context shall we do justice to its ramifications and, at the same time,
see clearly the significance of this historical retrospect. For the reception process now taking place and still before us is, like the reception
process at all times in church history, in the deepest sense a comprehensive and vital one. What is involved in the acceptance of the
statements on Baptism, Eucharist and Ministry is the *acceptance of
one another* as those whom Christ himself has accepted (Rom. 15:7).
What is required of us in accepting one another is to accept one
another as the Lord's messengers, that in the voice and form of the
others and in the documents and their binding claim on us we should
perceive the voice and figure of Christ himself.[29] For, each in our different way, we all have the right to say with Paul: "I have received of
the Lord that which I also deliver unto you" (1 Cor. 11:23).

Within this vital spiritual process, which is impossible without
penitence and conversion on all sides, an "official response" on the
part of the churches also has a significant and necessary place. It is
not to be expected that these official responses will simply agree in all
points with the statements. For they are thought of as responses
within a continuing process. They are responses which also presup-
pose an examination of the statements in the light of the one Word of
God which is authoritative for all of us.[30] As the churches prepare
their responses, however, they should not ignore the process of
change in which they themselves are in fact involved. This process of
change is one which will lead not to the loss of their own identity or
to the imposition of uniformity on legitimate difference, but to a new
and broader understanding of this identity. Seen in this light, the
process of the reception of the documents on Baptism, Eucharist and
Ministry points beyond itself to the fact that we are being led to an
ever fuller unity in the one apostolic faith,[31] and to the fact that, in
the strength of this growth, we may also grant one another full acceptance and fellowship at the Table of the Lord.

NOTES

1. Since Lausanne 1927.
2. Cf. H. Meyer, "Wer ist sich mit wem woruber einig? Uberblick uber die Konsenstexte der letzten Jahre", in P. Lengsfeld and H.G. Stobbe, eds., *Theologische Konsens and Kirchenspaltung*, Stuttgart, 1981, p.20. On the problem of reception in the context of the bilateral talks, see also "The Three Reports of the Forum on Bilateral Conversations", *Faith and Order Paper* No. 107, WCC, Geneva, 1981, p.38ff.
3. This is underlined in the report edited by P. Lengsfeld and H.G. Stobbe (see note 2) on the first academic consultation of the Societas Oecumenica and it is also repeatedly expressed at ecumenical gatherings, most recently for example by Philip Potter at the Faith and Order meeting in Lima, Peru.
4. H. Muhlen, *Morgen wird Einheit sein*, Paderborn, 1974, defines reception as "process of agreement" (p.101). Cf. "The Three Reports...", *op. cit.*, p.38.
5. On this, M. Garijo, "Der Begriff 'Rezeption' und sein Ort im Kern der katholischen Ekklesiologie", in P. Lengsfeld and H.G. Stobbe, *op. cit.*, pp.97ff., with reference to Y. Congar.
6. Cf. for example *Confessio Augustana*, Art. 28, 21.
7. Cf. M. Seils, "Die Problematik der Rezeption aus der Sicht evangelischer Kirchenleitung", in P. Lengsfeld and H.G. Stobbe, *op. cit.*, esp. pp.113f.. This is confirmed by a glance at the actual constitutions of evangelical churches in the German area.
8. Cf. the Faith and Order study "Wie lehrt die Kirche heute verbindlich?" (How does the church teach authoritatively today?) which was taken up very seriously in the German-speaking lands; on this the report of work of the German Ecumenical Study Committee in "Verbindliches Lehren der Kirche heute" (Beiheft z. *Okumenische Rundschau* 33) Frankfurt, 1978, as well as the workshop report from the GDR churches, English text in *The Ecumenical Review*, Vol. 33, No. 2, 1981, pp.147ff.
9. M. Luther, "Dass eine christliche Vesammlung oder Gemeinde Recht und Macht habe, alle Lehre zu urteilen, usw.", 1523 (that a Christian assembly or congregation has the right and power to judge all doctrine, etc.) in *Weim. Ausgabe*, 11, pp.408ff.
10. E. Lanne too points this out in his address on reception at the Faith and Order meeting in Lima.
11. On the NT evidence, cf. in addition to W. Kuppers, "Rezeption", in L. Vischer (ed.), "Konzile und die okumenische Bewegung", *WCC Studies* 5, Geneva, 1968, pp.82f., and H. Muhlen, *op. cit.*, p.105ff., the relevant NT works of reference.
12. This is emphasized by G. Sauter, "Konsens als Ziel und Voraussetzung theologischer Erkenntnis", in P. Lengsfeld and H.G. Stobbe, *op cit.*, esp. p.54ff.
13. Further careful consideration must be given to the question of what importance attached to church consensus and church reception in regard to the NT writings as canonical.
14. Cf. on this the works of G. Kretschmar, "Die Konzile der Kirche", in H.J. Margull, ed., *Die okumenische Konzile der Christenheit*, Stuttgart, 1961, pp.13-74; W. Kuppers, *op. cit.*, Y. Congar, "Die Rezeption als ekklesiologische

Realitat", in *Concilium* 8, 1972, pp.500-514; A. Grillmeier, "Konzil and Rezeption", in *Theologie and Philosophie*, 45, 1970, pp.321-352; and the article of A. Houtepen in this issue.

15. A. Grillmeier speaks here of "exogenous reception" (*op. cit.*, p.324).
16. On the Roman Catholic conception, see the article of A. Houtepen in this issue. On the Orthodox conception, cf. for example L. Stan, "Uber die Rezeption der Beschlusse der okumenischen Konzile seitens der Kirche", in *Konzile und die okumenische Bewegung, op. cit.*, pp.72-80; W. Hryniewicz, "Die ekklesiale Rezeption in der Sicht der orthodoxen Theologie", in *Theologie und Glaube*, pp.65, 1975, pp.250-265.
17. On this, cf. M. Seils, "Das okumenische Konzil in der lutheranischen Theologie", in H.J. Margull, *op. cit.*, pp.333-372.
18. Cf. M. Luther's famous and often repeated assertion that councils can err. Correspondingly G. Sauter, *op. cit.*, warns against a concept of truth whose only criterion is consensus in the sense of the coincidence of human opinions.
19. That is shown for instance in Articles 1 and 3 of the Confession of Augsburg as well as in the corresponding passages of the Confessio Helvetica Posterior and in the adoption of the Apostles' Creed by the Heidelberg Catechism.
20. Preface to the Book of Concord, in *Die Bekenntnisschriften der Ev. Luth. Kirche*, 1930 ed., Gottingen, 1955, pp.4f.
21. The constitution of the Lutheran World Federation, for example, mentions only the Confessio Augustana and Luther's Short Catechism.
22. On the change in interpretation of the Confessio Augustana, cf. U. Kuhn, "Die Zukunft einer Tradition — Vom Neulesen der Confessio Augustana als massgeblicher Gestalt christlicher Uberlieferung", in *Lutheran World Federation Report* 9, June 1980, pp.66ff. The attitude of the Reformed Churches to the sixteenth century confessional formularies also differs fundamentally from that of the Lutheran churches.
23. Naturally with the exception of the Leuenberg Agreement, already mentioned. The decrees of the union Councils of Lyons 1274 and Florence 1439 have of course *not* been ecumenically received.
24. An astonishing parallel to this in circumstances of separated churches, is represented by the ideas considered in the context of a possible recognition of the Confessio Augustana by the Roman Catholic Church. Cf. in this U. Kühn, "Die Frage einer katholischen Anerkennung der Confessio Augustana als Problem okumenischer Rezeption", in F. Hoffmann and U. Kühn, eds, *Die confessio Augustana in okumenischen Gesprach*, Berlin, 1980, pp.11-28.
25. This is rightly emphasized by G. Gasmann, "Rezeption in okumenischen Kontext", in *Okumenische Rundschau*, 26, 1977, pp.314-327; similarly F. Wolfinger, "Rezeption — ein Zentralbegriff der okumenischen Diskussion oder des Glaubenvollzugs?", in *Okumenische Rundschau*, 27, 1978, pp.14-21, as well as, "The Three Reports..." (*Faith and Order* 107), p.42.
26. In the sense of what A. Grillmeier terms "exogenous" reception; cf. also H. Muhlen, *op. cit.*
27. This can be shown particularly strikingly by the development of Roman Catholic thought and self-awareness in the twentieth century.
28. Cf. the address by E. Lanne already referred to.
29. So too H. Muhlen, *op. cit.*, p. 105f.; "The Three Reports,...", p.39.

30. G. Gassmann, *op. cit*, names as criteria of reception: holy scripture, church tradition, prevailing church practice, as well as sister churches and fellowship with them. Of course the question arises which of these criteria has priority in case of doubt.
31. So too E. Lanne in his address in Lima.

CATECHETICAL IMPLICATIONS

Ulrich Becker

Introduction

The importance of the Lima text for the movement for church unity has been justly stressed again and again. If conciliar fellowship requires also a common confession of the apostolic faith and a common witness to the world, then such work towards an agreed statement is a necessary and important step towards the goal of visible unity.

But at least as important as the reached agreement itself is the way to the formation of such a convergence. As it was pointed out in the report of the Faith and Order Standing Commission (1977):

> What is new here is a significant beginning in theological response by the member churches themselves. A transition is underway from documents agreed upon by theologians to agreement among member churches. The beginning is small, but the process towards consensus grows. It is not confined to the ecumenical centre; it embraces many initiatives and many conversations, bilateral and multilateral, which need to be drawn into fruitful relations with each other.
>
> It is worth noting that this whole effort throws new light on the Faith and Order mandate: to keep prominently before the churches the oneness of the Church of Jesus Christ. It shows that this mandate cannot mean, if it ever did, merely sending documents and reports on unity to the churches. Rather, it means helping the churches to participate in the consensus process and pointing out to the World Council of Churches the implications of the Churches' participation and response. [1]

• Ulrich Becker, formerly Professor of Theology and Religious Education at the University of Hanover, is at present Director of the Sub-Unit on Education at the WCC.

Such strong emphasis on the participation of the churches in the process of an agreed statement is indeed a new element, a transition, as was said, in the work towards consensus, but is such participation really possible within the churches? Who in the churches responded to the first text of an agreed statement?

The way in which the churches have responded since 1975 shows that little attention was given to the consequences of this agreed statement for the daily life of the church and the local church's participation in the consensus process was minimal.

Again the impression is, this process towards an ecumenical consensus on Baptism, Eucharist and Ministry is also in danger of remaining a matter for some specialists and its agreed statements risk remaining on the desks of the officers concerned without any consequences for the life of the church.

Therefore we would like here to bring two questions forward:
1. What are the possible consequences of the agreement on Baptism, Eucharist and Ministry for the churches' teaching in local congregations?
2. What are the experiences, questions, feelings, problems of people participating in catechetical activities on Baptism, Eucharist and Ministry which have also to be taken up in the consensus process?

Let us start with the second question.

I. Some ecumenical learning situations

There is an increasing awareness among us that there are theological and non-doctrinal problems, factors and viewpoints, which determine or at least influence ecumenical efforts in the local congregations positively or negatively and which are not taken seriously enough, if at all, in ecumenical or interconfessional dialogues and discussions. It is not possible here to deal with this extensively. In our context we have to confine ourselves only to a few ecumenical learning situations, from which we may get an idea of some of the theological and non-doctrinal problems, factors and viewpoints which can influence the agreement so far reached on Baptism, Eucharist and Ministry.

a) There is one ecumenical learning situation which has only recently begun to attract attention: the common curriculum material for religious instruction, prepared by different confessional families, or even by Christians and people of other faiths. Three examples:

— In French-speaking Switzerland, which covers totally or partially seven cantons, with an approximately 50-50 mixed Protestant and Catholic population, the Protestant and Roman Catholic churches came together on their own to produce a joint programme of biblical instruction for public schools. Since 1975 this has been introduced in nearly all schools of this area of Switzerland and children and teachers are no longer divided during biblical instruction.

— At a school in Alsace, France, where mentally-handicapped and normal children are being taught together, it was the former who led the way. It was the practice to divide religious instruction classes into Catholic and Protestant. The handicapped group understood the teaching about God the Father, Jesus Christ and the Bible, but they could not understand why friends in the same class had to be separated in order to learn such things. Earnest explanations by the teachers left them unconvinced. So finally it was decided to develop a common Christian catechetics for the school. Now Protestant and Roman Catholic children are being taught the faith together.

— In Ghana people went a dramatic step further, when the Government decided to prepare "A New Syllabus for Religious Education" for all primary schools and all the Junior Secondary Schools in the Public Educational System. The Christian Council of Ghana, the Roman Catholic Church, the Orthodox, Moslems and the Ahmadiyyah Movement joined in this effort to produce a unified syllabus, which was suggested for many reasons. One reason was the understanding that for quite a long time religious education had been mainly "sectarian", and that, as a consequence of this, there was also evidence of denominational teaching, both within the Christian and the Islamic traditions. It produced scholars whose knowledge of religion was narrow — and seemed to militate against the ever-growing call to citizens to live in mutual respect and cooperation with one another as one people with one destiny.

These are only three examples; there are many more. In the Office of Education of WCC a long list of such common curriculum material for religious instruction from all parts of the world is available. In some cases these examples are signs of a growing mutual understanding, growing mutual acknowledgement, and growing collaboration of churches which have been separated for centuries; in

other cases they come out of the strong request of a government or
society for a common Christian witness; in still other cases they are
signs of the awareness among people, among students on the local
level, in the congregations, schools and Sunday schools, that Christians have more in common than the traditional division and na-
tionalism would admit. Such syllabi have the tendency to bring to the
fore agreements and not disagreements, the common witness and not
the divided witness — also with regard to Baptism, Eucharist and
Ministry. Distinctions are made rather to interpret the history than to
describe the present situation. It could be a very interesting task to
find out the agreed statements on Baptism, Eucharist and Ministry
hidden in this curriculum material, which exists quite independently
of any ecumenical agreed statement. How can such an agreed statement on the local or regional level reinforce the agreed statement on
the ecumenical level, and vice versa?

   b) Another ecumenical learning situation is connected with the
first one: Christian teaching, in whatever form, and whether in
school or in church, has to be teaching that takes place the context of
the people. This context is, generally speaking, the context of the daily political, economic, social, personal challenges, the context of a
secular society and of a rapidly changing world in which ideological,
religious and societal pluralism dominates. All Christian teaching
and education must take this context seriously. It is the context in
which the whole people of God in today's world, be it in a minority
or in a majority situation, have to live and of which they are part —
influenced by it, annoyed with it and sometimes marginalized by it.
   In such a situation, a teaching-learning process can no longer start
only with a fixed catechism, but has to be open again and again to the
new changes, challenges, questions which the people of God, women
and men, young and old, clergy and laity, have to face. Such a
teaching-learning process is participatory and situation-oriented and
starts with the questions and needs of those whom it seeks to serve.
And therefore it will be obvious that the prevailing question is not
"What does the church or the churches teach about baptism and the
eucharist?" Rather it is, "What does it mean in my specific situation
that I am baptized or can take part in the Holy Communion? What is
the meaning of baptism and eucharist for my life, in view of the
challenges, hindrances, questions, doubts and sorrows I have to
face?" This could be the people's response to an agreed statement.

In other words, there is a need to state certain affirmations positively and in simple language.

c) The same is the case in an ecumenical learning situation, which is often found in our families. There are increasing numbers of married couples in our mobile societies, coming from different confessional backgrounds, who face the question of how they can together live as Christians and how they can educate their children in a Christian understanding of life and the world, despite the traditional distinctions in which they grew up. Where, among such couples or within such families, there is the desire to live a Christian family life, to take part in the life of a local congregation and to help one another to live as Christians, an agreement on basic Christian beliefs and also an agreement on Baptism, Eucharist and Ministry have already come into being, which cut right across confessional boundaries and which leave behind the old differences.

These people seem to support the statement in Lukas Vischer's preface to the first paper on the agreed statement: "Even more influential than all official studies and dialogues are the changes which have taken place in the life of the churches in recent decades. All the churches have to face up to the present, with its new elements and demands. All of them alike have to re-examine traditional convictions and practices. As a result of the liturgical revival and common biblical studies, a fellowship has come into being which cuts right across confessional boundaries and in which the old differences are in many respects seen in a different light. In the last analysis, almost the only function of dialogues and ecumenical conversations is to establish and consolidate this already existing fellowship."[2]

There are obviously such hidden agreed statements among students and teachers in schools, among Christians in the local congregation, who join in common missionary efforts and services, in common actions for social justice, common pastoral care and mutual visitations, and among parents and children in families. Very often they are also the result of the longing for Christian wholeness and simplicity, the result of their suffering under the churches' division, and a first answer to questions like these:

— Why can't the churches agree?
— Why can't they recognize each others' members and ministers?
— Why can't they give the world a common witness?
— Why can't Christians worship God together around the common faith?

The answers seem so simple, why are they taking so long to come? In the last analysis, almost the only function of dialogues and ecumenical conversations is to establish and consolidate this already existing agreement. Would it not be necessary to consider such agreed statements which have already grown up among people in the local congregations more seriously?

II. Starting point: learning communities

The earlier question "What are the possible consequences of the agreement on Baptism, Eucharist and Ministry for the teaching of the churches in the local congregations?" has already been answered to some extent by some suggestions and recommendations made by the Faith and Order Standing Commission which referred to actions being implemented by some churches. Five of them are in a special way related to our questions:

The revision of baptism catechesis through efforts by congregations to teach, learn and live along the lines of the common points which are becoming visible in the consensus process.

Regular weekly celebration of the eucharist by congregations which as a rule do not follow this practice.

An explicit invitation by churches which admit all persons who consider themselves to be Christian to their eucharistic table, so that the eucharistic sharing may be more complete; participation of church members in eucharistic celebrations other than one's own, in particular situations where doctrine and conscience permit it, even if the receiving of the elements is not possible.

Attendance and, where possible, *participation in one another's ordination ceremonies* by church members and ordained ministers. Such participation assists in visibly symbolizing the mutual sharing in ministry.

The recognition and incorporation of those elements listed for inclusion in liturgies of baptism, eucharist and ordination by churches and congregations which are involved in the development of new liturgies and in liturgical renewal.[3]

It is remarkable that these suggestions and recommendations in the first instance aim more at action than at teaching, and have in mind rather the experiences of people than their instruction. This seems to be essential for all further reflection on the catechetical implications. We have again learned that people (young and old) learn much less through the communication of ideas than through their concrete involvement on a local level, that they learn much less from teaching than from personal experience.

And nobody can say: "This is against the line of the catechetical tradition in our churches". Most of the old catechisms in our churches are didactical means which should serve the existing communities (families, congregations, worshipping communities etc.) in order to become a learning community. It was essential for them to start a joint learning process embracing all generations within an already existing community. And therefore the typical catechism question (for instance in the catechism of Martin Luther) "What does this mean?" is not so much a question about the cognitive content, but it aims rather at the lively reality of the biblical message as it appears in the life of the community itself, in its being and doing.

The difficulty in our present situation is that we have very often lost such communities, in families and in local congregations. Nor do learning communities exist any longer in the traditional form. So our teaching is directed at individuals — trying to teach and convince and change them individually, very often with doubtful results.

The alternative is to look for such learning communities again, and to discover them also among the new forms in which community life takes place at the present time. Obviously this is one of the conditions to deal also with the catechetical implications of the Lima text. The ecumenical learning situations to which we have referred are at least the starting point, and the hidden agreed statements which we have to find out more clearly are the point from which a bridge could be thrown to the published agreed statements. To build this bridge would also facilitate the interpretation and translation process of the agreed statements into various cultural, social and life contexts, and the development of supplementary materials, "which include, hymns, liturgies, stories and illustrations, and which can help people to experience the common faith to which they point".[4]

This is valid alike for children and adults, for young and old people. "It has yet to be demonstrated that adults learn and perceive in ways which are decisively different from those in which children learn. Everything that is important in the learning situation and process for the child is important for the adult. The generalisation that a person notices twenty per cent of what he hears, thirty per cent of what he sees, fifty per cent of what he both hears and sees, seventy per cent of what he himself says and ninety per cent of what he himself does is true, irrespective of the age of the person."[5]

III. New ways of teaching

In many of these learning situations the question of an agreed understanding of baptism and eucharist and ministry will come up automatically. Where, for example, a couple in a mixed marriage must decide on the denomination or the liturgy for the baptism of their child, or where in a mixed Protestant-Catholic discussion group the question of the authority of the pastor or teacher is raised. Or where a church has decided to admit all persons who consider themselves to be Christian to its eucharistic table. Also in the discussions about admitting children to Holy Communion, which is by no means only a discussion among theologians, church leaders and members of a synod, in churches formed or re-formed in the upheaval of the Reformation period of history, the agreed statement on eucharist will prove a very helpful guideline.

Interest in an agreed statement is also captured in a situation where people within a denominational congregation discover the diversity among themselves. For example, a particular church decided to build serious study into all its board and committee meetings as well as other church gatherings.

One evening the youth and adult choir had gathered to plan a "hymn sing" for Lent. They began by making large name tags which also involved each person's belief about the relationship between Jesus and God. Next they went around the room looking for those with whom they agreed. After forming groups, each group was to find a hymn which expressed their beliefs and write it on newsprint.

Following the exercise they saw the United Church of Christ filmstrip "The Council of Nicaea", and then discussed the Nicene Creed and summarized its contents. Christ is God; Christ is man; Christ is one. Then they reviewed the beliefs expressed in their hymns to make sure that each of these theological statements was present and a balanced orthodox understanding of Jesus Christ was affirmed. Putting the hymns in the order to be sung, they also wrote up short histories of each hymn and a summary statement of its theological affirmation. Not only had they created an exciting hymn sing in these three hours, but they had learned much about Christian theology.[6]

One could add: They had also learned much about diversity among Christians within one congregation and the need to overcome such diversities by agreed statements.

Against the background of such examples, it seems a much more difficult task to include common perspectives in catechetical material for the traditional instruction on the sacraments, be it in school, Sunday school, adult education, or above all in confirmation instruction. As long as such instruction is not linked to the experience of the celebration of the sacraments, included elements of the agreed statement will not change the situation of general indifference. For not only baptism (in the form of infant baptism) but also the Holy Communion, for which they should be prepared, is usually far removed from the experience and reality of candidates for confirmation unless the confirmation instruction has left the schooling-instructional paradigm and has really provided participation and common experience in some form. The starting point, here again, is the common experience — and thus again with the assumption that a congregational life exists in which the sacraments play an important role and are celebrated in such a way that the *whole* people of God can really take part in them.[7]

In other words, the celebration and liturgy of baptism and the celebration and liturgy of holy communion have to reflect the main affirmations of the agreed statement in the coloured variety of hymns, prayers, signs, details of participation, scripture readings, story-tellings, illustrations, etc., so that instruction and discussion on the agreed statement become a necessary consequence. But such instruction and discussion are only one component of the whole teaching. Teaching and learning take place in many ways. Very often church education has functionally equated the context of education with schooling and the means of education with formal instruction. This is a narrowing which needs to be overcome. To look for the catechetical implications of the agreed statement does not mean that we ask only how we include common perspectives in catechetical material. That will not necessarily mean that the total congregational life as the context or place for Christian education reflects these common perspectives in all their variety.

IV. Consequences of the convergence process

We come back once more to the convergence process itself. "What is new here", as it was pointed out in the Faith and Order Paper, "is a significant beginning in theological response by the member churches themselves. A transition is under way: from documents agreed upon by theologians to agreement among member churches." And later: "The process of widening and deepening the agreement on baptism, eucharist and ministry has been greatly stimulated by the responses and mutual exchange of the churches. In continuing this process, it is important that persons at all levels of church life (local, regional, national) and in all types of groupings (denominational, confessional, ecumenical) be encouraged to participate in reflection, exploration and action."

Such real or at least intended participation of the whole people of God in the convergence process has of course consequences for the teaching of the churches. If the convergence can only be achieved by participation in reflection, exploration and action, then the traditional pattern and ways of teaching have to be changed. The traditional schooling-instructional pattern, by which the teacher is encouraged to be with students in ways that assert control and power over them, excludes such mutual exchange and participation. Intended in the convergence process is an equal sharing of the living understanding of baptism, eucharist and ministry, a cooperative opportunity for reflection on the meaning and significance of these topics, expressed traditionally in different forms, ways and doctrines. So also each teaching, whether with children or with adults, has to follow this line, by which a teacher becomes a student and a student becomes a teacher and by which persons share their understandings in a historical, tradition-bearing community of faith. An emphasis on schooling and instruction makes it too easy to forget this truth. The way which was used in the process towards an ecumenical convergence on baptism, eucharist and ministry has again confirmed this truth!

NOTES

1. Towards an Ecumenical Consensus, Baptism, Eucharist, Ministry, *Faith and Order Paper* 84, 1977, p.3f.
2. *Faith and Order Paper* 73, 1975, p.6.
3. *Faith and Order Paper* 84, p.14.
4. Cf. *Faith and Order Paper* 84, p.13.
5. J.M. Sutcliffe, *Learning Community*, 1974, p.47.
6. *Will Our Children Have Faith?* New York, 1976, p.123.
7. Cf. e.g. the Faith and Order response: "Regular weekly celebration of the eucharist... as an important means of deepening eucharistic faith and experience and enriching the ecumenical dialogue", *loc. cit.*, p.14.

1987: LIMA AND BEYOND

WILLIAM H. LAZARETH

The World Council's Faith and Order Commission has recommended unanimously to the WCC Central Committee that the Fifth World Conference on Faith and Order be held in 1987. Why? To celebrate the 1200th anniversary of the last of the seven councils commonly recognized by the Eastern and Western churches to be truly ecumenical. How? By comparing and analyzing the churches' official replies to the Lima text on "Baptism, Eucharist and Ministry", and then by developing further those interdependent elements of the Church's visible unity in conciliar fellowship.

Already in 1967, at Bristol, England, Faith and Order shared the hope that it might "contribute towards creating the conditions which will enable all our churches to participate in a truly Ecumenical Council". Then, in 1975, the WCC Fifth Assembly in Nairobi, Kenya, was able to agree that the Council's primary purpose (and the Commission's sole aim) is "to call the churches to the goal of visible unity in one faith and in one eucharistic fellowship expressed in worship and in common life in Christ, and to advance towards that unity in order that the world may believe". The unity we seek was further described there as "a conciliar fellowship of local churches which are themselves truly united".

Building on these foundations, Faith and Order declared at its 1978 meeting in Bangalore, India, that "in order to reach visible unity, three fundamental requirements must be met: (1) full mutual recognition of baptism, the eucharist and the ministry; (2) common understanding of the apostolic faith; and (3) agreement on common ways of teaching and decision-making". Consequently it was agreed

---

• William H. Lazareth is Director of the Faith and Order Secretariat.

that study efforts in the coming years should focus on these three basic elements. So will this essay, as it documents current Commission research and programmes in preparation for the Fifth World Conference on Faith and Order in 1987.

I. Baptism, Eucharist and Ministry

Ecumenical history was made in January 1982 in Lima, Peru. At the triennial meeting of the World Council's Faith and Order Commission, about 100 theologians voted unanimously to transmit to the churches a major convergence document on "Baptism, Eucharist and Ministry".

The Lima text is potentially one of the most important documents of the ecumenical movement. Its preface outlines the process of its development, and announces plans for its official response in common reception as a basis for the churches' mutual recognition and eucharistic fellowship.

If the divided churches are to achieve the visible unity they seek, one of the essential prerequisites is that they should be in basic agreement on baptism, eucharist and ministry. Naturally, therefore, the Faith and Order Commission has devoted a good deal of attention to overcoming doctrinal division on these three themes. During the last fifty years, most of its conferences have had one or another of these subjects at the centre of discussion.

The three statements are the fruit of a 50-year process of study, stretching back to the first Faith and Order conference at Lausanne in 1927. The material has been discussed and revised by the Faith and Order Commission at Accra (1974), Bangalore (1978), and Lima (1982). Between the Plenary Commission meetings, the Standing Commission and its steering group on Baptism, Eucharist and Ministry under the presidency of Frère Max Thurian of the Taizé Community since 1979 have worked further on the drafting.

Where have these efforts brought us? As demonstrated in the Lima text, we have already achieved a remarkable degree of agreement. Certainly we have not yet fully reached "consensus" (*consentire*), understood here as that experience of life and articulation of faith necessary to realize and maintain the Church's visible unity. Such consensus is rooted in the communion built on Jesus Christ and the witness of the apostles. As a gift of the Spirit it is realized as a communal experience before it can be articulated by common efforts into words. Full consensus can only be proclaimed after the churches reach the point of living and acting together in unity.

On the way towards their goal of visible unity, however, the churches will have to pass through various stages. They have been blessed anew through listening to each other and jointly returning to the primary sources, namely "the Tradition of the Gospel testified in Scripture, transmitted in and by the Church through the power of the Holy Spirit" (Faith and Order World Conference, Montreal, 1963).

In leaving behind hostilities of the past, the churches have begun to discover many promising convergences in their shared convictions and perspectives. These convergences give assurance that despite much diversity in theological expression the churches have much in common in their understanding of the faith. The resultant text aims to become part of a faithful and sufficient reflection of the common Christian Tradition on essential elements of Christian communion. In the process of growing together in mutual trust, the churches must develop these doctrinal convergences step by step, until they are finally able to declare together that they are living in communion with one another in continuity with the apostles and the teachings of the universal Church.

This Lima text represents the significant theological convergence which Faith and Order has discerned and formulated. Those who know how widely the churches have differed in doctrine and practice on baptism, eucharist and ministry, will appreciate the importance of the large measure of agreement registered here. Virtually all the confessional traditions are included in the Commission's membership. That theologians of such widely different traditions should be able to speak so harmoniously about baptism, eucharist and ministry is unprecedented in the modern ecumenical movement. Particularly noteworthy is the fact that the Commission also includes among its full members theologians of the Roman Catholic and other churches which do not belong to the World Council of Churches itself.

In the course of critical evaluation the primary purpose of this ecumenical text must be kept in mind. Readers should not expect to find a complete theological treatment of baptism, eucharist and ministry. That would be neither appropriate nor desirable here. The agreed text purposely concentrates on those aspects of the theme that have been directly or indirectly related to the problems of mutual recognition leading to unity. The main text demonstrates the major areas of theological convergence; the added commentaries either indicate historical differences that have been overcome or identify disputed issues still in need of further research and reconciliation.

In the light of all these developments, the Faith and Order Commission now presents this Lima text (1982) to the churches. We do so with deep conviction, for we have become increasingly aware of our unity in the body of Christ. We have found reason to rejoice in the rediscovery of the richness of our common inheritance in the Gospel. We believe that the Holy Spirit has led us to this time, a *kairos* of the ecumenical movement when sadly divided churches have been enabled to arrive at substantial theological agreements. We believe that many significant advances are possible if in our churches we are sufficiently courageous and imaginative to embrace God's gift of church unity.

The Faith and Order Commission now respectfully invites all churches to prepare an official response to this text at the highest appropriate level of authority, whether it be a Council, Synod, Conference, Assembly or other body. In support of this process of reception, the Commission would be pleased to know as precisely as possible

— the extent to which your church can recognize in this text the faith of the Church through the ages;
— the consequences your church can draw from this text for its relations and dialogues with other churches, particularly with those churches which also recognize the text as an expression of the apostolic faith;
— the guidance your church can take from this text for its worship, educational, ethical, and spiritual life and witness;
— the suggestions your church can make for the ongoing work of Faith and Order as it relates the material of this text on Baptism, Eucharist and Ministry to its long-range research project, "Towards the Common Expression of the Apostolic Faith Today".

It is our intention to compare all the official replies received by 31 December 1984, to publish the results, and to analyze the ecumenical implications for the churches at the next World Conference on Faith and Order.

As concrete evidence of their ecumenical commitment, the churches are being asked to enable the widest possible involvement of the people of God at all levels of church life in the spiritual process of receiving this text. Here are two specific suggestions relating to its use in the worship, witness and study of the churches:

(1) *Growing Together in Baptism, Eucharist and Ministry* (Geneva, WCC, 1982) is a discussion guide prepared by this writer for lay study groups.

(2) *Baptism and Eucharist: Ecumenical Convergence in Celebration* (under preparation), edited by Fr Max Thurian, offers priests and pastors some appropriate resources and adaptable models for Christian worship. A wide variety of rites portray current liturgical renewal among the churches, including new ecumenical liturgies of Baptism and Eucharist that incorporate the elements recommended in the agreed text.

The materials may be used both for worship and for study. In so doing the hope is that there will be a common search by the churches to deepen their worship and spirituality, teach their doctrine, nurture their witness, and to engage in activities of justice and service while advancing Christian unity. Wherever possible all churches are encouraged to share and compare their study results across confessional, national and cultural boundaries.

(a) *Use in ecumenical contexts*
— in union negotiations
— in bilateral conversations
— in Councils of churches — national, regional and local
— in other ecumenical societies

(b) *Use within churches*
— in theological education
— in committees on church relations
— in church assemblies
— in councils, synods and conferences of ministers
— in lay study groups
— in regular acts of worship.

II. Towards the Common Expression of the Apostolic Faith Today

We have noted that it is the purpose of Faith and Order to call the churches to the goal of visible unity as a eucharistic and conciliar fellowship sharing the same apostolic faith. Therefore, as the churches now engage in the study and critical evaluation of our work on "Baptism, Eucharist and Ministry", the Commission agreed at Lima, 1982, to continue its own research activity with intensified interest in a long-range study process entitled "Towards the Common Expression of the Apostolic Faith Today".

In our present divided state, visible unity cannot be restored unless each church becomes aware of the painful situation of our divisions and takes decisions to overcome our disobedience to the will of Christ as expressed in his prayer for unity (Jn 17:1-26). These decisions will be genuine only to the extent to which they imply a resolve to do what the re-establishment of communion demands: conversion through a constant return to the source which is God as revealed in Jesus Christ through the Holy Spirit. Such a conversion requires an effort to express the content of the faith in such a way that the life of the community is consonant with the word of God.

At its Fifth Assembly in Nairobi in December 1975, the World Council of Churches, after its discussion of Conciliar Fellowship, adopted the following recommendation:

> We ask the churches to undertake a common effort to receive, reappropriate and confess together, as contemporary occasion requires, the Christian truth and faith delivered through the Apostles and handed down through the centuries. Such common action, arising from free and inclusive discussion under the commonly acknowledged authority of God's Word, must aim both to clarify and to embody the unity and the diversity which are proper to the church's life and mission. (Section II, 19).

As noted above, the same Assembly, in revising "The Constitution of the World Council of Churches", adopted the following statement as the first of the purposes of the Council:

> (i) To call the churches to the goal of visible unity in one faith and in one eucharistic fellowship expressed in worship and in common life in Christ, and to advance towards that unity in order that the world may believe (Art. III (1).

The intention of the Faith and Order Commission in formulating the following project is to help the World Council to fulfill its recommendation, and so to advance towards the realization of its first purpose.

A primary assumption of this project is the recognition of the special rank and function of the Nicene Creed. For, together with a growing convergence in our understanding of baptism, eucharist and ministry, the appeal for a common expression of the apostolic faith belongs to the movement towards the unity of the Church. In the attempt to work out such a common expression, it is impossible to disregard the special place of the Nicene Creed. It is the one common Creed which is most universally accepted as formulation of the apostolic faith by churches in all parts of the world, where it primarily serves as the confession of faith in the eucharistic liturgy.

The koinonia of the eucharistic community, which is united in Christ by baptism, is grounded on the apostolic proclamation of the crucified and risen Christ. This is documented by the scriptures, summarized in the creed of the church and is served by the minister who presides over the eucharistic celebration. The common understanding of the apostolic faith was expressed by the Ancient Church in the Ecumenical Creed of Nicea (325), complemented at Constantinople (381) and solemnly received at Chalcedon (451) as the authentic symbol of the Christian faith, witnessing to the fullness of the Christian faith and life and authoritative for the entire church.

The eucharist builds up the Church and visibly manifests its unity. The apostolic faith, fruit of the Holy Spirit, is the ground of that unity. The outward expression of this intimate relationship of faith and eucharistic celebration is therefore essential to the visible unity of the Church, so much so that without common recognition of the Nicene Creed as the ecumenical symbol of the apostolic faith, it is difficult if not impossible to understand how we are to advance "to the goal of visible unity in one faith and in one eucharistic fellowship expressed in worship and in common life in Christ ... in order that the world may believe" (WCC Constitution III (1)). Thus, together with a growing convergence in our understanding of baptism, eucharist and ministry, the appeal for common expression of the apostolic faith of the one, holy, catholic and apostolic Church as expressed in its Ecumenical Symbol of faith belongs to movement towards the unity of the Church.

It should be remembered how well this Creed has served millions of Christians, with whom we are also bound together in the unity of the Church, in the past. Its brief statement of the essential faith has provided at least formally a thread of unity down through the centuries. In one form or another, this creed has been used by the Orthodox churches, by the Roman Catholic and Anglican churches, and by most of the churches of the Protestant Reformation, and in all parts of the world. It has helped the churches to affirm their fundamental belief in God, in the Lord Jesus Christ and his saving action, in the Holy Spirit and the Church, and in the life of the Kingdom to come. Some have used it as a baptismal confession, others as a central standard of doctrine. It has been read and sung at the eucharist and other liturgical services and has been used as a statement of belief at the ordination of church ministers. As the product of a council received by the churches in a time of great confusion and strife, it has stood as a model of ecumenical confession, both in the method of its formulation and in the content of its definition. As such, it has inspired theologians, hymn-writers, preachers, and artists in all ages. It seems appropriate, therefore, to ask the churches when they try to express their common understanding of the apostolic faith today to recognize this Creed from the time of the early Church as the ecumenical expression of the apostolic faith which unites Christians of all ages in all places.

Such recognition would call each church to examine its beliefs and actions today in relation to that ecumenical Creed and so to express and interpret its meaning today theologically, ethically, liturgically, socially in terms understandable in that church's everyday life and in society.

We are convinced that any real progress among the divided churches towards the common expression of the apostolic faith today will require a twofold movement, towards unity in faith with the early Church, and towards unity in mission with the Church of the future. The word "towards" is important: both movements are actually, from our present divided situation, movements towards the future. Our hope then is that we can initiate a threefold study project, aiming:

a) to ask the churches to make a common recognition of the apostolic faith as expressed in the Ecumenical Symbol of that faith: the Nicene Creed;
b) to ask the churches how they understand its content today in their own particular situations of worship, fellowship and witness;
c) to ask the churches "to undertake a common effort to confess together, as contemporary occasion requires, the Christian truth and faith, delivered through the Apostles and handed down through the centuries".

We believe that this project will guide the churches to confess Christ in their life, and lead them towards the common celebration of the eucharist where "we proclaim the Lord's death until he comes" (1 Cor.11:26).

III. Stages on the way to conciliar fellowship

Faith and Order has contributed new theological insights on unity as a conciliar fellowship of local churches truly united, on baptism, eucharist and ministry, on authority in the Church and, in an initial way, on the nature of the Church. At the same time, several of the bilateral theological dialogues have begun to reach conclusions of considerable importance for the churches engaged in them.

The success of this work of developing the doctrinal content of unity has raised new expectations at the local level. People have begun to ask with some urgency how the implications of this success may be expressed structurally in each place, how the new understandings may be communicated to people at all levels, and how the growing communion may be made visible in witness, prayer and action. It becomes clear that the goal of unity and the way to it interact upon each other; a development of the one brings new insights and possiblities for the other. In each place, therefore, the instruments and structures for expressing the growing communion take on a new importance as the unity they seek to serve becomes both a more possible goal and a more urgent task.

The most widespread of these instruments are councils of churches. They are the place where churches interact in fellowship and where new theological understanding may be given concrete shape. Seen in this context, the growing Roman Catholic collaboration with councils of churches is indeed a significant development.

At the same time it has to be asked whether councils of churches could be expressing more actively the new understanding of unity and the growing fellowship. The question also arises whether the Roman Catholic Church could be taking more courageous steps in associating itself with councils of churches. Similarly, the countless informal types of ecumenical activity have to be taken into account. What impact do they have on, and what relationship do they have with, councils of churches? To explore these issues, the Faith and Order Commission and the Vatican's Secretariat for Promoting Christian Unity organized a consultation (Venice, February 1982) on the significance and contribution of councils of churches in the ecumenical movement.

A council of churches provides an ecclesial situation in which inherited values and elements of separated churches are tested and discerned and in which there is a real though imperfect experience of the future diversity of full conciliar fellowship (*concile*). Such a council (*conseil*) gives a new direction and impetus to the overall life, unity and mission of the church. Membership in a council of churches expresses a commitment to practise some real measure of mutual recognition and reconciliation at every level of church life.

In the history of the ecumenical movement, councils of churches were born almost by accident; but this birth eventually proved to be providential, a mark of the concrete action of God in history. Thus, although councils of churches are in no sense the only way towards unity, they can be called a providential and even a favoured way. Each council is shaped by the situation of its member churches, by the circumstances in which it came into being and by the tasks it has had to undertake.

The role of councils of churches is to be understood in the light of the importance of the local church (even though this may be understood variously by the member churches as diocese, parish or congregation). It is the assembly of Christians in unity in a given place — a unity which achieves its climax in the eucharistic celebration — which is the starting point for the growth of the Church of God. It is also in the local community, therefore, that the construction of unity or the common growth in unity must be rooted.

The growth of churches into a mature ecumenical fellowship and towards unity can often be seen to pass through several stages. It is possible to identify five main ones and to indicate where the fellowship of a council can give encouragement, support and direction.

— *Competition*: This is the stage where a church sees itself as entirely self-sufficient and does not, in any real way, acknowledge the role of other churches or its need of them (and so has few scruples in inviting Christians to transfer to it from other churches). A radical renewal of attitude is necessary before these churches are ready to engage in various forms of ecumenical collaboration.

— *Co-existence*: This is the stage where a church begins, more or less explicitly, to acknowledge that Christ can also be known in other churches, yet it still takes no initiative to enter into structured relationships.

— *Co-operation*: This is the stage where a church recognizes the other churches with sufficient warmth to be able to undertake certain tasks together, to engage with them in a real if limited partnership. Councils of churches, which come into existence when churches are prepared to go beyond mere co-existence, are instruments designed to help churches move through co-operation to deeper commitment.

— *Commitment*: This is the stage where it is felt that partnership in particular projects (e.g. through a council) no longer corresponds to the degree of mutual recognition between the churches. At this point, therefore, they enter into a general, lasting and deliberately open-ended agreement, under God, to do much of what they do as if they were limbs of the same body.

— *Communion*: This is the stage where it no longer makes sense to think of the fellowship as consisting of two or more separate entities, but where all separation can be overcome in the appropriate wholeness and singleness of the body of Christ.

Several of these stages will be marked by the kind of exchange known in general terms as "dialogue". At some point this may become more specifically a theological dialogue, whether multilateral or bilateral. This happens when a church, sensing that mere co-existence (or, sometimes, co-operation) is no longer enough, asks for a formal theological dialogue with one or more churches. The dialogue is usually carried out by qualified theologians and it tests whether there is suffcient unity in faith to allow the churches to move ahead to the later stages.

The stages do not succeed each other automatically; some churches may find themselves at different stages with different partners. These stages, however, are useful for marking the dynamism of the movement. We can even say that stages are indispensable. The divisions are too deep, and have lasted too long, for it to be possible to envisage a sudden unstaggered transition into unity. On the other hand, being able to mark the steps — even small ones — makes it possible to maintain the dynamism, to sustain the pace of advance, along a road which could otherwise seem too long.

It may be useful to mention some activities which, in many councils of churches, mark the growth from one stage to the next (e. g. from co-existence through cooperation to commitment) and are, themselves, part of the way towards the goal of unity.

— It seems to be a good pedagogical method to begin work together in those areas where people's needs are most keenly felt. Thus, councils often bring member churches together to plan ecumenically for the development of their community.

— The execution of community development programmes calls for skilled personnel. Hence the council has to encourage member churches to co-operate in an ecumenical training scheme for those who are to implement projects or carry out programmes. It should also encourage closer co-operation in theological training for the ordained ministry. It is of fundamental importance that the ministers and priests of the different churches involved come into close contact with one another during their years of theological education, and that as much of their curricula as possible be developed ecumenically.

— As a necesary step towards unity, the council may be able to encourage churches to agree on a mutual recognition of each other's baptism.

— In further and deeper mutual sharing, it would seem desirable that churches invite other members to their synods or conferences where important decisions are made.

— In sustaining this process of development, councils must be flexible and responsive to the various manifestations of growth which may appear, e.g., clarification of moral issues, questions of ministry, eucharist, authority.

— It will be important for councils to establish an evaluation process by which to measure the impact and effectiveness of these various steps, as well as to evaluate the commitment of the churches and the policies, programmes and structures of the council itself.

— All of the above steps must be undergirded by careful biblical and theological reflection. Only so will it have the spirit and the reserves to promote the growth in unity, discerning and facing new issues and challenges and calling the member churches to their prophetic role.

It appears indispensable to the advance towards unity that churches are able to mark irreversible steps; there are no ways back without the creation of new divisions, without shattering a new emerging community. A clear awareness of this condition considerably strengthens the commitment of churches to the ecumenical movement and to the councils of churches in particular.

APPENDIX I

The first drafts of 1967, 1970 and 1972

We reproduce here the first three drafts of "Baptism, Eucharist and Ministry". The earliest, on the eucharist, dates from October 1967, following the meeting in August of that year of the Commission in Bristol. In fact, it was there that the need was felt for putting on paper the points of agreement reached by the representatives of the churches in the course of the larger ecumenical gatherings. A provisional draft was composed on the basis of the results of Lund (1952), Montreal (1963) and Bristol (1967). This text was followed very soon by a more expanded document: "The Eucharist in Ecumenical Thought" which took up the structure and main lines of the provisional draft. This second draft was submitted to the working committee on Faith and Order at the Uppsala Assembly (1968) and recommended by it for study in the churches. It appeared in Study Encounter *IV, 3, 1968 and was part of the document presented in Louvain (1971) under the title "Beyond Intercommunion", of which it was appendix 3.*

For baptism, the same procedure was adopted and the first draft was edited in 1970 and underwent improvement until Accra (1974). Similarly for ministry, a draft was prepared in June 1972 for the Marseille meeting on the issue; this meeting drew up a new text for Accra.

We could compare these first drafts with the Lima text and thus measure the path covered on the way towards the expression of an agreement in the faith among churches. We would see that, while the texts on baptism and especially on ministry have greatly evolved, the one on eucharist has undergone a homogenous development as of the first draft which already contained all the elements later made explicit and specified.

Provisional draft of an ecumenical consensus on the Eucharist

Based on statements from Lund 1952, Montreal 1963 and Bristol 1967. Faith and Order, October 1967, FO/67:55

Preamble: Word, Baptism and Eucharist

Baptism, once performed and never repeated leads us into the continuous worshipping life of the "royal priesthood" (1 Peter 2:9) the people of God. In the Holy Eucharist or Lord's Supper constantly repeated and always including both word and sacrament we proclaim and celebrate a memorial of the saving acts of God (1 Cor. 11:23-6). What God did in the incarnation, life, death, resurrection and ascension of Christ he does not do again. The events are unique; they cannot be repeated or extended or continued. Yet in this memorial we do not only recall past events: God makes them present through the Holy Spirit who takes of the things of Christ and declares them to us, thus making us participate in Christ (1 Cor. 1:9).[1]

1. The Eucharist, as a meal and as the Lord's Sacrament

The Eucharist is the sacramental meal which Christ held with his disciples before his death on the cross and which he commanded them to hold until his return.

In this meal, the bread and the wine are the sacrament or the certain sign of the presence of Christ in person who sacrificed his life for all men and gives himself to them as true food; because of this the Eucharist is the sacrament of the body and blood of Christ, the sacrament of his real presence.[2]

Thus the Eucharist is the liturgical meal where the promise of the presence of the crucified and risen Christ is fulfilled and where the reality of Christ's presence bears its fruits of sanctification and unity.[3]

The Eucharist consists essentially of the proclamation of the Word of God, the prayer of thankgsgiving and intercession, the memorial of what God did for men, the words of Christ's institution of the sacrament, the prayer for the outpouring of the manifestation of his Kingdom.[4]

2. The Eucharist, thanksgiving to the Father

The Eucharist is a thanksgiving to the Father for everything which he accomplished in creation and redemption, for everything which he accomplishes now in the Church and in the world in spite of the sins of men, for everything that he will accomplish until the full manifestation of his Kingdom. Thus the Eucharist is the benediction (*berakah*) by which the Church expresses its thankfulness to God for all his benefits.[5]

The Eucharist is the sacrifice of praise by which the Church speaks on behalf of the whole creation and brings before God all things of value in the world. For the world God is reconciling to himself is present at every Eucharist: in the persons of the faithful and in the prayers they offer for themselves and for all men. As the faithful and their prayers are united in the Person of our Lord and to his intercession they are transfigured and accepted. Thus the Eucharist reveals to the world what it must become.[6]

3. The Eucharist, the memorial of Christ

The Eucharist is the memorial of Christ (*anamnesis*); that is to say the actualization of all that he accomplished for men from his incarnation until his ascension,[7] the participation of the church in his intercession for the world,[8] and the foretaste of his return which the Church awaits with zeal (*maranatha*).[9] The Eucharist is an act by which the sacrifice of the cross is proclaimed and takes effect in the Church and in the world.[10]

The memorial of Christ, as actualization and anticipation, is realized in thanksgiving and intercession. The Church proclaiming before God the mighty acts of redemption in thanksgiving beseeches him to give the benefits of those acts to every man. In thanksgiving and intercession, the Church is united with the Son, its great High Priest and Intercessor.[11]

By him, with him and in him we offer to the Father in the power of the Holy Spirit our praise, thanksgiving and intercession; with a spirit of poverty and repentance of heart we offer ourselves as a living and holy sacrifice, a sacrifice which must be expressed in the whole of our daily lives.[12]

The anamnesis of Christ is the basis and source of all Christian prayer. So our prayer relies upon and is united with the continual intercession of the risen Lord. In the Eucharist Christ empowers us to live with him and to pray with him as justified sinners joyfully and freely fulfilling his will.[13]

4. The Eucharist, the invocation of the Spirit

The Holy Spirit acts in the Eucharist for the accomplishment of Christ's promise.[14] It is because of Christ's promise in the words of institution and by the action of the Holy Spirit that the bread and wine are the sacrament of the body and blood of Christ.[15] The Eucharist is also an invocation of the Holy Spirit (epiklesis), so that he may sanctify and renew the Church, and lead it into all truth and empower it to fulfill its mission in the world and prepare for the Kingdom of God.[16]

5. The Eucharist, communion of the body of Christ

The Eucharist is communion in Christ present who nourishes the faith, the hope and the charity of the Church his body. The Eucharist is at the same time communion with the body of Christ which is the Church. Thus united to our Lord, and to the Church triumphant, and in fellowship with the whole Church on earth, we are renewed in the covenant sealed by the blood of Christ. In the Supper the Church also anticipates the marriage-supper of the Lamb in the Kingdom of God.[17]

The sharing of the common loaf and the common cup in a given place demonstrates the oneness of the sharers with the whole Christ, with all the other sharers in all times and places, and with the universal Church.[18]

Because of its catholicity the Eucharist is a radical challenge to the "demonic" tendencies in church life toward estrangement, separation and fragmentation. Lack of local unity in church or society constitutes a challenge to the Christians in that place. A mockery is made of the Eucharist when the walls of separation destroyed by Christ on his cross are allowed to persist: those between races, nationalities, tongues, classes, congregations and confessions, etc.[19]

6. The celebration of the Eucharist

Orders of Holy Communion usually include the following elements:

(a) A service of the word containing:
— the reading and preaching of the word,
— intercession for the whole Church and for the world.
(b) A service of the sacrament, having a shape determined by the actions of our Lord at the Last Supper:
— taking bread and wine to be used by God in this service,

— blessing God for creation and redemption and invoking the Holy
Spirit (or referring in some other way to the Holy Spirit), reciting
the words of institution whether before or within or after the
prayer of thanksgiving and saying the Lord's prayer,
— breaking the bread,
— giving the bread and the wine.

This list of liturgical items is not meant to exclude reference during
the service to many other important theological themes such as the
expression of contrition, the declaration of forgiveness of sins, the
affirmation of faith in credal form, the celebration of the communion of saints, the announcement of the Lord's coming and the self-
dedication of the faithful to God. We assume that the person who
presides will be someone recognized by his church as authorized to
do so.[20]

NOTES

1. The Report from Montreal 1963, p. 73, paragraph 116.
2. Lund, page 54, b. The Third World Conference on Faith and Order.
3. Report on the Holy Eucharist to the Faith and Order Commission, Bristol 1967,
   Section I,1.
4. Montreal, p.74, paragraph 118.
5. Montreal, p.74, paragraph 118. b. ii.
6. Bristol, Section II, 2.
7. Lund, p.54, a, Montreal, p.73, paragraph 116, Bristol I 1.
8. Montreal, p.73, paragraph 117, Bristol I 1.
9. Lund, p.54, c, Montreal, page 73, paragraph 117, Bristol, I 1.
10. Montreal, p.73, paragraph 117.
11. Bristol, I 2.
12. Montreal, p.73, paragraph 117.
13. Bristol, I 3.
14. Montreal, p.73, paragraph 116.
15. Bristol I 4.
16. Bristol, I 4.
17. Montreal, p.73, paragraph 117.
18. Bristol, II 1.
19. Bristol, II 4.
20. Montreal, p.74, paragraph 118.

Second draft on
"The Eucharist in ecumenical thought"
(Faith and Order, 1967)

Introduction

The Faith and Order Commission meeting at Bristol, England in August 1967, adopted the report of the section on "The Holy Eucharist", and accepted the following recommendation:

> That there be drawn up a resumé of the emerging ecumenical consensus on the Eucharist, drawing on the work of Lund, Montreal, Aarhus and Bristol, and on the work of regional groups and of individual scholars related to the ecumenical discussion of the Eucharist. On the basis of this resumé the draft of a popular booklet, perhaps with illustrations, should be prepared under the direction of the Secretariat. Booklets could then be printed separately in the language and idiom of the various countries, in consultation with representatives of National Councils of Churches and with experts in communication. In this way a wider public could be informed about ecumenical liturgical developments.

The resumé which follows is based on paragraphs produced by the Third and Fourth World Conferences on Faith and Order, at Lund in 1952 and Montreal in 1963, and by the Faith and Order Commission itself at Bristol in 1967, being drawn from the official records of these meetings.

The two World Conferences, and the Commission itself, were composed of scholars and churchmen, both lay and clerical, appointed or approved by the churches as their offical representatives for Faith and Order work. The substance of the paragraphs was produced by sections of these conferences, or of the commission, which were broadly representative of the major confessional families. In every case the section, in turn, had drawn upon the work of a theological or study commission that had laboured over several years, and upon the work of specialists in the field.

While the representatives of the churches, and the methods employed in each section or group, differed because of personalities and circumstances, the results of their labours have an official character which cannot be attributed to the writings of individuals or of other less representative groups, due to the fact that the section reports were in each case submitted for criticism and amendment to a plenary assembly widely representative of the churches. It should be recognized that this resumé represents a stage in a process and will probably be superseded by futher ecumenical consensus arrived at by a similar process. It will be continually subject to clarification, improvement and extension in the on-going work for Christian unity.

While we cannot be fully content with the consensus represented in this statement we believe that it reflects a degree of agreement that could not have been foreseen even five years ago, and that our future is bright with hope.

Preamble

"Baptism, once performed and never repeated, leads us into the continuous worshipping life of the royal priesthood, the people of God. In the Eucharist or Lord's Supper, constantly repeated and always including both word and sacrament, we proclaim and celebrate a memorial of the saving acts of God. What God did in the incarnation, life, death, resurrection and ascension of Christ, he does not do again; the events are unique, they cannot be repeated or extended ..."[1]; nevertheless, "Christ himself, with all he has accomplished for us and for all creation ... is present in the Eucharist."[2]

The Eucharist is essentially a single whole, consisting usually of the following elements in varying sequence:

proclamation of the Word of God, in different ways;
intercession for the whole Church and the world;
thanksgiving for creation and redemption;
the words of Christ's institution of the sacrament;
prayer for the gift of the Holy Spirit;
prayer for the Lord's coming and for the manifestation of his Kingdom;
the Lord's prayer;
the breaking of the bread;
the eating and drinking in communion with Christ and each member of the Church[3].

This list of liturgical items is not meant to exclude reference to others, such as "the expression of contrition, the declaration of forgiveness of sins, the affirmation of faith in credal form, the celebration of the communion of saints ... and the self-dedication of the faithful to God. We assume that the person who presides will be someone recognized by his church as authorized to do so."[4]

The Eucharist contains a great richness and variety of meaning. Individuals as well as ecclesiastical traditions hold (widely) varying views. No document could be a complete exposition of every aspect of eucharistic thought. Moreover any attempt to expound the Eucharist is bound to deal separately with different aspects, whereas the Eucharist is essentially a single whole. But this paper reflects the extent to which there is now a wide and growing agreement on many of the aspects of eucharistic thought.

1. The Eucharist, the Lord's Supper

The Eucharist is the sacramental meal, the new paschal meal of the people of God, which Christ, having loved his disciples until the end, gave to them before his death, shared with them after his resurrection and commanded them to hold until his return.

This meal of bread and wine is the sacrament, the effective sign and assurance of the presence of Christ himself. who sacrificed his life for all men and who gives himself, to them as the bread of life; because of this, the eucharistic meal is the sacrament of the body and blood of Christ, the sacrament of his real presence.

In the Eucharist the promise of the presence of the crucified and risen Christ is fulfilled in a unique way for the faithful, who are sanctified and unified in him, reconciled in love to be his servants of reconciliation in the world.

2. The Eucharist, thanksgiving to the Father

The Eucharist is the great thanksgiving to the Father for everything which he accomplished in creation and redemption, for everything which he accomplishes now in the Church and in the world in spite of the sins of men, for everything that he will accomplish in bringing his kingdom to fulfilment. Thus the Eucharist is the benediction (*berakah*) by which the Church expresses its thankfulness to God for all his benefits.[5]

The Eucharist is the great sacrifice of praise by which the Church speaks on behalf of the whole creation. "For the world which God has reconciled to himself is present at every Eucharist: in the bread and wine, in the persons of the faithful, and in the prayers they offer for themselves and for all men. As the faithful and their prayers are united in the Person of our Lord and to his intercession they are transfigured and accepted. Thus the Eucharist reveals to the world what it must become."[6]

3. The Eucharist, memorial (anamnesis) of Christ

"Christ instituted the Eucharist, sacrament of his body and blood with its focus upon the cross and resurrection, as the anamnesis of the whole of God's reconciling action in him. Christ himself with all he has accomplished for us and for all creation (in his incarnation, servanthood, ministry, teaching, suffering, sacrifice, resurrection, ascension and Pentecost) is present in this anamnesis as is also the foretaste of his Parousia and the fulfilment of the Kingdom. The anamnesis in which Christ acts through the joyful celebration of his Church thus includes this representation and anticipation. It is not only a calling to mind of what is past, or of its significance. It is the Church's effective proclamation of God's mighty acts. By this communion with Christ the Church participates in that reality.

Anamnetic representation and anticipation are realized in thanksgiving and intercession. The Church, proclaiming before God the mighty acts of redemption in thanksgiving, beseeches him to give the benefits of these acts to every man. In thanksgiving and intercession, the Church is united with the Son, its great High Priest and Intercessor.

The Anamnesis of Christ is the basis and source of all Christian prayer. So our prayer relies upon and is united with the continual intercession of the risen Lord. In the Eucharist, Christ empowers us to live with him and to pray with him as justified sinners joyfully and freely fulfilling his will."[7]

"With contrite hearts we offer ourselves as a living and holy sacrifice, a sacrifice which must be expressed in the whole of our daily lives. Thus united to our Lord, and to the Church triumphant, and in fellowship with the whole Church on earth, we are renewed in the covenant sealed by the blood of Christ."[8]

"Since the anamnesis of Christ is the very essence of the preached Word as it is of the Eucharist, each reinforces the other. Eucharist should not be celebrated without the ministry of the Word, and the ministry of the Word points to, and is consummated in the Eucharist."[9]

4. The Eucharist, gift of the Spirit

"The anamnesis leads to epiklesis, for Christ in his heavenly intercession prays the Father to send the Spirit upon his children. For this reason, the Church, being under the New Covenant, confidently prays for the Spirit, in order that it may be sanctified and renewed, led into all truth and empowered to fulfill its mission in the world.

Anamnesis and epiklesis... cannot be conceived apart from communion. Moreover it is the Spirit who, in our Eucharist, makes Christ really present and given to us in the bread and wine, according to the words of institution."[10]

The gift of the Holy Spirit in the Eucharist is a foretaste of the Kingdom of God: the Church receives the life of the new creation and the assurance of the Lord's return (maranatha).

"We agree that the whole action of the Eucharist has an epikletic character, i.e. that it depends upon the work of the Holy Spirit; we agree also that this aspect of the Eucharist should find expression in the words of the liturgy. Some desire an invocation of the Holy Spirit upon the people of God and upon the whole eucharistic action, including the elements: some hold that the reference to the Spirit may be made in other ways."[11]

"The consecration cannot be limited to a particular moment in the liturgy. Nor is the location of the epiklesis in relation to the words of institution of decisive importance. In the early liturgies the whole 'prayer action' was thought of as bringing about the reality promised by Christ. A recovery of such an understanding may help to overcome our differences concerning a special moment of consecration."[12]

5. The Eucharist, communion of the body of Christ

The eucharistic communion with Christ present, who nourishes the life of the Church, is at the same time communion with the body of Christ which is the Church. "The sharing of the common loaf and the common cup in a given place demonstrates the oneness of the sharers with the whole Christ and with their fellow sharers in all times and places. By sharing the common loaf they show their unity with the Church catholic, the mystery of redemption is set forth, and the whole body grows in grace."[13]

Because of its catholicity the Eucharist is a radical challenge to the tendencies towards estrangement, separation and fragmentation. Lack of local unity in church or society constitutes a challenge to the Christians in that place. A mockery is made of the Eucharist when the walls of separation destroyed by Christ on his cross are allowed to reappear in Church life: those between races, nationalities, tongues and classes.[14]

According to the promise of Christ, each faithful member of the Body of Christ receives in the Eucharist remission of sins and everlasting life, and is nourished in faith, hope and love.

Solidarity in the eucharistic communion of the body of Christ (agapè) and responsible concern of Christians for one another and the world should be given specific expression in the liturgies, for example, "in the mutual forgiveness of sins; the kiss of peace; the bringing of gifts for the communal meal and for distribution to the poor brethren; the specific prayer for the needy and suffering; the taking of the Eucharist to the sick and those in prison. In this agapeic realization of eucharistic fulness, the ministry of deacons and deaconesses was (in the early Church) especially responsible. The place of such a ministry between the table and the needy properly testified to the redeeming presence of Christ in the world. All these agapeic features of the Eucharist are directly related to Christ's own testimony as a Servant, in whose servanthood Christians themselves participate by virtue of their union with him. As God in Christ has entered into the human situation, so should eucharistic liturgy be near to the concrete and particular situations of men." [15]

6. The Eucharist, mission to the world

Mission is not simply a consequence of the Eucharist. Whenever the Church is the Church, mission must be part of its life. At the Eucharist the Church is supremely itself and is united with Christ in His mission.

The world is already present in the thanksgiving to the Father, where the Church speaks on behalf of the whole creation; in the memorial of Christ, where the Church united with its great High Priest and Intercessor prays for the world, in the prayer for the gift of the Holy Spirit, where the Church asks for sanctification and new creation.

Reconciled in the Eucharist, the members of the body of Christ are servants of reconciliation amongst men and witnesses of the joy of resurrection. Their very presence in the world implies full solidarity with the sufferings and hopes of all men, to whom they can be signs of the love of Christ who sacrificed himself on the cross and gives himself in the Eucharist.

The Eucharist is also the feast of the continuing apostolic harvest, where the Church rejoices for the gifts received in the world and welcomes every man of good will.

7. The Eucharist, end of divisions

"When local churches, no matter how humble, share in the Eucharist they experience the wholeness of the Church and reveal it in its fullness: its members, its faith, its history, and its special gifts. Eucharistic celebrations, therefore, are always concerned with the whole Church and the whole Church is concerned with every eucharistic celebration. Since the earliest days Baptism has been understood as the sacrament by which believers are incorporated into the body of Christ and are endowed by the Holy Spirit. When, therefore, the right of baptized believers and their ministers to participate in and preside over eucharistic celebrations in one church is called in question by those who preside over and are members of other eucharistic congregations, the catholicity of the Eucharist is obscured. On the other hand, insofar as a church claims to be a manifestation of the whole Church, it should recognize that the whole Church is involved in its pastoral and administrative regulations." [16]

"The question of intercommunion demands above all an inquiry about the nature, as well as the necessity, of the Ministry in general, and of Episcopacy in particular. The Churches should be urged to undertake a positive re-assessment of the Ministry, both as it is manifested in their own Order and in that of other churches. In particular, they should address themselves to the following questions:

a) The "Catholic" churches should ask whether the ministries of non-episcopal churches — quite apart from their possession of apostolic succession or their lack of it — do not in fact contain elements of value (such as charismatic or extraordinary ministries), and if so of what value such elements may be.

b) The "Protestant" churches, on the other hand, should reconsider, in the light of the ecumenical movement, the value of the commonly accepted ministry of the early Church and of pre-Reformation times.

c) "Protestant" as well as "Catholic" churches should further ask themselves whether, in spite of the widely divergent appearance of pre-Reformation and Reformation ministries, a measure of hidden identity may not in fact have been preserved. Does the fact that the Reformers rejected the name or title of a given ecclesiastical order necessarily prove that the reality behind the name was also rejected? Or again, does the fact that a name or title has been preserved, by itself, constitute a proof that the intended reality has been retained? In what cases is the rejection of episcopacy or of priesthood absolute and final? In what cases does the apparent rejection of the old ecclesiastical orders mean only the rejection of certain sociological forms and modalities? How far are they susceptible to the principle of 'economy'?"[17]

The best way towards unity in eucharistic celebration and communion is the renewal itself of the Eucharist in the different churches, in regard to teaching and liturgy. As the Eucharist is the new liturgical service Christ has given to the Church, it seems normal that it should be celebrated not less frequently than every Sunday, or once a week. As the Eucharist is the new sacramental meal of the people of God, it seems also normal that every faithful should receive communion at every celebration.

"As the churches in their eucharistic experience move toward the fulness which is in Christ, the problem of intercommunion will move toward its solution."[18]

NOTES

1. Montreal, No. 116;
2. Bristol, II 1;
3. See Montreal, No. 118;
4. Montreal, No. 118;
5. Montreal, No. 118, b II;
6. Bristol, III 2;
7. Bristol, II 1-3; see Lund, p. 54, a-c, and Montreal, No. 117;
8. Montreal, No. 117;
9. Bristol, II 5 a;
10. Bristol, II 4;
11. Bristol, Appendix 4;
12. Bristol, II 5 c;
13. Bristol, III 1;
14. See Bristol, III 4;
15. Bristol, IV 4;
16. Bristol, III 3;
17. Bristol, V 2;
18. Bristol, V.

First draft of an ecumenical agreement on baptism

As we have already undertaken for the Eucharist, we should now like to propose an ecumenical agreement on baptism, composed of texts accepted by the delegates to the Assemblies of the World Council of Churches and to the Faith and Order Conferences. We shall use the text and numbering of the volume "A Documentary History of the Faith and Order Movement 1927-1963", Ed. Lukas Vischer, The Bethany Press, St. Louis, Missouri 1963, and the official reports of the Montreal Conference on Faith and Order and of the Fourth Assembly at Uppsala. We shall adopt the following abbreviations for the quotations:

La   Lausanne Conference 1927
Ed   Edinburgh Conference 1937
Am   Amsterdam Assembly 1948
Lu   Lund Conference 1952
Ev   Evanston Assembly 1954
ND   New Delhi Assembly 1961
Mo   Montreal Conference 1963
Up   Uppsala Assembly 1968

1. Baptism, a sacrament instituted by Christ

"All the churches have based their sacramental doctrine and order upon their belief that, according to the evidence of the New Testament, the sacraments which they accept were instituted by Christ Himself. We are agreed that Baptism and the Lord's Supper occupied from the beginning a central position in the Church's common life, and take their origin from what was said and done by Jesus during his life on earth. Sacramental teaching and practice, therefore, are rightly founded upon the record of the New Testament".[1] "The Sacraments are Christ's gift to His Church".[2]

2. Baptism, participation in the death and resurrection of Christ

"The book 'One Lord, One Baptism' has clearly shown how wide is the agreement amongst the churches with regard to baptism.[3] There, attention is focused upon the baptism with which Jesus himself was baptised (Mark 10:38). This began with his acceptance of solidarity with sinners in his baptism in the Jordan and continued as he followed the path of the Suffering Servant through passion, death and resurrection. The Spirit that came upon Jesus comes also on the Church and unites his people with him in death and resurrection, in and through the baptismal action. Participation in Christ is the central meaning of baptism".[4] "The Church gladly confesses the Holy Spirit as the Lord and giver of life... In giving this life the Holy Spirit brings sinful men through repentance and baptism into the universal fellowship of the forgiven".[5]

3. Baptism, gift of the Spirit and incorporation into the Church

"We believe that in Baptism administered with water in the name of the Father, the Son and the Holy Spirit, for the remission of sins, we are baptised by one Spirit into one body.[6] Baptism is a gift of God's redeeming love to the Church; and administered with water in the name of the Father, the Son and the Holy Spirit is a sign and seal of Christian discipleship in obedience to our Lord's command.[7] All members of the visible Church are admitted by baptism.[8] This sacrament, which binds men to Christ in community, brings to an end all human estrangements in both Church and world based on differences of race or class."[9]

4. Faith and baptism

"Faith is — necessary — for the effectual reception of Grace."[10] "We all receive his gift of baptism whereby, in faith, we are engrafted in him even while we have not yet allowed it fully to unite us with each other."[11]

"When the element of faith expressed in an individual's explicit decision for and commitment to Christ is stressed (as in believers' baptism), baptism is seen as the crowning moment and goal of the faith which turns to the Lord. From such a point of view, the presence of personal faith in the recipient of baptism is considered essential. It must be held in mind, nonetheless, that this explicit decision is rooted in and declares Christ's faithfulness unto death, the decision of the Triune God for man. The personal decision of the individual has its setting within the life and faith of the Church, and through the life and witness of the whole Church declares the faithfulness of God, the ground of all decisions of faith."

"The practice of infant baptism occurs in a context in which stress is laid upon corporate faith, upon an environment of, rather than upon the explicit decision of the recipient of baptism. Here the whole community affirms its faith in God and pledges itself to provide such an environment of faith, in the home, and in the worship, instruction and witness of the Church."

"The necessity of the baptized himself to believe is in no way diminished, far less removed. The claim and promise of the gospel are laid on the child in baptism to which a response of obedience must be owned and which must be received by faith if the fruits of baptism are to be known and to flourish in his life. Thus in the baptism of infants, the rite does not take the place of faith, but demands it."[12]

"Though disagreement remains between those who practise infant baptism and those who practise believer-baptism, all would insist that personal commitment is necessary for reponsible membership in the body of Christ. For all, moreover, baptism is related not only to the individual but also to the Church, not only to momentary experience but to life-long growth of participation in Christ. Those who have been raised by the Holy Spirit to new life in Christ are led from baptism to confirmation (or its equivalent) and to Holy Communion. The life is necessarily one of continuing struggle but also of continuing experience of grace. In faith and obedience the baptized live for the sake of Christ, of his Church, and of the world which he loves."[13] "We urge ... that because many are baptized as a social custom only, the churches should reconsider the practice of administering baptism indiscriminately."[14]

5. Minister, form and place of baptism

The churches are in agreement that if the usual minister of baptism is an ordained minister (bishop, presbyter or deacon), there are cases where a believer can baptise[15].

"We have found general agreement that the following elements should find a place within any comprehensive order of baptism:
(a) an acknowledgement of God's initiative in salvation, of his continuing faithfulness, and of our total dependence on his grace,
(b) a declaration of the forgiveness of sins in and through Christ,
(c) an invocation of the Holy Spirit,
(d) a renunciation of evil,
(e) a profession of faith in Christ,
(f) an affirmation that the person baptised is a child of God and is incorporated into the body of Christ, whereby he becomes a witness to the Gospel

These will precede or follow baptism with water in the name of the Father and of the Son and of the Holy Spirit.

We make some practical recommendations to the churches:
(a) Baptism is not solely a matter of individual concern, but is intimately connected with the corporate worship of the Church. It should normally be administered during a public service of worship so that the members of the local congregation may be reminded of their own baptism, and may welcome into their fellowship those who are baptised and whom they are to nurture in the Christian faith.

(b) In order to make baptism more prominent in the life of the congregation, the sacrament might well be administered in public on great festival occasions, as was the practice of the early Church. The use of Easter as one such occasion would emphasise the link between baptism and dying and rising with Christ" [16].

6. The uniqueness and universality of baptism

"Through baptism and faith, Christians are brought into the life of the Church universal as well as into the visible community of the local church. Our common baptism is thus a basic bond of unity by which we are called as one people to confess and serve one Lord in each place and in all the world" [17].

7. Baptism as commitment and witness to Christ

"Mutual recognition of baptism (although it goes far) is not in itself a direct means of unity forthwith. This means that we must place our conceptions of baptism in a dynamic, forward-looking perspective and ask ourselves: Where does our baptism lead us? We all agree that baptism is both God's gift and human commitment, and that it supposes a growth into the 'measure of stature of the fullness of Christ' (Eph. 4:13). By this growth the baptised believers can even now visibly manifest to the world the new race of a redeemed mankind. Common witness to our churches, to the world, to those who have not yet heard the Gospel and to those who refuse it, is our common responsibility here and now. Fellowship in witness and service may help us to discover the meaning of God's gift to all the members of his people" [18].

8. Baptism and the eucharist

"All Churches should give attention to the relationship of their theology and practice of baptism to their theology and practice of the Lord's Supper" [19]. "We must learn afresh the implications of the one Baptism for our sharing in the one Eucharist" [20].

"Our ecumenical fellowship is essentially based upon the fact that we all want to be obedient to God's commandment in being baptised 'into the body' (1 Cor. 12:13). Our failure to share in the one Table of the Lord, to live and act as one visible and united body is an obvious contradiction of the baptismal gift that we all claim to possess.

This contradiction has been explained in some cases by unjustified rationalisations and must therefore be overcome. In other cases, it reflects an obvious lack of agreement as to the true nature of the fellowship into which baptism introduces us"[21].

"The first step is the serious recognition that through baptism we are one people serving the one Lord in each place. Baptism, once performed and never repeated, leads us into the continuous worshipping life of the 'royal priesthood' (1 Peter 2:9), the people of God". "In the Holy Eucharist or Lord's Supper, constantly repeated and always including both word and sacrament, we proclaim and celebrate a memorial of the saving acts of God"[22].

NOTES

1. Ed 64.
2. Ed 65.
3. *One Lord, One Baptism*, SCM Press, London, 1960.
4. Mo 111.
5. Up I, 8.
6. La 53.
7. In Edinburgh, 1937, Baptist delegates desired to add as follows: "As regards the above statement which has been passed by their brethren who practise infant baptism the Baptists could accept it as applying to the baptism of believers, i. e. of those who are capable of making a personal confession of faith. They believe that children belong to God and that no rite is needed to assure his grace for them." This statement of the Baptists was accepted also by a representative of the Disciples of Christ on behalf of that body.
8. Ed 87.
9. Mo 115.
10. Ed 69.
11. Ev 12.
12. *One Lord, One Baptism*, pp.63f., ND 36.
13. Mo 111; Am 15.
14. Up V,30.
15. See the implications of ED 83; cf. Up V, 30 b and c.
16. Mo 112-3.
17. Mo 154.
18. ND 35, 2, 9.
19. Lu 163.
20. Ev 27.
21. ND 34.
22. Mo 183, 116.

First draft of an ecumenical agreement on ministry
(Faith and Order, June 1972, FO/72:6)

Introduction

The world conference of Faith and Order in Lausanne in 1927 reached an unanimous agreement (*nemine contradicente*) concerning the ministry as follows:

1. The ministry is a gift of God through Christ to His Church and is essential to the being and well-being of the Church.
2. The ministry is perpetually authorized and made effective through Christ and His Spirit.
3. The purpose of the ministry is to impart to men that saving and sanctifying benefits of Christ through pastoral service, the preaching of the Gospel, and the administration of the sacraments, to be made effective by faith.
4. The ministry is entrusted with the government and discipline of the Church, in whole or in part.
5. Men gifted for the work of the ministry, called by the Spirit and accepted by the Church, are commissioned through an act of ordination by prayer and the laying on of hands to exercise the function of this ministry."[1]

After having stressed this fundamental agreement, the conference of Lausanne noted the important points of difference:

"These differences concern the nature of the ministry (whether consisting of one or several orders), the nature of ordination and of the grace conferred thereby, the function and authority of bishops, and the nature of apostolic succession."[2] In a final note of the report on the ministry (section V), the Lausanne Conference made some kind of classification of the confessional traditions with regard to the four theological problems mentioned above: the nature of the ministry, sacramental essence of ordination, the role of the bishop, and apostolic succession.[3] This classification can clarify our research and permit us to state the points where our thinking did not go forward, and the points where we have made progress towards unity.

Catholic and Orthodox tradition:
a) there have always been various grades of the ministry, each with its own function (bishops, presbyters, deacons);

b) ordination is a sacramental act of divine institution, and therefore indipensable, conveying the special charisma for the particular ministry;

c) bishops who have received their office by succession from the apostles are the necessary ministers of ordination;

d) the apostolic succession so understood is necessary for the authority of the ministry, the visible unity of the Church, and the validity of the sacraments.

Protestant tradition in the broader sense

a) essentially there is only one ministry, that of the Word and Sacraments;

b) the grace which fits men for the ministry is immediately given by God, and is recognised, not conferred, in ordination;

c) no particular form of ministry is necessary to be received as a matter of faith;

d) the ministries agreeable to the New Testament, are proved by their fruits and have due authority in the Church, and the sacraments ministered by them are valid.

Episcopal non-Catholic tradition

dd) the apostolic succession, as it is defined and stated by Catholics and Orthodox, is not a vital element of episcopacy; the historic episcopate is not essential.

Presbyterian Tradition

ddd) the apostolic ministry is transmissible and has been transmitted through presbyters orderly associated for the purpose.

This classification of the theological positions in 1927 still covers well the points of current views among the different churches. As concerns the ministry, have we made as much progress as we have seen in relation to baptism and eucharist? We are pressed by the urgency to find a solution, in view of the reconciliation of the ministries and of partaking in the same eucharist. The Louvain Report on the ministry has marked an important step which permits us to hope for an ecumenical agreement similar to those on baptism and eucharist.[4]

I. Christ, unique mediator between God and man: priest, prophet and king

"The redemptive work of Christ has its origin in the mission given by the Father to the Son, and willed by the Son with the Father in the Holy Spirit. In accordance with the purpose of God, prepared and foretold under the covenant with Israel, and by the power of the Holy Spirit, the Son became man, proclaimed the kingdom of God with power, was crucified, died, rose again, and lives eternally as Lord. In this person, this history and this work, God was in Christ has thus accomplished, he has accomplished once for all."[5]

"Jesus Christ is the king of the new people of God. He is 'the chief cornerstone in which the whole building, fitly framed together, grows up into a holy temple in the Lord'. He is the head of the Church which is his Body. Through his Spirit Jesus Christ himself is present in his Church. Christ lives in his Church and the Church lives in Christ. Christ is never without his Church; the Church is never without Christ. Both belong inseparably together, the king and his people, the keystone and the temple, the head and the body. As members of his body also. What has happened to Christ uniquely in his once-and-for-all death and resurrection on our behalf, happens also to the Church in its way as his body. As the Church is made a partaker in the crucified body of Christ, so also it is given to be partaker in the risen body of the same Lord. This means that the Church is called to continue the mission of Jesus Christ to the world, so that the way of Christ is the way of His Church."[6]

II. The Church, sign of the relation between Christ and the world: the royal and prophetic priesthood of the people of God

"The Lord Jesus Christ, through his word and spirit, calls his Church from the world. He forgives sins, delivers men from the lordship of the powers of destruction and gathers out of this broken world the one People of God, the community of the justified and sanctified whose citizenship is in heaven and whose life is hid with Christ in God.

Jesus Christ through his word and spirit sends his Church into the world to be the salt of the earth and the light of the world. That is, as prophet, priest and king he gives his Church to participate in his ministry of reconciliation, constraining it by his love to enter into his passion for the redemption of the world, and empowering it by his Spirit to proclaim the gospel of salvation to all nations, calling them to obey the will of God in all the areas of political and social and cultural life and to live out in the divisions of the world the life of the one people of God, so that through its witness Jesus Christ is at work among men as Saviour, and brings all things in subjection under himself as Lord and king of the world.

By calling and sending his people, by granting them manifold spiritual gifts for the ministry, Jesus Christ builds up his Church as the living temple of God. Thus the Church as the body of Christ 'grows up into him in all things who is the head from whom the whole body fitly joined together and compacted by that which every joint supplieth according to the effective working in the measure of every part, maketh increase of the body unto the edifying of itself in love'."[7]

"The Church, the people chosen by God, is the community of those who have been gathered in faith by the apostolic preaching and by the power of the Spirit and have been plunged into the waters of baptism. It belongs to Christ, as his own body confesses him, worships him and obeys him, as the redeemer of the world. Taken from the world and set in the world, it constitutes there the royal priesthood declaring the wonderful deeds of God, and offering to him as a sacrifice both worship and daily life."[8]

III. The Church in relation with the apostles: the apostolic succession

"In order that his redemptive work might be proclaimed and attested to the needs of the earth, and that its fruits might be communicated to man, Christ chose apostles, witnesses of his resurrection, and committed to them the word of reconciliation. Having clothed them with the Holy Spirit he sent them to gather all nations into the Church and to build it upon the one foundation which is no other than himself, and to inaugurate the ministry of the accomplished reconciliation for the salvation of all men. Thus the whole Church and its special ministry have their origin in the sending of the apostles.

The unique witness of the apostles to Christ is preserved by the Church in the New Testament. Their mission is continued by the Church and its ministry.[9]

"The orderly transmission of authority in ordination is normally an essential part of the means by which the Church is kept from generation to generation in the apostolic faith. All of us regard this continuity in the apostolic faith as essential to the Church."[10]

"The Church is by its very nature apostolic because it is the body of Christ, the envoy of the Father who sends it in its turn to the world in the power of the Spirit.

This apostolicity of the Church is based upon Christ's sending of the apostles as his ambassadors (2 Cor. 5:18-20). After the apostles the apostolic responsibility continues to be exercised in the Church on the basis established by the apostles and this exercise of responsibility must remain in every respect faithful to the deposit transmitted by them; there is an apostolic succession therefore.

This successsion should be understood in the context of the permanence of the Church in its entirety, which throughout history bears the responsibility of proclaiming the Gospel, celebrating the sacraments gathering men into fellowship with Christ, conducting a dialogue with the world with a view to mutually exchanging the gifts which the Lord bestows on each.

This apostolic succession is attested and signified by the continuity of transmissible elements in the apostolic responsibility such as the apostles entrusted to ministers instituted by the Lord, called by his Spirit, and recognized and ordained in the Church.

The fullness of the succession implies continuity in the transmission of the ministerial responsibility, fidelity of what is taught to the apostolic teaching and a life in accord with the Gospel and the requirements of the Church's mission.

In the Catholic Church continuity of ministerial responsibility is assured by the episcopate, and in the Reformed Churches by the presbyterate.[11] At this point two questions arise for the various churches:

a) How can the Catholic Church recognize a presbyteral succession and reconcile it with the episcopal succession?

b) How can the Reformed Churches rediscover the necessity of the episcopal succession without denying the gifts received through the presbyteral succession?"[12]

IV. The ministry, sign of the relation between Christ and church

"In order to build up the Church and to equip it for its mission, the Lord Jesus Christ has given ministers who, following the apostles and by the power of the Spirit, serve to the accomplished reconciliation ... by announcing, attesting and communicating that reconciliation by the means which the Lord has given.

All ministry in the Church is rooted in the ministry of Christ himself, who glorifies the Father in the power of the Holy Spirit. Christ stirs up, calls, strengthens and sends those whom he has chosen for the whole ministry of his Church and for the special ministry, making them the instrument of his message and of his work. Ministers are called to serve the work of the Lord by following him, by being conformed to him, and by announcing his name.

The special ministry thus reflects and serves the redemptive love of Christ.

a) Christ is Prophet; his Church is called to be his witness, announcing to the world by word and deed the good news of the word made flesh, of the accomplished reconciliation, and of the kingdom which comes. That it may truly be so, the ministers are set in its midst to proclaim him.

b) Christ is high priest; his Church is called to be the true priesthood in the world, holding out to all men the gift of the reconciliation which he has purchased, and offering up on behalf of all men both sacrifice of praise, thanksgiving and obedience, and the prayer of penitence and intercession. That it may truly be so, the ministers are set for the priestly service of the Gospel in the midst of the priestly people.

c) Christ is king; his whole Church is called to be the sign of his kingdom in the midst of the world, the evidence to men that the devil is conquered and that God reigns. That it may truly be so, the ministers are set in the midst to be the servants of the king, guarding his people in their unity one with another and with him, leading them in their spiritual warfare, and equipping them with all the armour of God.

In these ways the ministers are the servants of the servant of God and thus share in his suffering and in his joy."[13]

V. The distinctive character and content of ministry

The distinctive character of the Christian ministry is to be a service of Christ, prophet, priest and king, within the royal and prophetic priesthood of the baptized people, to help this people to grow in the fellowship of the Holy Spirit by means of the word and sacraments.

The ordained minister is at once ambassador, liturgist and pastor in Christ's name, according to three New Testament passages: 2 Cor. 5:18-20, Rom. 15:16 and 1 Pet. 5:1-4.

"Ministers are given to the Church as the Lord's messengers, watchmen and stewards, and as such they have to give an account to him of their stewardship."[14]

"Thus, the ordained minister:

a) gathers together and builds up the community for its mission in the world;

b) proclaims in word and deed the good news of God's reconciliation in Christ;

c) presides over the liturgical and sacramental life of the eucharistic community."[15]

This distinctive threefold function of the ministry within the universal priesthood of the baptized finds supreme expression in the celebration of the eucharist, at the heart of the Church's life.

"The ministry demonstrates that the congregation is not the proprietor of the rite it is engaged in performing, that it is not the master of the eucharist: it receives it from another, the living Christ present in his Church. While the minister remains a member of the congregation, he is also an envoy pointing to the initiative of God and a link between the local community and the other communities within the universal Church.

By their mutual relationships, the eucharistic congregation and its president give living expression to their dependence on the one Lord and high priest. In its relationship to the ministry, the congregation fulfils its royal priesthood as a gift of Christ the priest. In his relation to the congregation the minister fulfils his presidency as a service of Christ the Pastor."[16]

VI. The diversity of ministries

"Some churches recognize seven orders in the special ministry, some three, some only one. But the threefold pattern (bishop, presbyter, deacon) is also found (e.g. in the form of pastor, elder, deacon) in churches which normally speak of only one order in the special ministry. There is need both for discussion between the churches about these differing traditions, and also for self-examination within our churches about the way in which we have received and used the gift of ministry. For example, we must ask ourselves such questions as the following:

a) Granted that there is an essential ministry given to the Church by the Lord, does the traditional pattern of ministry, in our churches do justice to the variety of the gift of the Spirit?

b) Have churches which follow the pattern 'bishop, priest, deacon' in fact preserved the specific character of each of these orders of ministry as taught in their formularies? Do churches which have the pattern 'pastor, elder, deacon' (or some similar pattern) preserve the ministerial character of each? On what theological principle are elders (presbyters) or deacons included in, or excluded from, the special ministry?

c) While in all our churches men and women are set aside for limited periods for some forms of ministry, ordination to the special ministry is almost universally regarded as being for life. What are the grounds for this?

d) The following qualifications for the special ministry have by no means always been regarded as indispensable: academic training, full-time service, salary. Are they treated as indispensable in our churches today, and if so, on what grounds? How are these aspects of the ministry related to the fundamental theology of the ministry?" [17]

"There are several possibilities of more flexible forms of ministry in the light of experiments, for example:

a) The Church may ordain a man who works in a secular employment but has shown pastoral gifts, he will serve the local congregtion as a pastor, while continuing his secular work...

b) In some sectors of society which are impenetrable to existing forms of ministry (such as certain areas of industrial life, where groups of Christians are learning to work and witness in terms of the conditions of life there), the best way to ensure the full witness of the Gospel may be to ordain members of these groups to the ministry of word and sacraments after appropriate training, so that they may build up the body of Christ...

c) In a frontier situation, where there is no Christian community among the people, the Church may select a minister and send him into some secular employment so that he becomes a part of the community and within it seeks to witness and to form the community of God's people, the Church." [18]

VII. Ordination, sacramental epiklesis

"It may be said that the Church, in ordaining new persons to ministry in Christ's name, is attempting to follow the mission of the apostles and remain faithful to their teaching; ordination as an act attests the binding of the church to the historical Jesus and the historical revelation, at the same time recalling that it is the Risen Lord who is the true ordainer, who bestows the gift. In ordaining, the church attempts to provide for the faithful proclamation of the Gospel and humble service in Christ's name. The laying on of hands in ordination can be seen as the sign witnessing to the connection of the church and its ministry with Christ, binding the ministry to a conscious awareness of its anchorage and roots in the revelation accomplished in him, reminding it to look to him as the source of its commission."[19]

"The authority (*exousia*) of the ordained minister is not his own but is the sign and instrument of the authority of Christ received within the whole community.

Ordination is at one and the same time:

a) an invocation to God that he bestow the gifts of the Holy Spirit for ministry;
b) a sign of the granting of this prayer by the Lord;
c) a reception by the Church of the minister who is consecrated to the service of God;
d) a commitment by the minister to the ministry entrusted to him."[20]

Summing up, it can be affirmed, therefore, that there exists an ecumenical consensus that ordination is *epiklesis, sacramental sign and commitment.*

"The ordained ministry is permanent in virtue of its fundamental structure as service of the gospel, of the sacraments and of the congregation. The forms of ministry may vary according to the needs of the church and the missions which it entrusts. The ordained ministry may be interrupted by leave of absence, long or short, without any question of reordination in order for it to be resumed. While ordination signifies a difference of gifts between the minister and the priesthood of the baptized, it in no way separates the ministers from the people of God."[21]

Conclusion

"The church with all her ministries lives continuously in history as a pilgrim people among all the communities of mankind, in obedience to Christ and in a constant solidarity with the world. This means that the Church with repentance and renewal, with the hope and joy which Jesus gives, is always ready to be reshaped in the forms of its ministry according to his call at each stage of the pilgrim life."[22]

NOTES

1. Lausanne 34; we quote the references according to the numbering of L. Vischer, *Faith and Order*, St Louis, The Bethany Press, 1963.
2. La. 36.
3. La. 44-47.
4. Cf. the two consensus received at Louvain 1972.
5. Montreal 83.
6. Lund 10.
7. Lu. 14-16.
8. Mo. 86.
9. Mo 84-85.
10. Mo. 95.
11. "In the Episcopal churches this succession has been conceived at the same time as the succession of bishops in the principal sees of Christendom, handing down and preserving the Apostles doctrine, and as a succession by laying-on of hands. From early times this double succession has been associated with the stewardship of the sacraments, and is regarded by certain churches as constituing the sure and only guaranteee of sacramental grace and right doctrine."
    "The confessions of the Presbyterian and Reformed traditions are of the opinion that the true Apostolic Succession is manifested in a succession of ordination by presbyteries duly constituted and exercising episcopal functions, and in the succession of presbyters in charge of parishes, with special emphasis on the true preaching of the Word and the right administration of the Sacraments." Edinburgh 98-101.
12. Dombes 1972.
13. Mo. 87-89.
14. Mo. 98.
15. Louvain, final report of Committee III : Note on "The Ordained Ministry", *Faith and Order Paper* No. 59, pp.223-224.
16. Groupe des Dombes, *Vers une même foi eucharistique?*, Accord entre catholiques et protestants? Presses de Taizé, 1972, 35-35, pp.26-27.
17. Mo. 95.
18. Mo. 102.
19. Louvain, preparatory report, I, "The Ordained Ministry", *Faith and Order Paper* No. 59, pp.81-84.
20. Louvain, final report, Committee III, Note on "The Ordained Ministry", *Faith and Order Paper* No. 59, pp.223-224; cf. Lausanne 34 and Edinburgh 93.
21. Dombes 1972.
22. Mo. 103-104.

APPENDIX II

The eucharistic liturgy of Lima

Introduction

This liturgy was prepared for the plenary session of the Faith and Order Commission in Lima and was used for the first time there on 15 January 1982. It was also used in the Ecumenical Centre Chapel in Geneva on 28 July 1982 during the meeting of the Central Committee of the World Council of Churches, with Dr Philip Potter, the General Secretary, as the presiding minister. It will also be used at the Sixth Assembly of the World Council of Churches in Vancouver in 1983.

In composing this liturgy for the Lima Conference, the aim was to illustrate the solid theological achievements of the Faith and Order document, *Baptism, Eucharist and Ministry* (cited henceforth as BEM). The Lima liturgy is not the only possibility: the convergences registered in BEM could be expressed in other liturgical forms, according to other traditions, spiritualities or cultures. No "authority" attaches to this particular liturgy, save that accruing to it from the fact of its having been used on certain significant ecumenical occasions.

Celebration and celebrants

The Lima liturgy is characterized by its fullness and is perhaps more suitable for a particularly solemn celebration. It has already been used in a simplified form by a number of groups. Some examples of possible simplification will be given at the end of this introduction.

According to the indications given in the BEM document, the Christian liturgy should be regularly celebrated, at least every Lord's Day and on feast days. This eucharistic celebration will include the proclamation of the Word of God and the communion of the members of the Body of Christ in the power of the Holy Spirit (E31). The eucharistic liturgy thus consists of three parts. The introductory part unites the people of God in confession, supplication and praise (confession of sins, litany of the *Kyrie*, and the *Gloria*). The second part, the liturgy of the Word, begins with a prayer of preparation. It includes the three proclamations: of a prophet (first lesson), an apostle (second lesson), and Christ (the Gospel). Then the voice of the Church is heard in the sermon, making the eternal word contemporary and living. The sermon is followed by silent meditation. The faith of the Church is then summarized in the Creed and all human needs presented to God in the intercession. The third part, the liturgy of the eucharist, consists essentially of the great eucharistic prayer, preceded by a short preparation and followed by the Lord's Prayer, the sign of peace, and communion. We shall return to these elements in more detail. (They are listed in E27.)

The liturgy is an act of the community. This is even indicated in the etymology of the term "liturgy" — *leitourgia* — service of the people. It is not a clerical solo performance but a *concert* of the whole Christian community, in which certain of its members play a special part, in accordance with their different charisms and mandates. At ecumenical meetings, the liturgy of the Word will be shared by worship leaders (officiants) of several traditions, while the liturgy of the eucharist will associate as assistants of the principal celebrant those authorized by their own church to concelebrate on such occasions.

Normally the *presiding pastor* at the liturgy (bishop or presbyter, M29-30) gives the salutation, the absolution and the prayer; the pastor leads the liturgy of the Eucharist by praying the great eucharistic prayer: the preface, the *epiclesis* (I and II), the institution, the *anamnesis* and the conclusion; the pastor also offers the prayer of thanksgiving and gives the benediction. The *congregation* sings or says all the responses and the Amens; it recites together the confession, the Gloria (or it alternates with an officiant, unless it is sung), the Creed (said or sung) and the Lord's Prayer (said or sung). The biddings in the litany of the Kyrie and in the intercessions, the verses of the Gloria, the preparation and the mementos, the introduction to the Lord's Prayer and the prayer of peace, may be shared among *other officiants*. Three *readers* are assigned to read the lessons (the Gospel is read or sung by a deacon in the Orthodox, Roman Catholic and Anglican traditions); a *preacher* is assigned to deliver the sermon.

Sources and meanings

The entry hymn which accompanies the procession of the officiants, or even of the entire community, should preferably be a psalm, appropriate to the liturgical season or the festival being celebrated, punctuated by a suitable antiphon, simple enough for all to join in between the verses sung by the choir. On the first Sunday in Advent, for example, the entry hymn is Psalm 25, with the antiphon:

To you, Lord, I lift my heart;
They whose hope is in you will not be disappointed.

The psalm may, however, be replaced by a chorale or a hymn whose liturgical use is well-attested. In the Lutheran tradition, for example, the chorales mark certain Sundays. When the procession ends, the Gloria is sung ("Glory be to the Father and to the Son and to the Holy Spirit...") and the antiphon is repeated a last time.

The principal celebrant then gives the salutation, a custom which probably goes back to primitive liturgical usage, and the text for which is provided for us by St Paul (2 Cor. 13:13). It was restored to favour in the revised post-conciliar Roman Catholic liturgy, and it often forms part of Reformed and Lutheran celebrations.

The confession, said by the whole congregation, is followed by the absolution pronounced by the principal celebrant. Both have been taken from the *Lutheran Book of Worship* published by the Joint Lutheran Liturgical Commission for the churches in the United States and Canada.[1]

Slight alterations have been made in the English text to employ more inclusive language.

The litany of the Kyrie is a brief initial supplication. This litany derives traditionally from the Byzantine Liturgy which always begins with it. Here, however, it is shorter, containing only three petitions on the themes of baptism, eucharist and ministry, which take their cue from three New Testament passages: Eph. 4:3-5, 1 Cor. 10:16-17 and 2 Cor. 5:18-20. These petitions may be altered to suit the circumstances. Provision could also be made for penitential petitions in place of the confession, and these would then come immediately after the salutation.

The form used in the revised Roman Catholic liturgy is familiar:

Lord Jesus, sent by the Father
to heal and save us all,
have mercy on us.
— *Kyrie eleison.*

O Christ, who came into the world
to call all sinners,
have mercy on us.
— *Kyrie eleison.*

Lord, lifted up into the glory of the Father
where Thou dost intercede for us,
have mercy on us.
— *Kyrie eleision.*

May the almighty God
have mercy on us all;
may He pardon our sins
and bring us to eternal life.
— *Amen.*

The opening litany of the Orthodox Liturgy of St John Chrysostom could also be used.

This litany of supplication is followed by the hymn of praise: "Glory to God in the highest..." From the beginning of the liturgy, therefore, place is provided for the three fundamental attitudes of Christian prayer: penitence, supplication and praise.

The liturgy of the Word opens with prayer. In contemplation, preparation is made for hearing the Word of God. This prayer varies according to seasons, festivals and circumstances. Here it is based on the themes of the BEM document. It evokes Jesus' baptism in the River Jordan, the messianic *anointing* of Christ who is consecrated prophet, priest and king. It asks for a fresh outpouring of the Spirit upon the *baptized*, the deepening of desire for communion with Christ in the *eucharist*, and consecration to the *service* of the poor and those in special need of Christian love.

The first reading is taken either from the Old Testament, or from the Acts of the Apostles or the Book of Revelation. At Lima, the passage chosen was Ezekiel 47:1-9, on the water flowing from the source in the Temple, recalling the baptismal immersion which purifies, cleanses and gives life. The meditative hymn which follows is usually the fragment of a psalm, sung responsively. Appropriate verses to follow this Ezekiel passage about the life-giving water would be Psalm 42:2-3, 8-9, with the antiphon taken from Ezekiel 36:25:

I will sprinkle clean water upon you
and will cleanse you from all your uncleannesses.

The second reading is a short passage from one of the Epistles. At Lima it was 1 Peter 5:1-11, on the theme of ministry. The Alleluia then sounds out as an acclamation of welcome to the Gospel. For example:

Alleluia! Alleluia!
The disciples of Emmaus
recognized the Risen Lord
in the breaking of the bread. Alleluia!

The Gospel is then read by a deacon or a third reader. At Lima the Emmaus passage from Lk. 24:25-32 was read, on the theme of the eucharistic meal preceded by Christ's exposition of the Scriptures.

The sermon applies the message of the Word of God to our life today. It is the voice of the Church, echoing that of the prophets, apostles and Christ. A moment of silent recollection gives time for each to meditate on the Word received.

The Creed is then said or sung as a résumé of the history of salvation. Either the Nicaeno-Constantinopolitan (Nicene) Creed or the Apostles' Creed may be used. In an ecumenical spirit of fidelity to the original text of the Nicene Creed, we use here that form approved at the Council of Constantinople in 381, as was done at the Lima Conference and at the WCC Central Committee meeting in Geneva. The 1600th commemoration of this Council in 1981 by and large restored this primitive text to its rightful place of honour, reconciling East and West in the expression of fundamental faith.

The prayer of intercession unites the believing community, now nourished by the Word of God, in prayer for the needs of the Church and the world. The pattern and style adopted here are those of the litany of Pope Gelasius (+ 496) which reflects the Kyrie in use in Rome at the end of the fifth century.[2] The themes of the six intentions include the outpouring of the Spirit on the Church; the leaders of the nations, justice and peace; the oppressed and all the victims of violence; then (following the BEM themes) the unity of the churches in baptism; the communion of the churches around the one table; the mutual recognition of ministries by the churches.

The liturgy of the Eucharist begins with the presentation of the bread and wine, accompanied by two benedictions from the Jewish liturgy (also used in the revised Roman Catholic liturgy), and by a prayer inspired by the *Didache*. This preparation is completed by the very ancient eucharistic acclamation *"Maranatha"* ("Come, Lord!" or "The Lord is coming", 1 Cor. 16:22).

The great eucharistic prayer begins with a composite preface, which also take its themes from the BEM document. First of all, thanksgiving for creation is focused on the life-giving Word, giving life in particular to the human being who reflects the glory of God. In the fullness of time Christ was given as the way, the truth and the life. In the account of Jesus' life, the preface recalls the consecration of the Servant by baptism, the last supper of the eucharist, the memorial of the death and resurrection, and the presence of the Risen Saviour in the breaking of the bread. Finally, the preface refers to the gift of the royal priesthood to all Christians, from among whom God chooses ministers who are charged to feed the Church by the Word and sacraments and thereby to give it life.

In conformity with the Alexandrian and Roman traditions, the invocation of the Holy Spirit (the *epiclesis*) precedes the words of the institution of the Holy Supper.[3] The reminder of the work of the Holy Spirit in the history of our salvation is inspired by the liturgy of St James, (4th century). This is also used in the liturgy of the Evangelical Lutheran Church of France (1977, alternative VIII). The *epiclesis* asks for the Holy Spirit to be poured out, as on Moses and the prophets, on the Virgin Mary, on Jesus at the River Jordan, and on the apostles at Pentecost, to transfigure the thanksgiving meal, so that the bread and the wine become for us the Body and the Blood of Christ. The idea of transfiguration by the Spirit of life and fire is intended to point to the consecration of the bread and wine in a sacramental and mystical manner transcending all our understanding and all our explanation (E14-15). The congregation punctuates this *epiclesis* with the sung response: "Veni Creator Spiritus — Come, Creator Spirit!"

Just as the beginning of the *epiclesis* took up the themes of the preceding *Sanctus* (O God, Lord of the *universe*, you are *holy* and your *glory* is beyond measure), so too the beginning of the institution links up with the *epiclesis* and to its response, by referring to the Holy Spirit. This indicates the unity of the action of the Spirit and of Christ in the eucharistic mystery. The Holy Spirit accomplishes the words of the Son who, "on the night in which he was betrayed, took bread..." By the Holy Spirit, these historical words of Jesus become alive and contemporary: bread and wine become the Body and the Blood of Christ. "The Holy Spirit makes the crucified and risen Christ really present to us in the eucharistic meal, fulfilling the promise contained in the words of institution" (E14). The Holy Spirit "makes the historical words of Jesus present and alive" (E14). The blessing of the bread and the cup is accompanied, as in the Jewish liturgy, the passover meal in particular, by thanksgiving. The rendering of "Do this for the remembrance of me" is preferred in order to avoid the subjective idea of a mere souvenir. The eucharist is a memorial, an *anamnesis*, i. e. making present and alive the saving event of the cross and the presentation of Christ's unique sacrifice to the Father as an urgent prayer of the Church. The acclamation which concludes the institution has been adopted in many recent liturgical revisions: Roman Catholic, Anglican, Swedish, American Lutheran. It associates the congregation with the proclamation of the memorial. The *anamnesis* is the celebration of the "memorial of our redemption". The sacrifice of the cross and resurrection, made present and active for us today in the eucharist, is central in the *anamnesis*. But, as the BEM document says, what is recalled in thanksgiving in the eucharist is the whole existence of Christ (E6).

In the present liturgy, certain events are emphasized because they correspond to the BEM themes: the baptism of Jesus, his last meal with the apostles, his ministry as High Priest who makes intercession for us all. In the eucharist the whole people of God are united with Christ's unique priesthood, each member in accordance with the charism and ministry received. We present the memorial of Christ, i.e. we show forth to the Father the unique sacrifice of the Son as the urgent supplication of the Church and we say to God: "Do you remember the sacrifice of the cross and, in virtue of this unique sacrifice, source of all blessings, grant us and all human beings the abundance of blessings obtained for us in the work of salvation and liberation accomplished by Jesus Christ." This is the *anamnesis* or memorial, the making of the unique sacrifice livingly present and the intercession that the Father may remember Christ's work on our behalf. The eschatological acclamation is uttered as an act of faith affirming the coming of the Lord: "*Maranatha*"!

The eucharist, given in the Spirit to the church as a precious gift, is received by the Father as an intercession and a thanksgiving, one with the very offering of the Son which reestablishes us in the covenant with God.

In a very beautiful text of 1520, Luther showed how the intercession of Christ and the offering of the Church are intimately united in the eucharist:

It is not we who offer Christ, but Christ who offers us (to the Father). In this way, it is permissible, indeed helpful, to call the ceremony a sacrifice; not in itself, but because in it we offer ourselves in sacrifice with Christ. In other words, we lean on Christ with a firm faith in his covenant, and we present ourselves before God with our prayer, thanksgiving and sacrifice, only in the name of Christ and by his mediation... without doubting that He is our Priest in heaven before the face of God. Christ welcomes us, he presents us, ourselves, our prayers and our praise (to God); he also offers himself in heaven for us... He offers himself for us in heaven and with himself, he offers us.[4]

A second *epiclesis* then invokes the Holy Spirit on the congregation, a fresh outpouring consequent on communion in the Body and Blood of Christ. This effusion of the Spirit rallies together the Body of Christ, the Church, and inspires it to spiritual unity; it makes the congregation a living offering to the glory of God; it anticipates the coming Kingdom. Here, once again, the eucharistic prayer is punctuated by an acclamation: either the response "Veni Creator Spiritus", echoing the second *epiclesis*, or, once again, the eschatological *"Maranatha"*.

According to the Western tradition, this is where we mention all those for whom we wish especially to pray, remember those who preceded us in the faith, and all the cloud of witnesses by whom we are compassed about. These *mementos* make explicit our concern for the whole Christian community on which the Holy Spirit has just been invoked, which explains their location here after the second *epiclesis*. In a shorter liturgy they could be omitted and their content transferred to the moment of intercession (No 16). The wording of the *mementos* is inspired by the Eucharistic Prayer III in the draft text "Word, Bread and Cup".[5] After a final *"Maranatha"*, the eucharistic prayer is rounded off by a trinitarian conclusion, traditional in Western liturgies.

The introduction to the Lord's Prayer recalls the unity of all Christians in baptism, which incorporates them into the Body of Christ and gives them life by the one Spirit. This unity of Christians permits them to say together the prayer of the children of God, the Lord's Prayer. It also permits them to renew among themselves the peace of Christ and they give each other a sign of reconciliation and friendship.

The breaking of the bread during the *Agnus Dei* hymn is announced in the manner of the Reformed tradition: "The bread which we break is the communion in the body of Christ..." (1 Cor. 10:16).

In the prayer of thanksgiving we give thanks to God for the unity of baptism and the joy of the eucharist; we pray for full visible unity and for recogniton of the signs of reconciliaton already given; finally, we pray in hope that those who have already tasted of the meal of the Kingdom may also share the heritage of the saints in light (Col. 1:12). After the final hymn before the benediction, the presiding minister may give a brief message of dispatch on mission, for example, by repeating the central biblical text on which the sermon was preached.

Possible simplifications

This eucharistic liturgy may also be shortened in order to adapt it to different circumstances.

The introductory part may consist only of the hymn, the salutation, the litany of the Kyrie and the Gloria (1-2, 5-6), omitting the confession. It may even consist simply of a hymn — a psalm or Gloria — and then go straight into the prayer (1 or 6, then 7).

The liturgy of the Word always begins with a prayer, suited to the season, the festival or circumstances. There may be only two lessons instead of three: the first lesson or the Epistle, and always the Gospel. Between the two readings a psalm and alleluia, or simply the alleluia, may be sung. The sermon should always focus on some aspect of the message of the Word of God. The Creed has not always formed part of the eucharistic liturgy and it may be reserved for Sundays and feast days. A choice may be made between the intercession (16) and the *mementos* (25), using only one or the other. This would then give the simplified pattern: sermon, silence, preparation for the eucharist (13, 14, 17).

The liturgy of the Eucharist always begins with preparation (17). It necessarily includes the following elements: the preface (19) adapted to the season, festival or circumstances, and permissibly in a shorter version; the first and second *epiclesis* (21 and 24); the institution (22); the *anamnesis* (23) and the conclusion (26). The *mementos* may be omitted if already integrated in the intercession (16). The prayer of peace after the Lord's Prayer can be omitted, retaining only the announcement: "The peace of the Lord be with you always..." (28).

The prayer of thanksgiving may be a free prayer, provided it is always brief and well-structured. The liturgy ends with a final hymn, if possible, by a brief word of dispatch on mission, according to the occasion, and by the benediction.

The Eucharist at the centre of the community and its mission

The life of the first Christian community is described in the Acts of the Apostles as follows: "And they devoted themselves to the apostles' teaching and fellowship, to the breaking of the bread and prayers... And day by day, attending the temple together and breaking the bread in their homes, they partook of food with glad and generous hearts, praising God and having favour with all the people. And the Lord added to their number day by day those who were being saved" (2:42-47).

These verses epitomize the whole life of the Church through the ages. The Church will assume different faces through the centuries but only if these fundamental elements are found within it will it truly be the Church of Christ. We have here the model by which it will be able to measure this fidelity in the course of history. All periods of renewal in the Church will be due to the return to these original springs.

In this description of the primitive Christian community, seven elements may be discerned which must always be respected by the Church if it is to remain faithful to its origins and keep within the succession of Christ's purpose and of the apostolic foundation: the hearing of the Word of God, the celebration of the breaking of the bread, the offering of prayers, concern for communion as brothers and sisters, the sharing of material blessings, the unity of praising God and witnessing in the world, and the mission accomplished by the Lord who builds the church and increases it.

The Christian community is born of the hearing of the Word of God: the reading of the Bible and the preaching of the Word. Thanks to the meditation on this living Word, it is gradually built up and strengthened. The Holy Scriptures, read, preached and meditated on, distinguish the Christian community radically from every other human society or religious group. The increasing assimilation of the main themes of the Word transforms the community; it becomes a place of liberation, peace, joy, celebration, friendship, influence and hope... The Church cannot live unless it constantly returns to this life-giving source, the Word of God. This is why its worship is focused on the reading of the prophets and apostles, on the proclamation of the Gospel of Christ, on the preaching of and reverent reflection on the Truth in the Spirit. This Word of God feeds the Christian community and makes it grow; it makes it a centre of attraction and it sends it out into the world to announce the glad tidings.

On Easter evening, the Risen Lord, joining his disciples on their way to Emmaus, interpreted to them the things concerning himself in all the scriptures. His Word prepared their hearts to recognize him. But it was when he sat at table with them, when he took the bread, blessed it and gave thanks, that their eyes were opened and their hearts, set on fire by his Word, recognized him in the breaking of the bread (Lk. 24:27-32).

This is why, when the Church celebrates the presence of the Risen Lord in its midst, chiefly on the Lord's Day, it proclaims his Word and is fed in the thanksgiving Meal: it recognizes him in the Scriptures and in the Breaking of the bread. Thus the complete Christian liturgy includes the proclamation of the Word of God and the celebration of the Eucharist.

This proclamation and this celebration are surrounded by the prayers of the Church. The first Christians "devoted themselves to... the prayers" and "they attended the temple day by day". The primitive Church continued the discipline of Jewish prayers. It wished to observe day by day, with regularity, "the prayers of the hours", in the Temple in Jerusalem, which would be at the origin of the liturgy of the daily office. This liturgy included the singing of psalms, the reading of the Word, and intercessions. This regular offering of prayers by the Christian community seals the communion of the Church and constitutes a sacrifice of praise and intercession in which its communion with God is constantly renewed.

Brotherly and sisterly communion and concord are the consequences of this relationship between the community and its Lord by means of the Word, Eucharist, and Prayer. They are the marks of an authentic ecclesial life. They are expressed concretely in such actions as the *agape* meals when Christians take food together and share their material possessions with those in need. Joy and simplicity are the distinctive marks of this communion of solidarity among brothers and sisters. There is no contradiction between the praise of God and presence in the world; the one does not detach us from the other. The community whose primary work is the celebration of the praise of God is welcomed by the people around it, because it is one of brotherhood and sisterhood, simple and joyous.

The Eucharist is at the very heart of the Church's life. With the Word and the prayers, it creates the communion of brothers and sisters, their sharing with one another, and makes the community present for the world and radiant with Christ. The eucharist builds up the Church, in unity and for the world, and makes it the missionary Church.

MAX THURIAN

NOTES

1. *Lutheran Book of Worship*, Minneapolis, Augsburg Publishing House, Minister's Edition, 1978, p.195.
2. B. Capelle, "Le Kyrie de la messe et le pape Gélase", *Revue Bénédictine*, 1934, pp.136-138. A. Hamman, *Prières des premiers chrétiens*, Paris, Fayard, 1952, pp.349-352.
3. *Fragment of Der-Balyzeh* (sixth century), attesting the liturgy of St Mark; *Quam oblationem* of the Roman Canon and *epiclesis* of the new liturgical prayers. See my book, *Le mystère eucharistique*, Paris, Centurion-Taizé, 1981, pp.89-99, to be published by Mowbray, Oxford, 1983.
4. *WA* VI, 369.
5. Consultation on Church Union, USA.

THE EUCHARIST

Liturgy of entrance

1 ENTRANCE PSALM (with antiphon and Gloria Patri; or hymn)

2 GREETING*

P. The grace of our Lord Jesus Christ,
the love of God,
and the communion of the Holy Spirit
be with you all.

C. *And also with you.*

---

* P = Presiding Minister
C = Congregation
O = Another Celebrant

3 CONFESSION

 C. *Most merciful God,*
  we confess that we are in bondage to sin
  and cannot free ourselves.
  We have sinned against you
  in thought, word and deed,
  by what we have done
  and by what we have left undone.
  We have not loved you with our whole heart;
  we have not loved our neighbours as ourselves.
  For the sake of your Son, Jesus Christ, have mercy on us.
  Forgive us, renew us, and lead us,
  so that we may delight in your will
  and walk in your ways,
  to the glory of your holy name. Amen.

4 ABSOLUTION

 P. Almighty God
  gave Jesus Christ to die for us
  and for the sake of Christ forgives us all our sins.
  As a called and ordained minister of the Church
  and by the authority of Jesus Christ,
  I therefore declare to you
  the entire forgiveness of all your sins,
  in the name of the Father, and of the Son,
  and of the Holy Spirit.

 C. *Amen.*

5 KYRIE LITANY

 O. That we may be enabled to maintain the unity
  of the Spirit in the bond of peace and together confess
  that there is only one Body and one Spirit,
  only one Lord, one faith, one baptism,
  let us pray to the Lord.

              (Eph. 4:3-5)

 C. *Kyrie eleison.*

 O. That we may soon attain to visible communion
  in the Body of Christ, by breaking the bread
  and blessing the cup around the same table,
  let us pray to the Lord.

           (1 Cor. 10:16-17)

 C. Kyrie eleison.

O.   That, reconciled to God through Christ,
     we may be enabled to recognize each other's ministries
     and be united in the ministry of reconciliation,
     let us pray to the Lord.

                                                  (2 Cor. 5:18-20)

C.   *Kyrie eleison.*

6   GLORIA

Glory to God in the highest,
— And peace to God's people on earth.

Lord God, heavenly King, almighty God and Father,
— We worship you, we give you thanks.

We praise you for your glory.
— Lord Jesus Christ, only Son of the Father,

Lord God, Lamb of God,
— You take away the sin of the world: have mercy on us;

You take away the sin of the world: receive our prayer;
— You are seated at the right hand of the Father: have mercy on us.

For you alone are the Holy One,
— You alone are the Lord,

You alone are the Most High: Jesus Christ, with the Holy Spirit,
— In the glory of God the Father,

Amen.

Liturgy of the Word

7   COLLECT

P.   Let us pray:
     Lord God, gracious and merciful,
     you anointed your beloved Son with the Holy Spirit
     at his baptism in the Jordan,
     and you consecrated him prophet, priest and king:
     pour out your Spirit on us again
     that we may be faithful to our baptismal calling,
     ardently desire the communion of Christ's body and blood,
     and serve the poor of your people and all who need our love,
     through Jesus Christ, your Son, our Lord,
     who lives and reigns with you,
     in the unity of the Holy Spirit,
     ever one God, world without end.

C.   *Amen.*

8   FIRST LESSON (Old Testament, Acts or Revelation)

9   PSALM OF MEDITATION

10   EPISTLE

11   ALLELUIA

12   GOSPEL

13   HOMILY

14   SILENCE

15   NICENE — CONSTANTINOPOLITAN CREED (text of 381)

We believe in one God,
the Father, the Almighty,
maker of heaven and earth,
of all that is, seen and unseen.

We believe in one Lord, Jesus Christ,
the only Son of God,
eternally begotten of the Father,
Light from Light,
true God from true God,
begotten, not made,
of one Being with the Father;
through him all things were made.
For us and for our salvation he came down from heaven;
by the power of the Holy Spirit he became incarnate
from the Virgin Mary
and was made man.
For our sake he was crucified under Pontius Pilate;
he suffered death and was buried;
on the third day he rose again in accordance with the Scriptures;
he ascended into heaven.
He is seated at the right hand of the Father,
he will come again in glory
to judge the living and the dead,
and his kingdom will have no end.

We believe in the Holy Spirit,
the Lord, the giver of life,
who proceeds from the Father;

with the Father and the Son
he is worshiped and glorified;
he has spoken through the Prophets.
We believe in one holy catholic and apostolic Church.
We acknowledge one baptism for the forgiveness of sins.
We look for the resurrection of the dead,
and the life of the world to come. Amen.

16 INTERCESSION

O. In faith let us pray to God our Father,
his Son Jesus Christ
and the Holy Spirit.

C. *Kyrie eleison.*

O. For the Church of God throughout all the world,
let us invoke the Spirit.

C. *Kyrie eleison.*

O. For the leaders of the nations,
that they may establish and defend justice and peace,
let us pray for the wisdom of God.

C. *Kyrie eleison.*

O. For those who suffer oppression or violence,
let us invoke the power of the Deliverer.

C. *Kyrie eleison.*

O. That the churches may discover again their visible unity
in the one baptism which incorporates them in Christ,
let us pray for the love of Christ.

C. *Kyrie eleison.*

O. That the churches may attain communion
in the eucharist around one table,
let us pray for the strength of Christ.

C. *Kyrie eleison.*

O. That the churches may recognize each other's ministries
in the service of their one Lord,
let us pray for the peace of Christ.

C. *Kyrie eleison.*
(Spontaneous prayers of the congregation)

O. Into your hands, O Lord,
   we commend all for whom we pray,
   trusting in your mercy;
   through your Son, Jesus Christ, our Lord.

C. *Amen.*

Liturgy of the Eucharist

17   PREPARATION

O. Blessed are you, Lord God of the universe,
   you are the giver of this bread,
   fruit of the earth and of human labour,
   let it become the bread of Life.

C. *Blessed be God, now and for ever!*

O. Blessed are you, Lord God of the universe,
   you are the giver of this wine,
   fruit of the vine and of human labour,
   let it become the wine of the eternal Kingdom.

C. *Blessed be God, now and for ever!*

O. As the grain once scattered in the fields
   and the grapes once dispersed on the hillside
   are now reunited on this table
   in bread and wine,
   so, Lord, may your whole Church
   soon be gathered together
   from the corners of the earth into your Kingdom.

C. *Maranatha! Come Lord Jesus!*

18   DIALOGUE

P. The Lord be with you

C. *And also with you.*

P. Lift up your hearts.

C. *We lift them to the Lord.*

P. Let us give thanks to the Lord our God.

C. *It is right to give him thanks and praise.*

19   PREFACE

P.   Truly it is right and good to glorify you,
at all times and in all places,
to offer you our thanksgiving O Lord, Holy Father,
   Almighty and Everlasting God.
Through your living Word you created all things,
and pronounced them good.
You made human beings in your own image,
to share your life and reflect your glory.
When the time had fully come, you gave Christ to us
as the Way, the Truth and the Life.
He accepted baptism and consecration as your Servant
to announce the good news to the poor.
At the last supper
Christ bequeathed to us the eucharist,
that we should celebrate the memorial
of the cross and resurrection,
and receive his presence as food.
To all the redeemed Christ gave the royal priesthood
and, in loving his brothers and sisters,
chooses those who share in the ministry,
that they may feed the Church with your Word
and enable it to live by your Sacraments.
Wherefore, Lord, with the angels and all the saints,
we proclaim and sing your glory:

20   SANCTUS

C.   *Holy, Holy, Holy....*

21   EPICLESIS I

P.   O God, Lord of the universe,
you are holy and your glory is beyond measure.
Upon your eucharist send the life-giving Spirit,
who spoke by Moses and the prophets,
who overshadowed the Virgin Mary with grace,
who descended upon Jesus in the river Jordan
and upon the Apostles on the day of Pentecost.
May the outpouring of this Spirit of Fire
transfigure this thanksgiving meal
that this bread and wine may become for us
the body and blood of Christ.

C.   *Veni Creator Spiritus!*

22 INSTITUTION

P. May this Creator Spirit accomplish the words
of your beloved Son,
who, in the night in which he was betrayed,
took bread,
and when he had given thanks to you,
broke it and gave it to his disciples, saying:
Take, eat:
this is my body,
which is given for you.
Do this for the remembrance of me.
After supper he took the cup
and when he had given thanks,
he gave it to them and said:
Drink this, all of you:
this is my blood of the new covenant,
which is shed for you and for many
for the forgiveness of sins.
Do this for the remembrance of me.
Great is the mystery of faith.

C. *Your death, Lord Jesus, we proclaim!*
Your resurrection we celebrate!
Your coming in glory we await!

23 ANAMNESIS

P. Wherefore, Lord,
we celebrate today the memorial of our redemption:
we recall the birth and life of your Son among us,
his baptism by John,
his last meal with the apostles,
his death and descent to the abode of the dead;
we proclaim Christ's resurrection and ascension in glory,
where as our Great High Priest
he ever intercedes for all people;
and we look for his coming at the last.
United in Christ's priesthood, we present to you
this memorial: Remember the sacrifice of your Son
and grant to people everywhere the benefits
of Christ's redemptive work.

C. *Maranatha, the Lord comes!*

24   EPICLESIS II

> P.   Behold, Lord, this eucharist
>   which you yourself gave to the Church
>   and graciously receive it,
>   as you accept the offering of your Son
>   whereby we are reinstated in your Covenant.
>   As we partake of Christ's body and blood,
>   fill us with the Holy Spirit
>   that we may be one single body and one single spirit
>   in Christ,
>   a living sacrifice to the praise of your glory.

> C.   *Veni Creator Spiritus!*

25   COMMEMORATIONS

> O.   Remember, Lord,
>   your one, holy, catholic and apostolic Church,
>   redeemed by the blood of Christ.
>   Reveal its unity, guard its faith,
>   and preserve it in peace.
>   Remember, Lord, all the servants of your Church:
>   bishops, presbyters, deacons,
>   and all to whom you have given special gifts of ministry.
>   (Remember especially....)

>   Remember also all our sisters and brothers
>   who have died in the peace of Christ,
>   and those whose faith is known to you alone:
>   guide them to the joyful feast prepared
>   for all peoples in your presence,
>   with the blessed Virgin Mary,
>   with the patriarchs and prophets, the apostles and martyrs....
>   and all the saints for whom your friendship was life.
>   With all these we sing your praise
>   and await the happiness of your Kingdom
>   where with the whole creation,
>   finally delivered from sin and death,
>   we shall be enabled to glorify you
>   through Christ our Lord;

> C.   *Maranatha, the Lord comes!*

26 CONCLUSION

P. Through Christ, with Christ, in Christ,
all honour and glory is yours,
Almighty God and Father,
in the unity of the Holy Spirit,
now and for ever.

C. *Amen.*

27 THE LORD'S PRAYER

O. United by one baptism
in the same Holy Spirit and the same Body of Christ,
we pray as God's sons and daughters:

C. *Our Father, ...*

28 THE PEACE

O. Lord Jesus Christ, you told your apostles:
Peace I leave with you, my peace I give to you.
Look not on our sins but on the faith of your Church;
In order that your will be done,
grant us always this peace
and guide us
towards the perfect unity
of your Kingdom for ever

C. *Amen.*

P. The peace of the Lord be with you always

C. *And also with you.*

O. Let us give one another a sign of reconciliation and peace.

29 THE BREAKING OF THE BREAD

P. The bread which we break
is the communion of the Body of Christ,
the cup of blessing for which we give thanks
is the communion in the Blood of Christ.

30 LAMB OF GOD

C. *Lamb of God, you take away the sins of the world,
have mercy on us.*

*Lamb of God, you take away the sins of the world,
have mercy on us.*

*Lamb of God, you take away the sins of the world,
grant us peace.*

31   COMMUNION

32   THANKSGIVING PRAYER

> P.   In peace let us pray to the Lord:
> O Lord our God, we give you thanks
> for uniting us by baptism in the Body of Christ
> and for filling us with joy in the eucharist.
> Lead us towards the full visible unity of your Church
> and help us to treasure all the signs of reconciliation
> you have granted us.
> Now that we have tasted of the banquet
> you have prepared for us in the world to come,
> may we all one day share together
> the inheritance of the saints
> in the life of your heavenly city,
> through Jesus Christ, your Son, our Lord,
> who lives and reigns with you
> in the unity of the Holy Spirit,
> ever one God, world without end.

> C.   *Amen.*

33   FINAL HYMN

34   WORD OF MISSION

35   BLESSING

> P.   The Lord bless you and keep you.
> The Lord make his face to shine on you and be gracious to you.
> The Lord look upon you with favour and give you peace.
> Almighty God, Father, Son and Holy Spirit,
> bless you now and forever.

> C.   *Amen.*